Also by Ronald L. Smith

Who's Who in Comedy

The Bedside Book of Celebrity Sex Quizzes

The Stars of Stand-up Comedy

Comedy on Record

Cosby

Johnny Carson

Let Peas Be with You

Poe in the Media

The Stooge Fan's I.Q. Test

Sweethearts of Sixties TV

THE COMEDY QUOTE DICTIONARY

the
COMEDY
QUOTE
dictionary

Ronald L. Smith

DOUBLEDAY

NEW YORK LONDON TORONTO SYDNEY AUCKLAND

PUBLISHED BY DOUBLEDAY
a division of Bantam Doubleday Dell Publishing Group, Inc.
666 Fifth Avenue, New York, New York 10103

DOUBLEDAY and the portrayal of an anchor with a dolphin
are trademarks of Doubleday,
a division of Bantam Doubleday Dell Publishing Group, Inc.

Book Design by Liney Li

Library of Congress Cataloging-in-Publication Data

The Comedy quote dictionary / [compiled by] Ronald L. Smith.—1st ed.
p. cm.
Includes index.
1. American wit and humor. 2. Comedians—United States—
—Interviews. I. Smith, Ronald L. 1952–
PN6162.C654 1992
818'.540208—dc20   91-31396
                                                            CIP

ISBN 0-385-41691-1

April 1992

1 3 5 7 9 10 8 6 4 2

FIRST EDITION

TO MY FATHER

Outside of a dog, a book is man's best friend.
Inside of a dog, it's too dark to read.

—Groucho Marx

THE COMEDY QUOTE DICTIONARY

introduction

Now that you've finished thumbing through the jokes and have some questions, or nothing better to do, you've noticed the introduction.

There's no reason for an introduction, technically. You already know this is a book of quotable twentieth-century humor and wit. And you can surely do without the filler of a hand-wringing essay on how "we need more humor in the world."

However, if you want to know about the "ground rules" for who was chosen and why, etc., read on.

WHO are the people I've quoted? Twentieth-century people who have made humor their business: stand-up comedians, authors of funny books (sometimes called "humorists"), cartoonists, and the odd raconteur. In this imperfect world, people have not conveniently dropped dead at the turn of each century, so a decision had to be made on several wits, including Mark Twain and Ambrose Bierce. Since they did most of their writing in the nineteenth century, even if they lived into the first decade of the twentieth, they are omitted.

WHERE did I get the material? From interviews with the hundreds of performers I've met while editing comedy magazines and writing books on comedians, from attending comedy clubs, from books, and from my collection of thousands of records and tapes made from the 1960s to the 1990s.

HOW I chose the final jokes was subjective, based on what material "read" funny without the benefit of a funny face, funny voice, or cartoon drawing.

As you're browsing you may ask **WHY** a particular joke was attributed to a specific comedian when you heard someone else tell it. This question requires some explanation.

Much to the chagrin of gag writers and comedians, great jokes are often stolen or "switched." Some well-known comedians actually believe they're entitled to do this because only *they* can tell the joke properly! To add insult to injury, sometimes the joke becomes more popular told by this other, more famous comic, and it becomes permanently attributed to that person. As Oscar Levant once said, "It doesn't matter who says it first, it's who gets credit for it last that counts."

This really isn't new. Throughout history people have borrowed or improved on classic lines. It wasn't Charles Darwin who first described "the survival of the fittest"; it was Herbert Spencer. Well before Franklin Roosevelt talked about having nothing to fear but fear itself, Henry David Thoreau had said, "Nothing is so much to be feared as fear"; Francis Bacon had said, "Nothing is terrible except fear itself"; and Michel de Montaigne had said, "The thing I fear most is fear." And before John F. Kennedy it was pop guru Kahlil Gibran who asked, "Are you a politician asking what your country can do for you, or a zealous one asking what you can do for your country?"

Often (especially in the 1950s and 1960s) comics bought the same joke from an all-purpose "funnyman's gag book" and none of them technically deserves the credit. One well-worn and feeble "public domain" gag: "These new filter cigarettes—you don't have to worry about cancer but you get a hernia inhaling 'em!" It appears, with slight changes, on albums by everyone from Jackie Vernon and Phyllis Diller to Davy Bold and Pearl Williams.

It's unfortunate that anonymous gag writers have remained anonymous. Only in rare cases when a gag writer becomes famous do the jokes retroactively become attributed to him. When Rodney Dangerfield was temporarily out of the business, working as a paint salesman, he wrote gags for other comics. Henny Youngman made popular the one about the guy who heard bad news from his doctor and said he wanted a second opinion. The doctor said, "You're ugly too." In such a case where the gag writer is known, that credit is given.

Over the years I've met hundreds of comedians and heard many woeful tales of joke theft. Jackie Mason had the best attitude. When I asked him about another well-known comic who obviously stole some of Jackie's gags (and even had the nerve to record them almost verbatim from an earlier Mason album), Jackie said, "The audience is buying our personalities, not jokes. It doesn't really hurt me."

Sometimes a humorist gently "lifts" a gag, the time and situation making it hard to resist. In one of the first episodes of Roseanne Barr Arnold's sitcom, critics delightedly quoted her line about kids: "Now I know why some animals eat their young." They thought it was an original. It was—it was *originally* used in the film *Mildred Pierce* and spoken by Eve Arden.

Tracking down the origin of a joke isn't easy. Broadway columnist Earl Wilson once tried and reported the problem. He told of another columnist, Paul Denis, attributing a gag to Groucho Marx in his December 1947 column. Denis mentioned that a contestant from Liverpool was on Groucho's show and he cracked, "Isn't that where they make Carter's Little Liverpools?"

It was a fairly terrible pun, but the man who actually wrote it wanted credit: author Max Shulman complained to Denis that the joke appeared in his book *The Zebra Derby*, published in January 1946. Then Denis received another letter. It was from Bennett Cerf, who said the gag was lifted from *his* 1945 book, *Laughing Stock*, and that it was told by Harry Hershfield. According to Wilson, the joke was eventually traced back to 1909.

Most comedians start with completely original material, but the demand for fresh jokes wears them down. So a Joan Rivers, Jay Leno, Johnny Carson, Phyllis Diller, or Rodney Dangerfield buys gags and honestly acknowledges it. The important thing to remember here is that even if a joke isn't actually written by the performer who delivers it, the joke could not have been created for that performer if that performer hadn't established a style via original material. In cases involving comedians who buy a large quantity of material, every effort was made to use older jokes from the days before they could afford to buy gags, or jokes that the stars definitely wrote or ad-libbed.

Before any perfectionists out there get upset about all this, think about how many times you've told a joke you didn't make up. You heard it on TV or on a record, or read it in a book like this one, and then told it to someone else—without crediting the original source. Some comedians are no different from you. And since their lives depend on telling funny jokes, they sometimes feel justified borrowing a gag "in the heat of the moment," relying on memory to adapt what seems like a fresh ad-lib.

Care was taken to try to authenticate familiar jokes. It wasn't easy. In some cases several comics legitimately thought of the same easy gag at the same time. In others, lazy columnists or jokebook editors simply attributed an anonymous joke to a favorite comedian, or even to a completely witless actor or politician. Attempting to sort through these problems can be difficult. Once a movie producer came up to W. C. Fields and asked to buy all rights to the quote "Everything I like to do is either illegal, immoral, or fattening." Fields accepted a check. Later, the producer approached Fields and demanded the money back. "I found out that quote was originally spoken by Alexander Woollcott!" the man roared. "Well," drawled Fields, "I never said I wrote it. I just said I'd sell you all rights *I* had to the joke."

WHEN you look through the book, a few gags here and there will definitely test your sense of humor. Sometimes you'll fail the test. I tried to avoid obvious racial, stereotypical, or sexual jokes (mostly because there are plenty of paperbacks for stuff like that), but since a lot of humor comes from anger, fear, hostility, and frustration, there is no way of avoiding humor that might offend someone. To quote Red Skelton: "If I said something to offend you, I didn't mean it." And to quote Homer and Jethro: "Keep those cards and letters—don't bug us with 'em."

Most of the people quoted in the book are well known to a general audience. There is only one example of name duplication and this is noted in the text (Dave Barry the modern columnist and author is different from Dave Barry the stand-up comic who worked primarily in the 1950s and 1960s). For the benefit of non-comedy scholars, here's a breakdown of some of the quoted comedians and humorists by category:

Writers include: Stephen Baker, Roger Bower, Marshall Brickman, Irvin S. Cobb, Will Cuppy, Jack Douglas, Bruce Feirstein, Corey Ford, Jane Goodsell, Ray Hand, Samuel Hoffenstein, Frank Jacobs (Mad magazine), Charlie Kadau (Mad magazine), Garrison Keillor, Doug Kenney, Alexander King, Tom Masson, Luke McCluke (newspaper columnist James Syme Hastings), P. J. O'Rourke, F. S. Pearson 2d, Anne Eva Ricks, Frank Ridgeway, Herb Sargent, Charles Simmons, Roger Simon, Robert Paul Smith, Frank Sullivan.

British humorists include: Dolly Allen, Ronnie Barker, Alan Bennett, Jasper Carrott, Billy Connolly, Jilly Cooper, Ronnie Corbett, Quentin Crisp, Ben Elton, Dame Edna Everage (Barry Humphries), Simon Fanshawe, Michael Flanders, Harry Graham, Hattie Hayridge, Kit Hollerbach, Spike Milligan, Sandy Powell, Hal Roach (Irish comedian, not the American comedy producer), The Sea Monster (Jo Brand), Donald Swann, Jack Warner, Robb Wilton.

Comedians of radio and vaudeville include: Goodman Ace, Benny Rubin, "Senator" Ed Ford, The Great Gildersleeve (Harold Peary), Senator Claghorn (Kenny Delmar), Joe Laurie, Jr., Molly McGee (Marion Jordan), Colonel Lemuel Stoopnagle (Frederick Taylor), James Thornton, Cal Tinney.

Comedians of nightclub comedy, 1950s–1970s, include: Lou Alexander, "Uncle Dirty" Altman, Dr. Murray Banks, Pete Barbutti, Sandy Baron, Gene Baylos, Larry Best, Ed Bluestone, Davy Bold, Rod Brasfield, Jethro Burns (of Homer and Jethro), Pat Buttram, Archie Campbell, Jean Carroll, Jack Carson, Bobby Clark, Jackie Clark, Del Close, Leroy "Sloppy" Daniels, Severn Darden,

Selma Diamond, the Duke of Paducah (Whitey Ford), Herb Eden, Jimmy Edmondson (Professor Backwards), Totie Fields, Homer Haynes (of Homer and Jethro), Bert Henry, Billy Holliday, Jimmy Joyce, Bob Kaliban, Milt Kamen, Adam Keefe, Dave Ketchum, James Komack, London Lee, Sam Levenson, Hal McKay, Bob Melvin, Jan Murray, Mike Preminger, Ray Scott, Harvey Stone, Bub Thomas, Pearl Williams.

Young comedy club stars of the 1980s and 1990s include: Gabe Abelson, Max Alexander, Larry Amoros, Andy Andrews, Tom Arnold, Rhonda Bates, Gerry Bednob, Mike Binder, Scott Blakeman, Tommy Blaze, Jordan Brady, Billy Braver, Larry "Bubbles" Brown, Audrey Buslik, Brett Butler, Drew Carey, Judy Carter, Tim Cavanagh, Jimi Celeste, Jeff Cesario, Blake Clark, Ray Combs, Billiam Coronel, Rick Corso, Wayne Cotter, Ben Creed, Barry Crimmins, Danny Curtis, Ron Darian, Johnny Dark, Evan Davis, Ellen DeGeneris, Mark Dobrient, Bob Dubac, Rick Ducommon, Mike Dugan, Will Durst, Dave Edison, Lorne Elliott, Billy Elmer, Chas Elstner, Bill Engvall, Steve Epstein, David Feldman, Peter Fogel, Diane Ford, Glenn Foster, John Fox, Jeff Foxworthy, Dan French, Stevie Ray Fromstein, Brad Garrett, Dr. Gonzo (John Means), Jack Graiman, Anthony Griffin, Geechy Guy, Karen Haber, Rhonda Hansome, Bob Harris, Allan Havey, Jon Haymen, Bill Hicks, Stephanie Hodge, Billy Jaye, Jeffrey Jena, Richard Jeni, Jenny Jones, Diana Jordan, Hiram Kasten, Jonathan Katz, Bobby Kelton, Brian Kiley, Bill Kirchenbauer, Danny Koch, Sue Kolinsky, Cathy Ladman, Angela LaGreca, Valerie Landsburg, Wendy Liebman, "Noodles" Levenstein, Emily Levine, George Lopez, Bernadette Luckett, Bill Maher, Linda Maldonado, Henriette Mantel, Norm McDonald, Brian McKim, Tom McTeague, Michael Meehan, John Mendoza, Beverly Mickins, George Miller, Larry Miller, Maureen Murphy, Jimmy Myers, Susan Norfleet, Cary Odes, Ellen Orchid, Tamayo Otsuki, Jackson Perdue, Monica Piper, Paula Poundstone, Marc Price, Alan Prophet, Colin Quinn, Greg Ray, Larry Reeb, Brian Regan, Mike Reynolds, Rick Reynolds, Ron Richards, John Riggi, Kevin Rooney, Chris Rush, Lenny Rush, Joan St. Onge, Jim Samuels, Drake Sather, Robert Schimmel,

Steve Scrovan, Ross Shaffer, Steve Shaffer, Ronnie Shakes, Jeff Shaw, Wil Shriner, Jack Simmons, Sara B. Sirius, Carol Siskind, Daryl Sivad, Bobby Slayton, Tommy Sledge, Bruce Smirnoff, Margaret Smith, Jonathan Solomon, Spanky (Steve McFarlin), Dan Spencer, Barry Steiger, Abby Stein, Jeff Stilson, Fred Stoller, Tony Stone, Glen (Mr. Bullhorn) Super, Jimmy Tingle, Greg Travis, Stu Trivax, J. J. Wall, George Wallace, John Wing, Lizz Winstead, Anita Wise, Dennis Wolfberg, David Wood, Bob Zany.

Cartoonists and comic-strip artists include: Charles Addams, Tom Armstrong ("Marvin"), Dave Berg, Bo Brown, Mark Cullum, Jim Davis, Chon Day, Fontaine Fox ("Toonerville Trolley"), Dana Fradon, Walt Handelsman, Johnny Hart ("BC"), Bill Hoest ("The Lockhorns"), Syd Hoff, Stan Hunt, Phil Interlandi, S. Kelley, Gary Larson, Mell Lazarus, H. (Henry) Martin, Donald McGill, Frank Modell, Gardner Rea, Brian Savage, Mick Stevens, Thaves, Walt Wetterberg, Rowland P. Wilson, Tom Wilson ("Ziggy").

Actors

Some of the greatest love affairs I've known have involved one actor—unassisted.

WILSON MIZNER

A barman in a bar in New York sees a guy sitting at the end of the bar who looks very glum and lonely and he says, "Why don't you talk to someone? You look real lonely," and the guy says, "I have an IQ of 181. I can't find anyone to talk to." And a guy sitting on a stool there says, "Hey, I'm 179, let's talk." So the barman gets them together, gives them a vodka, and they start talking about negative energy and entropy, why it was that Karpov kept moving that rook in the sixteenth game of the world chess championship, and where atomic physics is going.

Meanwhile the barman's gone down the bar and he sees somebody else. He says, "What's your IQ?" The guy says, "I have the same problem. I'm 153." Somebody says, "156!" The barman gets them together, and they talk about the latest Woody Allen movie, where you can get fresh pasta, and BMWs.

Then the barman sees one guy right down on the end and he's just sitting there. He says, "What's your IQ?" And the guy says, "It's 61." He says, "Is there anyone with the same IQ?" And another guy says, "I'm 56." The barman says, "Well, get together, talk!" The man says, "What are we going to talk about?" He says, "I

don't know—been to any auditions recently?"
JOHN CLEESE

Adages and Axioms

Nobody ever sees you eat a tuna fish sandwich.
DAVID BRENNER

Nobody says, "Can I have your beets?"
BILL COSBY

A fool and his money are soon parted, but nobody can part a two-dollar toupee.
FRED ALLEN

A fool has no business inside a balloon.
HERB SARGENT

Time wounds all heels.
JANE ACE

Two is company. Three is fifty bucks.
JOAN RIVERS

The further you get into the suburbs the bigger women's hairstyles get.
BILLY JAYE

You all know that Patrick Henry said, "Give me liberty or give me death." But you've never been told his complete statement. It went like this: "Give me liberty or give me death; preferably in that order."

And we are told in the Scriptures that at the beginning of time the Lord said, "Let there be light." But I've checked this out with a number of eminent biblical scholars. The Lord's complete statement was as follows: "Let there be light. Well, maybe not all day."

Everyone, I think, remembers Voltaire's famous line about freedom of speech. The version of it that you are familiar with is actually based on a faulty translation. What Voltaire actually said was this: "I do not agree with what you say, sir, though I will defend to the death your right to say it. But for now . . . shut up!"
STEVE ALLEN

Horace Greeley did not say, "Go West, young man." He said, "It's the first door on the left, kid."

JACK DOUGLAS

If at first you don't succeed, try, try again. Then quit. No use being a damn fool about it.

W. C. FIELDS

Imitation is the sincerest form of television.

FRED ALLEN

You can lead a horse to water—but before you push him in, just stop and think how a wet horse smells.

GEORGE GOBEL

Don't count your boobies until they are hatched.

JAMES THURBER

Never go to a doctor whose office plants have died.

ERMA BOMBECK

A good listener is usually thinking about something else.

KIN HUBBARD

Show me a man with both feet on the ground and I'll show you a man who can't put his pants on.

JOE E. LEWIS

The best things in life are free. And the cheesiest things in life are free with a paid subscription to *Sports Illustrated*.

JOHNNY CARSON

I don't know much about art, but I know when somebody is getting away with murder.

BILL HOEST

I don't mind a man going around telling lies about me, but he'll hear from me if he dares to tell the truth!

JIMMY SAVO

Sex is one of the most beautiful, wholesome, and natural things that money can buy.

STEVE MARTIN

Don't let a man put anything over on you except an umbrella.

MAE WEST

Oh, give me a home where the buffalo roam—and I'll show you a house full of dirt.

MARTY ALLEN

If her lips are on fire and she trembles in your arms, forget her. She's got malaria.

JACKIE KANNON

If your eyes hurt after you drink coffee, you have to take the spoon out of the cup.

NORM CROSBY

Honesty is the best policy, but insanity is a better defense.

STEVE LANDESBERG

A journey of a thousand miles occasionally begins with the realization that a thousand miles is one hell of a long journey.

MICK STEVENS

The cost of living's goin' up and the chance of living's goin' down.

FLIP WILSON

Everywhere is walking distance if you have the time.

STEVEN WRIGHT

Advertising

Advertising may be described as the science of arresting the human intelligence long enough to get money from it.

STEPHEN LEACOCK

Agents

A bank robber hits the biggest bank in LA. He's planned this heist for years and everything goes like clockwork, but as he's running out of the bank he notices one security camera aimed right at him. A minute later a huge manhunt for him is on. He manages to keep out of sight for a few days but he can tell from the news that it's only a matter of time before he's discovered.

Suddenly, he gets a brilliant idea. He jumps in his car, races down to the William Morris agency, and forces them at gunpoint to sign him to a five-year contract. He is never seen or heard from ever again.

JIMMY MYERS

There's a sophisticated area of the business called "pending." When you call your agent about a particular job, he never says he can't get you the job.

He says you are "pending" for the job. In the same sense that an acne-covered high school student holding a *Playboy* magazine is "pending" to make it with the centerfold model.

RICHARD JENI

Shakespeare said, "Kill all the lawyers." There were no agents then.

ROBIN WILLIAMS

When I first got into show business they told me, "You must get a press agent." So I got an agent, a hundred dollars a week. I took five weeks, a hundred a week. The first week, nothing in the paper. I said, "What's happening—a hundred dollars—" He said, "They're talkin' about ya, baby, they're talkin' about ya!"

Two more weeks go by, it's three hundred dollars. I'm scared. He says, "They're talkin' about ya, baby." The end of the fifth week, forget about it, five hundred dollars, a life savings. Nothing. I walk into his office. I'm angry, I'm mortified, I'm embarrassed. I said, "What does this mean? Five hundred dollars—nothing—"

He said, "They're talkin' about ya, baby."

I said, "They're talking about me? What are they saying?"

He said, "They're saying—whatever happened to Will Jordan . . ."

WILL JORDAN

Aging

From birth to age 18, a girl needs good parents, from 18 to 35 she needs good looks, from 35 to 55 she needs a good personality, and from 55 on she needs cash.

SOPHIE TUCKER

Certainly it's nicer to refer to middle age as "maturity," but, like calling green beans *haricots verts à l'anglaise*, the difference is academic . . . How in the world did you get so old so young? Why, you don't even feel grown-up, much less mature. Where are the wisdom and character you'd expected to acquire by this time? What happened to the tact and sophistication you should have picked up over the years?

Where, for that matter, is the nest egg you should have salted away and the portfolio of stocks you'd planned to secure. Here you are, clearly retarded for your age . . .

As for books like *Life Begins at Forty,* they're comforting to read, but they're about as close to the truth as near beer. You don't see any books titled *It's Fun to Be Twenty* because everyone already knows that. And who'd buy them? Twenty-year-olds are out living it up, not sitting at home reading about it.

JANE GOODSELL

He's so old that when he orders a three-minute egg, they ask for the money up front.

MILTON BERLE

Most women are not so young as they are painted.

MAX BEERBOHM

I've reached that age when a good day is one when you get up and nothing hurts.

H. MARTIN

A woman past 40 should make up her *mind* to be young, not her face.

BILLIE BURKE

I am the oldest living white man, especially at seven in the morning.

ROBERT BENCHLEY

As we grow older, our bodies get shorter and our anecdotes longer.

ROBERT QUILLEN

You may be certain that age is galloping upon you when, after a feminine voice over the telephone says, "Do you know who this is?" you say, "No," and hang up the receiver.

FRANKLIN P. ADAMS

Senior citizens! This is good news: of memory, hearing, all the faculties—the last to leave us is sexual desire and the ability to make love. That means that long after we're wearing bifocals or hearing aids, we'll be making love. But we won't know with whom.

JACK PAAR

My grandfather's a little forgetful, but he likes to give me advice. One day he took me aside and left me there.

RON RICHARDS

I said to my old husband, "I'm gonna take you out into the country for a picnic. Do you like the country?" He said, "Sure I do. When I was a little boy, I used to live in the country." I said, "When you was a little boy *everybody* lived in the country."

MOMS MABLEY

He's so old his blood type was discontinued.

BILL DANA

I have reached an age when I look just as good standing on my head as I do right side up.

FRANK SULLIVAN

My, my—65! I guess this marks the first day of the rest of our life savings.

H. MARTIN

In all of the theories about why so many people have attacks of wackiness when they reach middle age—resign from the bank to go live in a van with a teenage mushroom gatherer, and that sort of thing—one factor has been neglected: When someone reaches middle age, people he knows begin to get put in charge of things, and knowing what he knows about the people who are being put in charge of things scares the hell out of him. If he's one of the people put in charge of things himself, it may scare him all the more.

CALVIN TRILLIN

Middle age occurs when you are too young to take up golf and too old to rush up to the net.

FRANKLIN P. ADAMS

She was 102. She didn't have wrinkles, she had pleats . . . There's one advantage to being 102. There's no peer pressure.

DENNIS WOLFBERG

Middle age is a time of life That man first notices in his wife.

RICHARD ARMOUR

With women, the aging thing's terrible. We just fall apart. First thing that goes on you is your butt . . . BAM . . . once it's down there it's not coming back up. Remember when you were young, you used to walk down the beach in the summertime pulling your little pants down over your firm

15

round buttocks? Now I spend my summers trying to push my butt flaps back up into my shorts . . . At a certain age you quit lookin' behind you. I'm getting dressed, pulling up my pantyhose, I catch myself in the mirror. I look back there thinking: My Lord! Who's that ugly man with the jowls sneakin' up on me!

STEPHANIE HODGE

He's so old he gets winded playing checkers.

ED WYNN

I don't think it's fair to call people middle-aged just because they're not so young anymore.

SYD HOFF

She was so old when she went to school they didn't have history.

RODNEY DANGERFIELD

The only time in our lives we like to get old is when we're kids. If you're less than 10 years old you're so excited about aging you think in fractions: "How old are you?" "Six and *a half!*" You're never 36 and *a half.*

"Four and a half—going on five." You're going on . . . the greatest day of your life: you *become* 21. But you *turn* 30. It makes you sound like bad milk. Then you're *pushing* 40. It's all slipping away. Then you *reach* 50. "My dreams are gone!" You become 21, you turn 30, you're pushing 40, you reach 50: and you *make it* to 60. By then you've built up so much speed you HIT 70. After that?

It's day by day. You hit Wednesday. In your 80s you hit lunch. My grandmother won't even buy green bananas. It doesn't end there. In the 90s you start going backward. "I was just 92." Then a strange thing happens. If you make it over a 100 you become a kid again: "I'm 104. And a half."

LARRY MILLER

You know how you tell when you're getting old? When your broad mind changes places with your narrow waist.

RED SKELTON

My grandmother's 90. She's dating. He's 93. It's going great. They never argue. They can't hear each other.

CATHY LADMAN

We're going to find out tonight who the oldest lady in the audience is. And we have a marvelous present for her. When we find the oldest lady, we're going to give her . . . the oldest man.

The first time we tried this was about ten years ago. We had a very nice lady in our audience. She was 87 years old, as I recall. We introduced her that evening to a man from Chicago who was 96, and shortly thereafter, believe it or not, they were married. It was a lovely story. And that wasn't the end of it either.´ I read in the paper recently where that woman has just given birth to a beautiful 47-year-old baby boy!

STEVE ALLEN

At the retirement center for senior citizens, Wrinkle City, if everyone happens to smile at once it's automatically declared Halloween. The residents are so elderly it's considered a good deed for a Boy Scout to help an old lady cross her legs.

PAT McCORMICK

The biggest myth, as measured by square footage, is that as you grow older, you gradually lose your interest in sex. This myth probably got started because younger people seem to want to have sex with each other at every available opportunity including traffic lights, whereas older people are more likely to reserve their sexual activities for special occasions such as the installation of a new pope.

But does this mean that, as an aging person, you're no longer capable of feeling the lust that you felt as an 18-year-old? Not at all! You're attracted just as strongly as you ever were toward 18-year-olds! The problem is that everybody your *own* age seems repulsive.

DAVE BARRY

An elderly couple went to the doctor for their annual checkup. The wife waited in the reception room while the husband went in to be examined.

The doctor, kibitzing with him, said, "Sam, how's your sex life?" "I'll tell you the truth," he said, "the first time is great. But the second time, I start to sweat something terrible." The doctor said, "Just a second. The second time? At 85—

that's remarkable." He said, "Sam, excuse me for a minute."

The doctor walked into the reception room and talked to the guy's wife. He said, "Honey, I have to ask you this. I was talking to your husband and I asked him how his sex life was. He tells me the first time is great, but the second time he starts to sweat something terrible."

The wife says, "He wouldn't lie to you. In January it's cold. In July it's hot."

PHIL STONE

The secret of staying young is to live honestly, eat slowly, and lie about your age.

LUCILLE BALL

A man is as old as the woman he feels.

GROUCHO MARX

I'm beginning to appreciate the value of naps. Naps are wonderful, aren't they? Sometimes now I have to take a nap to get ready for bed.

MARSHA WARFIELD

People tell me, "Gee, you look good." There are three ages of man: youth, middle age, and "gee, you look good." But I don't let old age bother me. There are three signs of old age. Loss of memory . . . I forget the other two . . . My doctor said I look like a million dollars—green and wrinkled.

RED SKELTON

Yesterday morning the Baptist preacher was out to the hospital visiting Aunt Pet. She explained to him that she had all sixteen of her teeth pulled at one time. She didn't have no teeth.

While the preacher was talking to her, he was eating some peanuts that was in a bowl on the nightstand. He'd talk and he'd eat. He visited, then he got up and said, "Mrs. Ledbetter, I'll be back to see you tomorrow, and I'll bring you more peanuts."

She said, "No! No, I can't chew 'em. So don't bring me no peanuts till I get me some teeth. My gums are too tender now. What I do now is just suck the chocolate off of them peanuts and put the peanuts back in the bowl right there."

JERRY CLOWER

One of the nicest things about golf is you can play it for years and years. There were these two old friends who'd been playing together since they were kids, every Saturday morning and Sunday afternoon. Old Lester was 82 and his friend Ralph was 81. One day, standing on the 8th tee, Lester suddenly gave up. He just couldn't do it anymore. He turned to his old pal Ralph and said, "Ralphie old boy, I'm afraid I'm gonna have to quit. I just can't see anymore. I hit the ball, but I don't know where it goes."

Ralph said to him, "But you can't quit. We've been playing together all these years. It wouldn't be the same without you."

"What can I do?" said Lester.

"You just leave it up to me. You go ahead and hit the ball, and I'll keep my eye on it."

So Lester teed one up and let it fly. They stood silently for a few seconds. And then Lester spoke. "Well, Ralph, sounded pretty good. Did you see where it went?"

Ralph said, "Of course I did!"

Lester said, "Well? Where did it go?"

And Ralph thought for a few seconds and said, "I forget."

BOB KALIBAN

Airplanes and Flight

Airline tickets have small print on them. It says, "Schedules are subject to change without notice." I missed my plane in Houston by fifteen minutes. And believe me, I noticed it.

MARK DOBRIENT

The Concorde was great. It travels at twice the speed of sound. Which is fun except you can't hear the movie till two hours after you land.

HOWIE MANDEL

I love when the stewardess says, "Your seat cushion becomes a flotation device." Well, why doesn't the plane just become a boat?

STEVE SHAFFER

Those preflight safety instructions: "Your seat cushion can be used as a flotation device."

Folks, if we're crashing, my seat cushion's gonna be used as a toilet!

TOM PARKS

I'm giving up flying. I was at the airport and I saw a sign: "Take out insurance." I thought: If the lobby's that dangerous, imagine what it's like in the plane.

CORBETT MONICA

You know what a stewardess is. That's a girl who asks you what you want, then straps you in the seat so you can't get it.

JIMMY EDMONDSON

(PROFESSOR BACKWARDS)

I'm not thrilled about flying. . . . We don't know how old the airplanes are and there's really no way for us to tell, 'cause we're laymen. But I figure if the plane smells like your grandmother's house, get out. That's where I draw the line.

GARRY SHANDLING

He was a little "off," I think is the term . . . One day he said to me, "I'm gonna fly." I said, "I believe ya can, Maynard, I've seen ya do a lot of wild things. I think you can fly." We went up to Willard's Bluff . . .

He Scotch-taped a hundred forty-six pigeons to his arms.

He said, "I know I can do it . . . I know I can." I said, "Don't repeat yourself, just do it." He was airborne for a good twenty seconds. Then some kid came from outta nowhere, threw a bag of popcorn in the stone quarry, and he bashed his brains out.

JONATHAN WINTERS

A chap was sealed in a rocket ship and shot upwards to see how high he could go. He was told to keep track of the altitude, so he kept counting, 20,000, 30,000, 100,000, 500,000. When he got this far, he said to himself, "Jesus Christ!" And a very soft voice answered back: "Yesssss?"

EDNA PURVIANCE

There's the stealth plane, the invisible plane. What good is an invisible airplane gonna do? Enemy looks down on their radar and says, "Well, there's no aircraft here. But there's two little guys in a sitting position at 40,000 feet!"

WILL DURST

What is a stealth bomber? It's a bomber that doesn't show up on radar and you can't see it. Then we don't need one.

ROBIN WILLIAMS

I had the chance to go to London a couple of months back. Had kind of a weird flight over there, though, 'cause one of the flight attendants got very angry with me. I didn't eat all of my dinner. She said, "Sir, you really shouldn't waste all that food. There are people starving on Air-India."

TIM CAVANAGH

Have you ever been frisked on a plane trip? They frisk you and then, on the plane, they serve and everybody has a steak knife!

SHELLEY BERMAN

I took an economy flight. There wasn't any movie, but they flew low over drive-ins.

RED BUTTONS

They sent for me to come down to Washington in an airplane . . . Sure enough, no sooner I got on the plane they strapped me down. The stewardess come by. I say, "Honey, my ears is all stopped up." Ohh, I was so sick!

She say, "Here's some chewing gum." I chewed that. That ain't unstopped 'em. I said, "Do something for me, honey, I'm dyin'." She said, "Drop your jaws." And I misunderstood her. They grounded me in Baltimore!

MOMS MABLEY

There ought to be an FAA requirement that crying babies have to go into the overhead compartment.

BOBBY SLAYTON

I'm on a plane and it hits me: When did it become a federal regulation that you have to have at least seven crying babies on every flight? I just want to know: Where are they going? Why are they on planes? They have no appointments, they were born just days ago. Our times are so hectic that babies are born and go, "I just popped out of the womb, I gotta dry up, learn to breathe—I'll be on the two o'clock, it's the best I can do . . ."

PAUL REISER

The airlines banned smoking on their flights. Now if they can do it on their landings.

BARRY CRIMMINS

I think I embarrassed the lady next to me on the plane. It was one of those flights that you sleep on. And I sleep in the nude.

JOHNNY DARK

I got a wonderful tribute at the airport. They fired twenty-one shots in the air in my honor. Course, it would've been nicer if they'd waited for the plane to land . . . On champagne flights, some stewardesses serve too much. Once I got on as a passenger and got off as luggage.

BOB HOPE

Two men jump from an airplane. The first pulls the cord —and the chute works perfectly. The second pulls the cord—and nothing happens. He keeps falling straight down. As he passes his friend, the guy gets mad, unbuckles the harness, and shouts, "So, you wanna race, eh?"

CHARLIE CALLAS

I once went for a job at one of the airlines. The interviewer asked me why I wanted to be a stewardess, and I told her—it would be a great chance to meet men. I was honest about it! She looked at me and said, "But you can meet men anywhere." I said, "Strapped down?"

MARTHA RAYE

I think I agree with the old lady who said if God had intended us to fly he would never have given us the railways.

MICHAEL FLANDERS

If you don't drink, when you wake up in the morning that's the best you're gonna feel all day.

MARTIN MULL

Let's get out of these wet clothes and into a dry martini.

ROBERT BENCHLEY

Father was coming up the stairs with five gallons of elderberry wine, and he slipped and fell clear down into the basement. Fortunately, he didn't spill a drop—he kept his mouth closed.

CHARLEY WEAVER (CLIFF ARQUETTE)

I was in love with a beautiful blonde once. She drove me to drink. That's the one thing I'm indebted to her for.

W. C. FIELDS

Alcohol *kills* brain cells. Brain cell: "Did you bring the oxygen?" Blood cell: "The oxygen? Oh boy, let's see. I was in the lungs. I headed toward the head. And . . . I stopped to party with friends . . . I just forgot." We take the only organ in our body that won't grow back and we kill it for fun!

CAREY ODES

Alcohol is good for you. My grandfather proved it irrevocably. He drank two quarts of booze every mature day of his life and lived to the age of 103. I was at the cremation—that fire would not go out.

DAVE ASTOR

There was a couple drinking doubles. And the waitress goes over and says, "Miss, your hus-

band just slid under the table." She said, "My husband just walked in that door."

SLAPPY WHITE

Whiskey and women'll kill you. I know. They killed my brother. He couldn't get either one so he just laid down and died.

THE DUKE OF PADUCAH

(WHITEY FORD)

I'll quit drinkin' just as soon as I can find some better way to get it down.

JETHRO BURNS

Bill Paley just walked into my dressing room with two bottles of champagne and opened them up and said, "Let's have a drink. Bottoms up." And I said to him, "Isn't that an awkward position?"

GRACIE ALLEN

I envy people who drink—at least they know what to blame everything on.

OSCAR LEVANT

The drinking age should be 18. When you're 18 years old you're old enough to vote. You should be old enough to drink.

Look at who we have to vote for! You *need* a drink.

MARC PRICE

Beer commercials are so patriotic: "Made the American Way." What does that have to do with America? Is that what America stands for? Feeling sluggish and urinating frequently?

SCOTT BLAKEMAN

Allergies

My allergy tests suggest that I may have been intended for some other planet.

WALT WETTERBERG

America

This finance magazine says most Americans don't plan for a rainy day. Of course we do. We just plan to get wet.

MARK CULLUM

In what other country than American can a person like me say to a person like you, "Why don't you get out of America?"

STANLEY MYRON HANDELMAN

Animals

What really happened to the buffaloes is just what you might expect if you've ever seen one in a zoo—the moths got into them.

WILL CUPPY

Stuffed deer heads on walls are bad enough, but it's worse when you see them wearing dark glasses and having streamers around their necks and a hat on their antlers, because then you know they were enjoying themselves at a party when they were shot.

ELLEN DeGENERIS

Ants can carry twenty times their own body weight, which is useful information if you're moving out and you need help getting a potato chip across town.

RON DARIAN

A myth is a moth's sister.

STAN LAUREL

Look at that ugly little bee. Makes honey. I'm a nice-looking person and all I can do is make a little wax with my ears.

MILT KAMEN

All creatures must learn to co-exist. That's why the brown bear and the field mouse can share their lives and live in harmony. Of course, they can't mate or the mice would explode.

BETTY WHITE (in *The Golden Girls*)

People who do not understand pigeons—and pigeons can be understood only when you understand that there is nothing to understand about them—should not go around describing pigeons or the effect of pigeons.

Pigeons come closer to a zero of impingement than any other birds . . . No other thing can be less what it is not than a pigeon can . . . The pigeon is just there on the roof being a pigeon, having been, and being, a pigeon, and, what is more, always going to be, too. Nothing could be simpler than that . . .

There is nothing a pigeon can do or be that would make me feel sorry for it or for myself or for the people in the world, just as there is nothing I could do or be that would make a pigeon feel sorry for itself . . . No other thing in the world falls so far short of being able to do what it cannot do as a pigeon does. Or being unable to do what it can do, too, as far as that goes.

JAMES THURBER

Some months ago I saw a man breaking a loaf of whole-wheat bread and tossing the pieces at pigeons. I was curious and I asked him, "Why whole-wheat bread?" He very seriously answered, "Everybody gives them white bread or cake; this is how they'll remember me."

HAL LINDEN

As of yet there have been no deaths attributed to the killer bees in Texas. However, two bees were caught this week planning a murder.

DENNIS MILLER

Apathy

Scientists announced today that they have discovered a cure for apathy. However, they claim no one has shown the slightest bit of interest in it.

GEORGE CARLIN

When Grandmama fell off the boat
And couldn't swim (and wouldn't float),
Matilda just stood by and smiled.
I almost could have slapped the child.

HARRY GRAHAM

April

April diverts our attention from life's inevitabilities and focuses it on the potentialities. In April, if the glands still work

properly, it is possible to see the world as it might be if only it were not the world.

RUSSELL BAKER

Arizona

Sunday morning in Arizona is just like Sunday morning in Connecticut, only more bow-legged.

JACK DOUGLAS

Armed Forces

My brother just got out of the Marines. They made a man out of him . . . paid for the operation and everything.

STU TRIVAX

The Army spent two billion dollars for flyswatters to send to Alaska. When the flyswatters got up there they found there wasn't no flies in Alaska. So the Army spent four billion dollars more to raise flies to ship to Alaska so's they could use them flyswatters! That's how the Army works, son!

SENATOR CLAGHORN (KENNY DELMAR)

They're gonna cut back on the troops by 100,000 in Europe. Could you imagine what a loser you gotta feel like when you get laid off by the Army?

JACK COHEN

You have to have a physical before you get into the Army. A doctor looks in one ear, another doctor looks in the other ear, and if they can't see each other, you're in. And if they can see each other, you become an MP.

JOE E. BROWN

We had a colonel named Fat Ass Johnson. That wasn't his real name . . . but they called him Fat Ass Johnson. No one ever called him Fat Ass Johnson to his face. I once called him that on the phone. You see, I was working in the motor pool. That's where they keep trucks and jeeps and vehicles like that.

Now, the phone rings. The sign said, "Recruits, do not answer phone." I didn't know what's a recruit, so I said hello.

A voice said, "Soldier, what vehicles have you got available?" I said, "Six trucks, seven jeeps, an MA armored car, a half-track, and Fat Ass Johnson's command car."

He said, "Have you any idea who you're talking to?"

I said, "No, sir."

He said, "This is Colonel Johnson!"

I said, "Colonel, do you have any idea who you're talking to?"

He said, "NO."

I said, "Bye-bye, Fat Ass!"

BUDDY HACKETT

Asians

There was a hijacking this afternoon. They hijacked a bus filled with Japanese tourists. But thank God, they got over two million pictures of the hijackers.

JAN MURRAY

It's dishonor if Japanese man late. It means he has cheap watch.

TAMAYO OTSUKI

A holdup man walks into a Chinese restaurant. He says, "Give me all your money." The man says, "To take out?"

HENNY YOUNGMAN

Babies

The baby is great. My wife and I have just started potty training. Which I think is important, because when we wanna potty-train the baby we should set an example.

HOWIE MANDEL

There is only one beautiful child in the world, and every mother has it.

STEPHEN LEACOCK

Those signs—that "Baby on Board" crap—doesn't it make you want to hit the car harder?

SUE KOLINSKY

Lord have mercy, Mrs. Tugwell just had her sixteenth young 'un. She said she had so many young 'uns she'd run out of names—to call her husband.

MINNIE PEARL

Ivy and Herbert have just had another baby, and they asked me to go along and see the little stranger. They asked me what I thought it was. I got it in three guesses.

Herbert says it will be a member of Parliament when it grows up, because it can say so many things that sound good and mean nothing.

JACK WARNER

I'd hate to be a new baby being born into this world today. There seems to be so much trouble everywhere. If I were a new baby, I don't think I could stand knowing what I was going to have to go through. That's why they don't show them any newspapers for the first two years.

CHARLES SCHULZ ("Peanuts")

Every baby resembles the relative who has the most money.

LUKE McLUKE (JAMES SYME HASTINGS)

Two women were talking about that recent birth of quintuplets. One woman says, "Did you know that happens only once in four million times?" The other says, "My God, when did she ever have time for her housework?"

BILL BARNER

I remember a lot of things before I was even born. I remember going to a picnic with my father and coming home with my mother.

FOSTER BROOKS

When I was born, my family was so poor my mother couldn't afford to use talcum powder on me. So she used to douse me with kitchen baking soda . . . About once every month I'd break out in a severe case of cookies."

WOODY ALLEN

Two working-class expressions that seem to be creeping upwards are: "Baby needs changing," as though you were fed up with her already, and "I've potted Sharon," as though she were a shiny red billiard ball. Confusion is also caused by the term "putting down." The upper classes "put down" sick or senile dogs . . .

The middle classes "put down" children for school, but when the working classes say, "I've put Sharon down," it means they've put her to bed. When they say, "I mind children," it doesn't mean they dislike them, but that they look after them.

JILLY COOPER

I read an article in a magazine: women 49 years old having their first child. Forty-nine! I couldn't think of a better way to spend *my* golden years. What's the advantage of having a kid at 49? So you can both be in diapers at the same time?

SUE KOLINSKY

Bachelors

Bachelors know more about women than married men. If

they didn't, they would be married too.

H. L. MENCKEN

I'm single because I was born that way.

MAE WEST

A bachelor is a man who never makes the same mistake once.

ED WYNN

I think—therefore I'm single.

LIZZ WINSTEAD

Ballet

You go to the ballet and you see girls dancing on their tiptoes. Why don't they just get taller girls?

GREG RAY

I was a ballerina. I had to quit after I injured a groin muscle. It wasn't mine.

RITA RUDNER

Banks

When your life flashes before you, do you think that includes every trip you made to the bank?

CAROL LEIFER

I bank at a women's bank. It's closed three or four days a month due to cramps.

JUDY CARTER

I went to the bank and went over my savings. I found out I have all the money that I'll ever need. If I die tomorrow.

HENNY YOUNGMAN

The banks have a new image. Now you have "a friend." Your friendly banker. If the banks are so friendly, how come they chain down the pens?

ALAN KING

My girlfriend's father died of throat trouble. They hung him. He used to work in a bank. But no matter how much the boss likes you, if you work in a bank you can't bring home samples.

EDDIE CANTOR

A record number of savings-and-loan failures left America with a nationwide shortage of flimsy toaster ovens, cheap pocket calculators, and ugly dinnerware.

P. J. O'ROURKE

Baseball

I saw this guy at the baseball game all year, holding up a sign: "John 13." I looked it up. It said, "Go, Mookie!"

ALLAN HAVEY

I feel terrible about what they do to the umpires. The first time they go out on the field the band strikes up "Oh, say, can you see."

GOODMAN ACE

Baseball has been called the National Pastime. It's just the kind of game anyone deserves who has nothing better to do than try to pass his time.

ANDY ROONEY

Bat Day seems like a good idea, but I question the advisability of giving bats in the Bronx to 40,000 Yankee fans.

AARON BACALL

Ralph Hunker's daddy made the first baseball glove in history. Made it out of genuine cowhide. Of course, he cheated a little. He made it out of the part of the cow that already had the fingers in it.

PAT BUTTRAM

Bathroom

Who invented the brush they put next to the toilet? That thing hurts!

ANDY ANDREWS

We have only one bathroom, so you'll have to take pot luck.

FRANK SULLIVAN

The Beach

I was walking along the ocean. That's generally where you'll find the beach. Looking for ashtrays in their wild state.

RONNY GRAHAM

I have a large seashell collection, which I keep scattered on beaches all over the world.

STEVEN WRIGHT

Beards

A short while after I began to wear a beard I was accosted by a Morality One lady in a state of righteous indignation. "That beard is disgusting," she said. "Why did you decide to grow it?"

"But, madam, I didn't," I replied. "I never decided to grow a beard. When I was twelve years old, God decided I should have a beard, and the next morning there it was on my face—but I took a razor and cut it off. The next morning God put it back, but I cut it off again. We went on like that day after day—with God putting a beard on my face every night and me cutting it off every morning. After thirty-eight

years of this, I simply decided to let God have his way."

ALLAN SHERMAN

Beauty

I'm tired of all this nonsense about beauty being only skin-deep. That's deep enough. What do you want—an adorable pancreas?

JEAN KERR

Mudpacks aren't good for the complexion. Did you ever see a pretty pig?

JACK E. LEONARD

American showgirl Carol Gale initiated a malpractice suit after a plastic surgeon accidentally injected her with Silly Putty instead of silicone. Carol claimed that overnight she went from a 34B to a 42 long."

DICK MARTIN

I don't have anything against face lifts, but I think a good rule of thumb is that it's time to stop when you look permanently frightened.

SUSAN FORFLEET

All God's children are not beautiful. Most of God's children are, in fact, barely presentable. The most common error made in matters of appearance is the belief that one should disdain the superficial and let the true beauty of one's soul shine through. If there are places on your body where this is a possibility, you are not attractive—you are leaking.

FRAN LEBOWITZ

Birth

The best thing is not to be born. But who is as lucky as that? To whom does it happen? Not to one among millions and millions of people.

BROTHER THEODORE

People are giving birth underwater now. They say it's less traumatic for the baby because it's in water. Then it comes out into water. I guess it probably would be less traumatic for the baby, but certainly more trau-

matic for the other people in the pool.

ELAYNE BOOSLER

She's screaming like crazy . . . You have this myth you're sharing the birth experience. Unless you're passing a bowling ball, I don't think so. Unless you're circumcising yourself with a chain saw, I don't think so. Unless you're opening an umbrella up your ass, I don't think so!

ROBIN WILLIAMS

I was born by C-section. This was the last time I had my mother's complete attention.

RICHARD JENI

I told my mother I was going to have natural childbirth. She said to me, "Linda, you've been taking drugs all your life. Why stop now?"

LINDA MALDONADO

In the natural childbirth classes my wife and I took, the birthing process was represented by a hand puppet being pushed through a sock. So, at the actual birth, I was shocked to see all this blood. The thing I had prepared myself for was a lot of lint.

STEVE SCROVAN

Telegram to Mary Sherwood after the birth of her child: "Dear Mary, we all knew you had it in you."

DOROTHY PARKER

"Delivery" is the wrong word to describe the childbearing process. Delivery is: "Here's your pizza. Takes thirty minutes or less." "Exorcism," I think, is more apt: "Please! Get the hell out of my body!"

JEFF STILSON

I want to have children, but my friends scare me. One of my friends told me she was in labor for thirty-six hours. I don't even want to do anything that feels good for thirty-six hours.

RITA RUDNER

In this day and age women can have kids for other women through surrogate motherhood. Is this the ultimate favor or what? I think I'm a good friend. I'll help you move. Okay. But whatever comes out of me after nine months, I'm keeping. I don't care if it's a shoe.

SUE KOLINSKY

Oh, what a tangled web we weave when first we practice to conceive.

DON HEROLD

Mother didn't make it to the hospital. I was born on the bus. Mother was furious when she had to open her pocketbook the second time.

JACK DOUGLAS

We delivered our child via natural childbirth, the procedure invented by a man named Lamaze—the Marquis de Lamaze, a disciple of Dr. Josef Mengele, who concluded that women could counteract the incredible pain of childbirth through breathing. I think we can all agree that breathing is a reasonable substitute for anesthesia. That's like asking a man to tolerate a vasectomy by hyperventilating.

Lamaze expects the husband —me—to be there, so that I can witness this festivity. I did not want to be there. This was remarkably *painful* for my wife. There was nothing my presence could really do to relieve her pain. In other words, I didn't see why *my* evening should be ruined too.

DENNIS WOLFBERG

They call us "coaches." The job is to remind your wife to breathe. Think about that for a second. You realize exactly how worthless I am in this thing? When was the last time *you* had to be reminded to breathe? It's like saying, "Digest!" . . . My baby, "Hesitation Klein," took twenty hours of labor to come out. They used a plunger at the end.

ROBERT KLEIN

Birth Control

Contraceptives should be used on all conceivable occasions.

SPIKE MILLIGAN

There's a new birth-control pill for women. You put it between your knees and keep it there.

BILL BARNER

They've got a new birth-control pill for men now. I think that's fair. It makes a lot more sense to take the bullets out of the gun than to wear a bulletproof vest.

GREG TRAVIS

I'm Catholic . . . My mother and I were unpacking and she found my diaphragm. I had to tell her it was a bathing cap for my cat.

LIZZ WINSTEAD

I practice birth control, which is being around my sister's children. You want to run right out and ovulate after you play with them for five minutes.

BRETT BUTLER

A guy goes into a drugstore on a Friday and says, "Give me a gross of those safes." He comes back Monday and says, "There were only 143 in that gross." The clerk says, "I'm sorry I spoiled your weekend, sir."

PEARL WILLIAMS

The new birth-control implants have some side effects: bloating, pimples, and mood swings

. . . Well, that'll certainly keep me from getting pregnant.

S. KELLEY

I was involved in an extremely good example of oral contraception two weeks ago. I asked a girl to go to bed with me and she said no.

WOODY ALLEN

B*lacks*

This fellow standing on the corner, a colored fellow (I always stick to race). And he's standing on the corner, and he looks up and he says, "Lord, why did you make me so dark?"

And the Lord says, "The reason I made you so dark is that when you're running through the jungle, the sun would not give you sunstroke."

He says, "Lord! Why did you make my hair so coarse?" He said, "Well, the reason I did that is so that when you're running through the jungle, your hair would not get caught in the brambles."

He said, "Lord, why did you make my legs so long?" He said, "The reason I made your legs long, my son, is so that when you're loping through the jungle in quest of the wild beast, you would run very fast and swiftly." He said, "My son, do you have any further questions?"

He said, "Yeah, Lord! What the hell am I doing here in Cleveland?"

GODFREY CAMBRIDGE

This fella, he joined the integrated church down in one of them foreign countries, Alabama or Mississippi or one of them foreign countries, and the time comes for him to be baptized, you know. So this minister ducked him down in the water, brought him up, and said, "Do you believe?"

He said, "Yessir, I believe."

Ducked him down again, held him a little longer, said, "Do you *believe?*"

He said, "Y-yes, I believe."

Ducked him down there again, held him a little longer, raised him up, and said, "*Do you believe?*"

He said, "Y-y-yessir, I believe. I believe you tryin' to drown me!"

MOMS MABLEY

Black folks have the coolest names—Arsenio, Oprah. When I was a kid, next to Mickey Mantle my favorite player was a guy named Cleon Jones of the Mets. You just know Cleon is gonna be a black guy. You know he's not gonna be my accountant, Cleon Goldberg. Or my dentist, Mookie Brody.

And when my wife was thinking up names for the baby, and she's got this yuppie book, *Jason and Jennifer,* I said why can't we be black and just make up a name? That's what black people do. You guys could be making love in the back seat of a Toyota. And name the kid Tercel.

BOBBY SLAYTON

Black names are always bizarre. Black names sound more like products you'd find in the drugstore. My name is Advil, this is my wife, Cloret. Tylenol, you wanna turn the TV down, it's givin' me a headache! And the twins, Murine and Visine . . .

DARYL SIVAD

Cold weather makes it very nice for race relations. Last month when it was 15 below zero in Chicago, I walked out of a nightclub. A drunk walked up to me and said, "Why don't you go back to Africa where you belong and take me with you!"

DICK GREGORY

You are a white. The Imperial Wizard. Now, if you don't think this is logic you can burn me on the fiery cross. This is the logic: You have the choice of spending fifteen years married to a woman, a black woman or a white woman. Fifteen years kissing and hugging and sleeping real close on hot nights. With a black, black woman or a white, white woman. The white woman is Kate Smith. And the black woman is Lena Horne. So you're not concerned with black or white anymore, are you? You are concerned with how cute or how pretty. Then let's really get basic and persecute ugly people!

LENNY BRUCE

I think we all can agree racial prejudice is stupid. It really is. Because if you spend time with someone from another race and really get to know them, you can find other reasons to hate them.

BERNADETTE LUCKETT

I said, "Why aren't there more black people on TV?" They said, "We got you on TV." I said, "I know it, but I get tired of watching basketball games." I heard one of them say, "I heard the Negroes are sweeping the country." I said, "Yes, it's one of the few jobs we can get."

JAMES WESLEY JACKSON

I was on the bus, and the bus was crowded, and I pushed and shoved. And I was standing beside a white fella, about six foot three, 250 pounds, broad shoulders. He looked down at me and said, "Are you a member of the NAACP?" And I said no. He said, "Do you belong to CORE?" I said no. He said, "Are you a follower of Martin Luther King?" I said no. He said, "Well, do you believe in Black Power?" I said I don't believe in none of that stuff. He said, "Then get off my damn foot!"

SLAPPY WHITE

It makes no damn difference, black or white. Turn off that light, sweetie, it comes down to a case of who washed.

NORMA MILLER

B lindness

If blind people wear sunglasses, why don't deaf people wear earmuffs?

SPANKY (STEVE McFARLIN)

Deprived of sight, unable to read, this is perhaps the greatest loss to the blind person. I'm blind, but I am able to read thanks to a wonderful new system known as broil. I'm sorry— I'll just feel that again . . .

PETER COOK

A blind man comes into a drugstore and starts knocking things off the shelf with his cane. The owner says, "Can I help you?" He says, "No, thanks, just looking."

GALLAGHER

Boating

The captain. He's a real son of the sea. He first became interested in ships when his mother approached him. "John, your father wants you to build a boat at once," she said. "Where is Father?" inquired John. "In the middle of the lake, drowning," was the reply. He told me he had the sea in the blood, and believe me, you can see where it gets in.

SPIKE MILLIGAN

Books

This is not a novel to be tossed aside lightly. It should be thrown with great force . . .

This must be a gift book. That is to say, a book which you wouldn't take on any other terms.

DOROTHY PARKER

I can't understand why a person will take a year to write a novel when he can easily buy one for a few dollars.

FRED ALLEN

I know of no sentence that can induce such immediate and brazen lying as the one that begins: "Have you read . . ."

WILSON MIZNER

I just got out of the hospital. I was in a speed-reading accident. I hit a bookmark.

STEVEN WRIGHT

Why pay a dollar for a bookmark? Use the dollar *as* a bookmark.

FRED STOLLER

I went to a bookstore and I asked the woman behind the counter where the self-help section was. She said, "If I told you, that would defeat the whole purpose."

BRIAN KILEY

I can read a book twice as fast as anybody else. First I read the beginning, and then I read the ending, and then I start in the middle and read toward whichever end I like best.

GRACIE ALLEN

Bores and Dullards

Linda is a real master at making a long story short . . . she interrupts me.

DAVE BERG

If your monthly phone bill includes over seventy-five dollars' worth of calls to *Entertainment Tonight* 900-number opinion polls, get a life . . . If you always make a point to sit up front on a bus so you can "chat" with the driver . . . get a life! If you still own and operate a CB radio and you are not a licensed interstate truck driver . . . get a life! If you are on a first-name basis with all of the security guards at your local shopping mall . . . *Get a life!*

CHARLIE KADAU

I believe in living life one doldrum at a time.

TOM WILSON ("Ziggy")

He's a punishment that's waiting for a suitable crime.

ED GARDNER

Boston

Then here's to the city of Boston,
The town of the cries and the groans,
Where the Cabots can't see the Kobotschniks
And the Lowells won't speak to the Cohns.

FRANKLIN P. ADAMS

Bullfighting

There is surely nothing more beautiful in this world than the sight of a lone man facing single-handedly half a ton of angry pot roast.

TOM LEHRER

A bull is heavy, violent, abusive, and aggressive, with four legs and great sharp teeth—whereas a bullfighter is only a small greasy Spaniard.

ERIC IDLE

Did you ever attend a Polish bullfight? The arena becomes

very solemn. The local clergy appears and he consecrates the animal. And everyone stands up and shouts, "Holy cow!" Wanna hear something worse? Then the people complain, because no matter where you put them, they're sitting behind a Pole!

PETE BARBUTTI

Bus

A woman on the Fifth Avenue bus was being a nuisance. Every five minutes she'd pester the driver, "Are we on Riverside Drive yet?" She kept asking, getting on his nerves, but he kept his temper. When he didn't respond after she asked yet again, she cried, "How will I know when we come to Riverside Drive?" He said, "By the big smile on my face, lady, by the big smile on my face."

FRANK SULLIVAN

Look at all the buses now that want exact change, *exact* change. I figure if I give them

exact change, they should take me *exactly* where I want to go.

GEORGE WALLACE

During the Depression era my mother found out how to save money. She used to cheat bus drivers. She got on a bus with a transfer a day old. And the driver said, "Lady, this is from yesterday." And she said, "You see how long I've been waiting for the bus?"

BOB MELVIN

California

Living in California adds ten years to a man's life. And those extra ten years I'd like to spend in New York.

HARRY RUBY

Everybody in Los Angeles is in therapy. It's a good thing they don't have parking spaces for the emotionally handicapped. There'd be no place to park.

JACKSON PERDUE

So you call this California, the land of golden sunshine, do you? Well, let me tell you something. Every day of every year the sun shines on New York three hours before it shines on you, so all California gets is New York's secondhand sunshine. Think that one over.

JAMES THORNTON

Los Angeles is a great place. Where else can you smell the air and see it coming at you at the same time? You want to see blue water you have to look in the toilet bowl.

JACKIE GAYLE

There are two million interesting people in New York and only seventy-eight in Los Angeles.

NEIL SIMON

What with the Los Angeles earthquake, massive forest fires, beach erosion, freeway shootings, and ozone-layer de-pletion that's giving every Malibu volleyball player whole-body melanoma, it looks like God has finally gotten serious about destroying California. Sources close to the Lord say the so-called yuppie shows of the new TV season were the last straw.

P. J. O'ROURKE

California is a fine place to live in—if you happen to be an orange.

FRED ALLEN

Capital Punishment

Just as the prisoner was being strapped into the electric chair, the priest said, "Son, is there anything I can do for you?" The prisoner said, "Yeah, when they pull the switch, hold my hand."

DICK GREGORY

I believe in the death penalty for terrorists. Not only that, I believe in execution with humiliation. As this guy is frying in the electric chair, we crack two eggs on top of his head. A future deterrent for the crime, and food for thought.

PETER FOGEL

Priests will walk you to the gas chamber—while telling you to read the Bible, which says, "Thou shalt not kill." That's a little weird.

MURRAY ROMAN

Liberals think you can reform an ax murderer. They don't want to kill anything. They want to change the Listerine labels: *Rehabilitate* the germs that can cause bad breath."

MARC PRICE

There's a lot of morons out there and this gotta be stopped. If you look at the death penalty—we've got to start thinning out the herd and murder might be the only way to do it.

This guy in Texas is going to get the electric chair. He's borderline psycho, borderline retarded. He's not like either one. He's like a singer/actress—can't do either one really well but dabbles in both fields. All these guilty liberals are saying, "You can't kill crazy people, they're crazy. They don't know what they did."

Well, if they don't know what they did, then they don't know you're gonna kill 'em! Put 'em in the electric chair and tell 'em it's a ride.

BOBBY SLAYTON

Cars

Some people have a lot of vanity. They say, "I only wear glasses when I drive." If you only need glasses when you drive, then drive around with a prescription windshield!

BRIAN REGAN

I bought myself a new car and the first thing I done was grease it all over—so the finance company can't get a hold of it.

ROD BRASFIELD

The fancier a car is named, the more gas it is burning.

FRANK JACOBS

Anybody abuse rental cars? If I'm really bored I'll take one to Earl Scheib and have it painted

43

for $29.95. This really messes up their paperwork for months and months. The thing that bothers me is when you have to return one with a full tank of gas. It makes everybody mad. They say bring it back full. You know what I do now? I just top it off with a garden hose.

WIL SHRINER

My license plate says PMS. Nobody cuts me off.

WENDY LIEBMAN

Anybody in the audience with a New York license plate BL 75836745895947362847456578392610284 will you kindly move it. Your license plate is blocking traffic.

BILL DANA

A woman was out driving with her husband. She was speeding along at about fifty. Suddenly a motorcycle cop appeared alongside and told her to pull over. The cop looked at her. "Hmmm!" he said, "I'm going to put you down for fifty-five." She turned to her husband. "See! I told you this hat makes me look old."

JOE LAURIE, JR.

Some people say a front-engine car handles best. Some people say a rear-engine car handles best. I say a rented car handles best.

P. J. O'ROURKE

I like doing things to help people. People don't wear their seat belts anymore. I figure, I'll make fuzzy clothes and make seats out of Velcro.

ANDY ANDREWS

Americans are broad-minded people. They'll accept the fact that a person can be an alcoholic, a dope fiend, a wife beater, and even a newspaperman, but if a man doesn't drive there's something wrong with him.

ART BUCHWALD

Since 1952 I wanted to drive a Caddy. That's what I drive: a '52 Caddy.

BOB MELVIN

What does it take to get a cabdriver's license? I think all you need is a face. This seems to be their big qualification. And a name with eight consonants in a row. Have you ever checked out some of the names on the license? The *o* with the line through it? What planet is *that* from? You need a chart of the elements just to report the guy: "Yes, Officer, his name was Amal—and then the symbol for boron!"

JERRY SEINFELD

I don't like the idea that people can call you in your car. I think there's news you shouldn't get at sixty miles per hour. "Pregnant? Whooaaaah!" But if we're gonna have car telephones, I think we definitely should have car telephone answering machines: "Tom's at home right now. But as soon as he goes out, he'll get back to you."

TOM PARKS

A hundred years ago we were much smarter; then you lived until you died and not until you were just run over.

WILL ROGERS

I passed a car dealership. I looked in the window and I saw the most beautiful cars. And a fellow came out and said, "Come on in, they're bigger than ever and they last a lifetime!" He was talking about the payments.

CORBETT MONICA

Television sets are becoming very popular in automobiles these days. My uncle has a television set in his automobile, but it led into a little trouble. You see he was sitting in the car watching television while his wife was driving on the thruway at sixty miles per hour. And then the commercial came on, and he stepped out to go to the bathroom.

JACKIE CLARK

I had a brand-new Mercury. I loaned it to my brother last week. I said, "Treat it as if it was your own." He sold it.

JIMMY EDMONDSON

(PROFESSOR BACKWARDS)

And take the new Buskirk cars. The ad says they're now rolling off the assembly line. If they could keep them on the assembly line they'd have a better car.

HENRY MORGAN

At the University of Illinois they think they've developed a new source of fuel for energy.

They think they can make fuel from horse manure. I ain't lyin'. I read it in the paper today. Now, I don't know if your car will be able to get thirty miles to the gallon, but it's sure gonna put a stop to siphoning.

BILLY HOLLIDAY

I see an article in the paper that says 25 percent of all men propose to their wives in an automobile. That's like I say—more accidents happen in a car than any other way.

THE DUKE OF PADUCAH

(WHITEY FORD)

Some guy came running in the other night and said, "Somebody stole my car!" I said, "Did you see him?" He said, "No, but I got his license plate."

BILL BARNER

Never lend your car to anyone to whom you have given birth.

ERMA BOMBECK

Cats

I don't like cats. I prefer dogs, because dogs don't care. If a dog can do it, you could watch. You can't say that about cats. You only get to *hear* cats! Cats are like Baptists. You know they raise hell, you just can't catch 'em at it!

JIM STAFFORD

I found out why cats drink out of the toilet. My mother told me it's because it's cold in there. And I'm like: *How* did my mother know *that?"*

WENDY LIEBMAN

Garfield's Law: Cats instinctively know the precise moment their owners will awaken . . . then they awaken them ten minutes sooner.

JIM DAVIS

I'm used to dogs. When you leave them in the morning, they stick their nose in the door crack and stand there like a portrait until you turn the key eight hours later. A cat would never put up with that kind of rejection. When you returned, she'd stalk you until you dozed off and then suck the air out of your body.

ERMA BOMBECK

It is said that cats are untrainable. That is not totally accurate. Appearances to the contrary, cats do pay attention to the instructions they receive. They listen closely to what you have to say and sometimes even wait for you to finish your sentence. They understand plain English as well as anybody. How else would it be possible for them to so uncannily do just the opposite?

STEPHEN BAKER

A lady lost her cat, and took the cat in a little casket up to a big church and said, "I want you to bury my cat." And they run her off. She went to another church, and they run her off. She took the cat to a Baptist church on the edge of town, and told the preacher she couldn't find nobody to hold a service for her dead cat. And the man talked to her bad. "How dare you think that we bury cats?" She said, "Well,

I'm frustrated and I'm prepared to give two thousand dollars to whoever gives a service for my cat." And the preacher said, "Lady, why didn't you tell me your cat was a Baptist?"

JERRY CLOWER

The clever cat eats cheese and breathes down rat holes with baited breath.

W. C. FIELDS

Cats are intended to teach us that not everything in nature has a purpose.

GARRISON KEILLOR

We have two cats. They're my wife's cats, Mischa and Alex. You can tell a woman names a cat like this. Women always have sensitive names: Muffy, Fluffy, Buffy. Guys name cats things like Tuna Breath, Fur Face, Meow Head. They're nice cats. They've been neutered and they've been declawed. So they're like pillows that eat.

LARRY REEB

Cats sit in laps because it's warm there. They don't care if it's you or the radiator, so it certainly was a compliment when the owner said the cat liked me. Who had this cat met that it was comparing me to? The maid? Another cat? Here's an animal which can't read, that hasn't been out of the house in God knows when, lives on free milk and garbage, and this bum has an opinion? Two years old, doesn't have a cent. No clothes. Owns one rotten rubber ball. For big entertainment it scratches on the upholstery. And this green-eyed impoverished snob likes me? Thanks a group.

HENRY MORGAN

I saw a commercial the other day for cat food. It said, "All natural food for your cat." All natural food. But cat food is made out of horsemeat. That's how it works in nature—the cat right above the horse on the food chain . . . Matter of fact, every time my kitty feels a little cooped up in his environment I take him down to the racetrack, let him stalk some prey.

NORM McDONALD

A famous art collector is walking through Greenwich Village when he notices a mangy old cat lapping milk from a saucer in front of a store. And the collector does a double take when he sees the saucer. He knows it's very old and very valuable. So he saunters casually into the store and offers to buy the cat for two dollars.

But the store owner says to him, "I'm sorry, but the cat isn't for sale."

And the collector says, "Please. I need a hungry old tomcat around the house to catch mice. I'll give you ten dollars for him."

And the owner says, "Sold," and takes the ten dollars. Then the collector says, "Listen, I was wondering if, for the ten dollars, you might include that old saucer. The cat seems to be used to it. It'll save me a dish."

And the owner says, "Sorry, buddy. That's my lucky saucer. So far this week, I've sold sixty-eight cats!"

SOUPY SALES

I gave my cat a bath the other day . . . they love it. He sat there, he enjoyed it, it was fun for me. The fur would stick to my tongue, but other than that . . .

STEVE MARTIN

Celibacy

The last woman I was in was the Statue of Liberty.

WOODY ALLEN

Just remember, so long as you don't hurt anybody, or talk badly about them, or take advantage of them sexually, you'll always be disappointingly dull.

ERIC IDLE

Cheapness

He read in the paper that it takes ten dollars a year to support a kid in India. So he sent his kid there.

RED BUTTONS

A Scot was down to his last dollar. He came to America and filed to find work. There was none for him. Discouraged, he went to the harbor and looked out to sea, dreaming of the money he'd spent to come to America. As he sat on the dock, he saw a diver come up, unscrewing the headpiece of his deep-sea helmet and taking a deep breath. The Scot looked at him and said, "Well, well, if I had known that, I would've walked over myself!"

DANNY KAYE

My father originated the limbo dance—trying to get into a pay toilet.

SLAPPY WHITE

He had an awful dizzy spell. He dropped a dime in a revolving door and it took him five minutes to find it.

BOB HOPE

A chronic borrower begged an old friend to lend him a hundred dollars. "I'll pay it back the minute I return from Chicago," he promised. "Exactly what day are you returning?" the friend asked. The man shrugged. "Who's going?"

MYRON COHEN

You heard about the man who quit playing golf, then took it up again fourteen years later? He found his ball.

BOB KALIBAN

Chess

What I don't like about chess is the way you have to sit and pretend to think.

GARDNER REA

Children

I don't have any kids. Well . . . at least none that I *know* about. I'd like to have kids one day, though. I want to be called Mommy by someone other than Spanish guys in the street.

CAROL LEIFER

There's no such thing as a tough child—if you parboil them first for seven hours, they always come out tender.

W. C. FIELDS

Growing up, I was a little guy. My father enrolled me in a local martial arts academy. So once a week I got beat up in a more formal setting.

JONATHAN KATZ

If your parents didn't have any children, there's a good chance that you won't have any.

CLARENCE DAY

What are kids, really, but little stupid people who live in your house and don't pay rent?

RICK REYNOLDS

I was overjoyed when the family could join me in New York for a couple of months in the summer, and I wanted to make sure the children didn't get sore at me for jerking them out of Oklahoma right during vacation time—which, in spite of the heat, is naturally the best time of the year to them. So I told my wife, "Even if I'm at work, keep the kids amused."

That accounts for my wife taking them to New York's famous Natural History Museum, with all its stuffed animal exhibits—mounted zebras, lions, hippopotamuses, elephants, mountain goats, and so on.

That night I asked Linda what she had seen. When she proved hesitant, I said, "Come on, you don't have to make it a long story. Just name it. What did you see?"

Her eyes twinkled. "I saw a dead circus."

CAL TINNEY

When my mom got really mad, she would say, "Your butt is my meat." Not a particularly attractive phrase. And I always wondered, "Now, what wine goes with that?"

PAULA POUNDSTONE

A tornado touched down, uprooting a large tree in the front yard and demolishing the house across the street. Dad went to the door, opened it, surveyed the damage, muttered "Darn kids!" and closed the door.

TIM CONWAY

Kids—they're not easy, but there has to be some penalty for sex.

BILL MAHER

Can you remember when you didn't want to sleep? Isn't it inconceivable? I guess the definition of adulthood is that you want to sleep . . .

Adults are always asking little kids what they want to be when they grow up—'cause they're lookin' for ideas.

PAULA POUNDSTONE

In order not to influence a child, one must be careful not to be that child's parent or grandparent.

DON MARQUIS

In America, there are two classes of travel: first class and with children.

ROBERT BENCHLEY

Alligators have the right idea. They eat their young.

EVE ARDEN (in Mildred Pierce)

Any kid will run any errand for you, if you ask at bedtime.

RED SKELTON

As a kid, I used to have a lemonade stand. The sign said, "All you can drink for a dime." So some kid would come up, plunk down the dime, drink a glass, and then say, "Refill it."

I'd say, "That'll be another dime." "How come? Your sign says—" "Well, you had a glass, didn't you?" "Yeah." "And that's all you can drink for a dime."

FLIP WILSON

During this past Christmas while I was on a shopping spree in a department store I heard a little five-year-old talking to his mother on the down escalator. He said, "Mommy, what do they do when the basement gets full of steps?"

HAL LINDEN

A man gets on a train with his little boy, and gives the conductor only one ticket. "How old's your kid?" the conductor says, and the father says "He's four years old." "He looks at least twelve to me," says the conductor. And the father says, "Can I help it if he worries?"

ROBERT BENCHLEY

Little kids are tough. I saw a little kid, I gave him an orange. His mother said, "What do you say to the man?" The kid looked at me and said, "Peel it."

BILL BARNER

A door is something you're on the wrong side of when you're too short to reach the knob. When you are tall enough to reach the knob, a door is something you have left open if it's supposed to be closed, or closed if it's supposed to be open. You can't win. Whichever you do, you have done it wrong. So close all open doors and open all closed doors. You will still be wrong but you will be busy.

ROBERT PAUL SMITH

Pro: Children ask better questions than do adults. "May I have a cookie?" "Why is the sky blue?" and "What does a cow say?" are far more likely to elicit a cheerful response than "Where's your manuscript?" "Why haven't you called?" and "Who's your lawyer?"

Con: Even when freshly washed and relieved of all obvious confections, children tend to be sticky. One can only assume that this has something to do with not smoking enough.

FRAN LEBOWITZ

Never raise your hands to your kids. It leaves your groin unprotected.

RED BUTTONS

A woman came to ask the doctor if a woman should have children after 35. I said 35 children is enough for any woman!

GRACIE ALLEN

The other day my wife brought home a toy for our baby boy. It was a small wooden mailbox with three openings in it: a square one, a round one, and a triangular one. The set was completed by three wooden objects, each of which could fit only into its proper hole. The combination is described as "educational," for obvious reasons. It's brand name is Playskool.

A few days earlier I had bought the baby another educational toy: a tiny functional piano, the brand name of which is Famus.

Someday when my son is going to *skool* and has become *famus* for his daring and strangely phonetic approach to spelling, he will be thankful that we gave him only educational toys.

STEVE ALLEN

Once upon a time, a four-year-old boy was visiting his uncle and aunt. He was a very outspoken little boy and ofttimes had to be censured to say the right thing at the right time. One day at lunch, when his auntie had company, the little boy said, "Auntie, I want to tinkle." Auntie took the little boy aside and said, "Never say that, Sonny. If you want to tinkle, say, 'I want to whisper.'" And the incident was forgotten.

That night, when Uncle and Auntie were soundly sleeping, the little boy climbed into bed with them. He tugged at his uncle's shoulder and said, "Uncle, I want to whisper." And Uncle said, "All right, Sonny, don't wake Auntie up. Whisper in my ear." The little boy was sent back to his parents the next day.

GEORGE JESSEL

Translations from the Child
"I don't know why. He just hit me."
He hit his brother.
"I didn't hit him. I just sort of pushed him."
He hit his brother.
"I didn't do anything."
He hit his brother.
"Mo-m-m-my!"
His brother hit him.
ROBERT PAUL SMITH

Children are stupid. That's why they're in school. I'd lecture for an hour about percentages and interest rates and at the end I'd ask one simple question, "You put ten grand in a bank for one year at $5\frac{1}{2}$ percent and what do you get?" Some kid would always yell out, "A toaster."
JEFFREY JENA

God said be fruitful and multiply. It was a punishment! Each time you multiply you get a fruit. With brain damage!
BILL COSBY

Christmas

The price of Christmas toys is outrageous—a hundred dollars, two hundred dollars for video games for the youngsters. I remember a Christmas years ago when my son was a kid. I bought him a tank. It was about a hundred dollars, a lot of money in those days. It was the kind of tank you could actually get inside and ride in.

He played in the box it came in.

It taught me a very valuable lesson. Next year he got a box. And I got a hundred dollars' worth of scotch.
JOHNNY CARSON

At Christmastime, even Santa Claus wouldn't give you love or hope unless you met his impossible conditions: "Have you been a good boy all year?" Damn him! Damn Santa Claus —has anybody ever been a good boy all year? . . . "He's making a list, and checking it twice, He's gonna find out who's naughty or nice." Who the hell did he think he was? J. Edgar Hoover?

ALLAN SHERMAN

My boss at Christmas was a lot of fun: "I want you to look in your pay envelopes and you'll know that I keep the Christmas spirit around here. Because in each and every pay envelope you'll find . . . snow."

DAVE KETCHUM

The Supreme Court has ruled they cannot have a Nativity scene in Washington, D.C. This wasn't for any religious reasons. They couldn't find three wise men and a virgin.

JAY LENO

I never believed in Santa Claus because I knew no white man would be coming into my neighborhood after dark.

DICK GREGORY

From up on the rooftops there arose such a clatter,
I ran from my bed to see what was the matter.
I ran to the window and threw up.

TOM SMOTHERS

Let me see if I've got this Santa business straight. You say he wears a beard which hides his face, has no discernible source of income, and flies to cities all over the world under cover of darkness? You sure this guy isn't laundering illegal drug money?

TOM ARMSTRONG ("Marvin")

I already have a hundred gifts to distribute at Christmas— my Christmas seals have arrived . . . I wanted our street to have the prettiest Christmas decorations in the neighborhood, so I strung colored balls from house to house all the way down the block. And I did all the electric wiring myself. If you'd like further information, just drive down Moorpark Street in North Hollywood. We're the third pile of ashes from the corner.

BOB HOPE

The stockings were hung by the chimney with care—and oh what a terrible smell filled the air.

JETHRO BURNS

Santa Claus has the right idea. Visit people once a year.

VICTOR BORGE

Santa Claus? You have to look very carefully at a man like this. He comes but once a year? Down the chimney? And in *my* sock?

PROFESSOR IRWIN COREY

I must say, when the doorman where I live puts up the Christmas tree in the lobby, he has the same friendly smile for those who have remembered him at Christmas and those who have not. Except that when he trims the tree, if you have not, there you are on the tree, hanging in effigy.

SELMA DIAMOND

Probably the worst thing about being Jewish during Christmastime is shopping in stores, because the lines are so long. They should have a Jewish express line: "Look, I'm a Jew, it's not a gift. It's just paper towels!"

SUE KOLINSKY

Clichés

I can tell I'm getting older. I'm starting to use "old people" clichés. The other day I actually told someone I slept like a baby. Like I woke up hungry every two hours with a mess in my pants.

JACK GALLAGHER

Did you ever hear someone say this: "It was more fun than a barrel of monkeys"? Did you ever smell a barrel of monkeys?

STEVE BLUESTEIN

My father said, "Bring along your best girl." This is something you say to a pimp!

BILL MAHER

It's a rare person who wants to hear what he doesn't want to hear.

DICK CAVETT

When people sit in front of you at a movie theater, never say, "Sit down in front." People don't bend that way.

JETHRO BURNS

English is a language in which grown people see nothing peculiar about telling a child, "Sit down and sit up."

RUSSELL BAKER

Nothing in life is "fun for the whole family."

JERRY SEINFELD

What's this claim about things being "untouched by human hands"? What's wrong with human hands? Mention a better kind of hand.

HENRY MORGAN

I don't understand some phrases. Take "I look forward to seeing you." Why don't you listen forward to looking me? One night a woman came to me after a concert and said, "I haven't laughed so much since my husband died." My own English isn't too good. Somebody remarked to me, "Spring in the air, Mr. Borge." And I jumped eight feet.

VICTOR BORGE

I lost my job. No, I didn't really *lose* my job. I know where my job is, still. It's just when I go there, there's this new guy doing it . . . I lost my girl. No, I didn't really *lose* my girl. I know where my girl is, still. It's just when I go there, there's this new guy doing it.

BOB GOLDTHWAIT

Where do clichés come from? My grandfather says, "You just tell a couple of jokes and you're riding the gravy train?"

First of all, it's hard to write jokes. Second of all, what *is* a gravy train? I didn't know they were actually hauling gravy by rail. People gather around big mounds of mashed potatoes waiting for the 5:15 gravy train to show up?

RICH HALL

College

Does college pay? Of course. If you're a halfback or a basketball player they pay you very well. College athletes are always saying to me, "When should I turn pro?" And I say not until you've earned all you can in college.

WILL ROGERS

I majored in nursing. I had to drop it. I ran out of milk.

JUDY TENUTA

I was thrown out of NYU. On my metaphysics final I looked within the soul of the boy sitting next to me.

WOODY ALLEN

A father, Princeton alumnus, was quite a grouch. His son had finished his first term and said that his grades were next to the top of his class. "*Next* to the top?" the father exclaimed. "What do you mean? I'm not sending you to college to be NEXT! Why aren't *you* the top?"

The son was crestfallen. He studied harder, and the next semester he announced to his father that he was indeed the top of his class. The father looked at him for a moment and shrugged. "At the head of your class, eh? Well, that's a fine commentary on Princeton University!"

ALAN YOUNG

Five-Minute University teaches you in five minutes what the average college student re-members five years after he or she's out of school . . .

Say, if you want to take Spanish, what I teach you is "*Cómo está usted.*" That means "How are you." And the response is "*Muy bien.*" That means "Very well." And believe me, if you took two years of college Spanish, five years after you're out of school, "*Cómo está usted*" and "*Muy bien*" is about all you're gonna remember.

So in my school that's all you learn . . . Economics? "Supply and demand." That's it . . .

FATHER GUIDO SARDUCCI
(DON NOVELLO)

If you've never met a student from the University of Chicago, I'll describe him to you. If you give him a glass of water, he says, "This is a glass of water. But *is* it a glass of water? And if it *is* a glass of water, *why* is it a glass of water?" And eventually he dies of thirst.

SHELLEY BERMAN

I took a course at Cal once called Statistical Analysis. And there was a guy in the course who used to make up all his computations and he never used Sigma. He used his own initials. 'Cause he was the standard deviation.

MORT SAHL

My whole freshman year I wore brown and white shoes. Actually they were impractical, because the white one kept getting dirty.

DICK CAVETT

I have a daughter who goes to SMU. She could've gone to UCLA here in California, but it's one more letter she'd have to remember.

SHECKY GREENE

I went to college—majored in philosophy. My father said, "Why don't you minor in communications so you can wonder out loud?" So I did. I got out of school, landed a job as a morning DJ on an all-philosophy radio station: WYMI. "Good morning, it's 8:05 on YMI. For those of you just waking up— what's the point, really?"

MIKE DUGAN

Some students were watching the chemistry professor give a demonstration of the properties of various acids.

"Now," said the professor, "I'm going to drop this silver dollar in a glass of acid. Will it dissolve?"

"No, sir," answered one of the students.

"No?" repeated the prof. "Then perhaps you can explain to the class why it won't dissolve."

"Because," the student said, "if the silver dollar would dissolve, you wouldn't drop it in."

FANNY BRICE

College is the best time of your life. When else are your parents going to spend several thousand dollars a year just for you to go to a strange town and get drunk every night?

DAVID WOOD

Committee

A conference is a gathering of important people who singly can do nothing, but together can decide that nothing can be done.

FRED ALLEN

A committee is a small group of the unqualified appointed by the unthinking to undertake the utterly unnecessary.

FIBBER McGEE (JIM JORDAN)

Cooking

I don't know about microwave ovens. Food should not get hotter as you're eating it. It can't be good for you . . . Maybe it's just mine. I've got a cheap microwave. It doesn't have a door. It just cooks whatever's around, and when I get dizzy, I know lunch is ready.

BILLIAM CORONEL

I can't cook. I use a smoke alarm as a timer.

CAROL SISKIND

Bachelor cooking is a matter of attitude. If you think of it as setting fire to things and making a mess, it's fun. It's not so much fun if you think of it as dinner . . . Nomenclature is an important part of bachelor cooking. If you call it "Italian cheese toast," it's not disgusting to have warmed-over pizza for breakfast.

P. J. O'ROURKE

I thought my mother was a bad cook, but at least her gravy used to move about.

TONY HANCOCK

Every time I go near the stove, the dog howls . . . In our house, we have Alka-Seltzer on tap. If you cook like I do, the best thing I can tell you is not to be sensitive. Here are some of the insults I've had to over-look: When Fang passes my gravy, he says, "One lump or two?" Once I sent a treat to the Boy Scouts and the leader awarded a merit badge to any-one who could eat it. When I entered a cake at the county fair, it was the only one awarded a black ribbon . . . But now I can boil water— when I don't forget and use the colander.

PHYLLIS DILLER

Ever since Eve started it all by offering Adam the apple, woman's punishment has been to have to supply a man with food and then suffer the consequences when it disagrees with him.

HELEN ROWLAND

My husband says I feed him like he's a god; every meal is a burnt offering.

RHONDA HANSOME

My wife's not the worst cook in the world, but she keeps on burning the coffee. You would too if you kept pouring it through the toaster all the time.

JACK E. LEONARD

I idolized my mother. I didn't realize she was a lousy cook until I went into the Army.

JACKIE GAYLE

She's the only girl in the world who can burn a stove . . . Eating her cooking is like playing Russian roulette. I never know which meal is going to kill me.

HARVEY STONE

I got brown sandwiches and green sandwiches. It's either very new cheese or very old meat.

NEIL SIMON *(The Odd Couple)*

Cosmopolitan

I was reading *Cosmopolitan* and there was a woman on the cover and I thought maybe I should change my image. Maybe I should be more like that woman on the cover. How she's posed with the blouse open to the navel, the skirt slit up the side. And underneath, the caption: "How to Avoid Sexual Harassment."

MAUREEN MURPHY

I read in *Cosmo* that women like to have whipped cream sprayed over their breasts. Unfortunately, my girlfriend has silicone implants. So I use nondairy topping.

JEFF SHAW

Crime and Crooks

Ludlow Bean was arrested the other day for stealing a woman's change purse. He told the judge that he hadn't been feeling well, and he thought the change would do him good.

CHARLEY WEAVER (CLIFF ARQUETTE)

New Orleans is the only city in the world you go in to buy a pair of nylon stockings they want to know your head size.

BILLY HOLLIDAY

You think New York is bad? You ought to go to Detroit. You can go ten blocks and never leave the scene of the crime.

RED SKELTON

A cement mixer collided with a prison van on the Kingston Bypass. Motorists are asked to be on the lookout for sixteen hardened criminals.

RONNIE CORBETT

A man was about to go on trial for murder and he didn't feel that his chances for acquittal were very good, so he decided to get to one of the jurors. After sizing them up, he decided to bribe one little guy who didn't look any too bright. And he was successful. This little dope would take a bribe. The dope said to the man, "What do you want me to do?"

The man said, "I want you to oppose the death penalty."

The dope said, "How do I do that?"

"You just hold out for a verdict of manslaughter."

"Okay."

After the trial, the jury was charged and they retired. They were out deliberating for about four days. Meanwhile the man was on tenterhooks. Finally, they returned with a verdict. And the verdict was manslaughter.

The man was delighted with the verdict and as soon as he could he met the dope to pay him off. He said, "I'm tremendously obliged to you. Did you have a hard time holding out for a verdict of manslaughter?"

"Yeah. The other eleven guys wanted to acquit you!"

ROGER BOWER

I have six locks on my door, all in a row, and when I go out I only lock every other one.

'Cause I figure no matter how long somebody stands there, picks the locks, they're always locking three.

ELAYNE BOOSLER

I was walking through the park. I had a very bad asthmatic attack. These three asthmatics attacked me. I know . . . I should've heard them all hiding.

EMO PHILIPS

A murderer is only an extroverted suicide.

GRAHAM CHAPMAN

I don't buy temporary insanity as a murder defense. 'Cause people kill people. That's an animal instinct. I think breaking into someone's home and ironing all their clothes is temporary insanity.

SUE KOLINSKY

Critics

Has anybody ever seen a drama critic in the daytime? Of course not! They come out after dark, up to no good.

P. G. WODEHOUSE

Cynicism

No matter how cynical you get, it's impossible to keep up.

LILY TOMLIN

In this best of all possible worlds, everything is in a hell of a mess.

BROTHER THEODORE

If penicillin is such a wonder drug, how come it can't cure bread mold?

RON SMITH

There is always a comforting thought in time of trouble when it is not our trouble.

DON MARQUIS

I was going to buy a copy of *The Power of Positive Thinking*, and then I thought: What the hell good would that do?

RONNIE SHAKES

How many of those dead animals you see on the highway are suicides?

DENNIS MILLER

As long as the world is turning and spinning we're gonna be dizzy and we're gonna make mistakes.

MEL BROOKS

Some people think a horseshoe's gonna bring 'em lotsa luck.
A horseshoe is a lucky sign of course.
For every set of horseshoes human beings use for luck
Somewhere in this world's a barefoot horse.

ALLAN SHERMAN

Go to bed. What you're staying up for isn't worth it.

ANDY ROONEY

If this is to be the winter of our discontent, then I expect I'll need a new coat of some kind.

H. MARTIN

I've been looking forward to this evening about as much as I'd look forward to having my prostate examined by the Incredible Hulk.

JAN MURRAY

Do you feel that excitement of being a woman in the '90s? Maybe it's just static cling.

RHONDA HANSOME

We should live and learn, but by the time we've learned, it's too late to live.

CAROLYN WELLS

Deteriorata: Go placidly amid the noise and waste and remember what comfort there may be in owning a piece thereof. Avoid quiet and passive persons unless you are in need of sleep. Rotate your tires. Speak glowingly of those greater than yourself and heed well their advice, even though they be turkeys; know what to kiss and when. Consider that two wrongs never make a right but that three do. Wherever possible, put people on hold. Be comforted that in the face of all aridity and disillusionment and despite the changing fortunes of time, there is always a big future in computer maintenance . . . Be assured that a walk through the ocean of most souls would scarcely get your feet wet. Fall not in love therefore; it will stick to your face . . . Reflect that whatever misfortune may be your lot, it could only be worse in Milwaukee. You are a fluke of the universe; you have no right to be here, and whether you can hear it or not, the universe is laughing behind your back. Therefore make peace with your God whatever you conceive him to be—Hairy Thunderer or Cosmic Muffin. With all its hopes, dreams, promises, and urban renewal, the world continues to deteriorate. Give up.

TONY HENDRA

Men have a much better time of it than women; for one thing, they marry later; for another thing, they die earlier.

H. L. MENCKEN

Progress is what people who are planning to do something really terrible almost always justify themselves on the grounds of.

RUSSELL BAKER

There were four million people in the Colonies and we had Jefferson and Paine and Franklin. And now we have 240 million and we have Bush and Quayle. What can you draw from this? Darwin was wrong!

MORT SAHL

All modern men are descended from a wormlike creature, but it shows more on some people.

WILL CUPPY

The Plain People are worth dying for until you bunch them and give them the cold Once-Over, and then they impress the impartial Observer as being slightly Bovine, with a large Percentage of Vegetable Tissue.

GEORGE ADE

Down with everything that's up.

MALCOLM MUGGERIDGE

It is a sin to believe evil of others, but it is seldom a mistake.

H. L. MENCKEN

Dating

Why are women wearing perfumes that smell like flowers? Men don't like flowers. I've been wearing a great scent. It's called New Car Interior.

RITA RUDNER

I met this guy who said he loved children, then I found out he was on parole for it.

MONICA PIPER

Whenever I want a really nice meal, I start dating again.

SUSAN HEALY

I was out on a date recently and the guy took me horseback riding. That was kind of fun, until we ran out of quarters.

SUSIE LOUCKS

I can remember her just as if it were yesterday . . . Our first meeting. It was in the park. She coyly dropped her handkerchief. And as I picked it up, she was embarrassed. Her nose was still in it.

JACKIE GLEASON

He came up to my table, he goes, "Hey, darling, you're okay in my book." Yeah. Apparently not a best-seller. He wouldn't let up either. He took my glasses off and he said, "Without your glasses, why, you're beautiful." I said, "Without my glasses, you're not half bad either."

KIT HOLLERBACH

My friend Sappo was real depressed. He said, "I can't get any girls." I said, "Don't worry, listen, tomorrow we're going swimming. What you do is you put a big potato in your bathing suit. That way you'll attract girls." Come the end of the day he came up to me and said, "No girls came up to talk to me. I did what you said, I put the potato in my bathing suit." I said, "Sappo, next time put it in the front!"

GEORGE "GOOBER" LINDSEY

I want a good girl . . . and I want her bad.

DONALD McGILL

I just broke up with someone, and the last thing she said to me was: "You'll never find anybody like me again." And I'm thinking: I should hope not! Isn't that why we break up with people? If I don't want you, why would I want someone just like you! Does anybody end a bad relationship and say, "By the way, do you have a twin?"

LARRY MILLER

I wouldn't mind being the last man on earth—just to see if all of those girls were telling me the truth.

RONNIE SHAKES

A date is a job interview that lasts all night. The only difference between a date and a job interview is that there are not many job interviews where there's a chance you'll end up naked at the end of it.

JERRY SEINFELD

I know a girl who broke every date she had—she went out with them.

BOB MELVIN

A little woman fell in love with a man 90 years old—until she made a date with him. She goes out with him that night, and a friend says the next morning, "How did you like him?" She says, "I had to slap his face three times!" The friend says, "Why, did he get fresh?" She said, "No, I thought he was dead."

MICKEY KATZ

I've been on so many blind dates I should get a free dog.

WENDY LIEBMAN

When I think of some of the men I've slept with—if they were women, I wouldn't have had lunch with them.

CAROL SISKIND

I hate blind dates, but a friend says he could set me up, so I said, "Okay." But you should have seen this girl. It was like she hadn't taken a bath in a month. She was so dirty that somebody had written "wash me" across her forehead.

BOB ZANY

How many of you ever started dating someone 'cause you were too lazy to commit suicide? This guy says, "I'm perfect for you, 'cause I'm a cross between a macho and a sensitive man." I said, "Oh, a gay trucker?"

JUDY TENUTA

I was dating this girl for two years—and right away the nagging starts: "I wanna know your name."

MIKE BINDER

I hate singles bars. Guys come up to me and say, "Hey, cupcake, can I buy you a drink?" I say, "No, but I'll take the three bucks."

MARGARET SMITH

I remember the first time I picked up my girlfriend at her parents' place. Her father said to me, "Make sure you have my daughter home by midnight." I said, "Don't worry, if it looks like I'm not getting anywhere, I'll have her home by ten."

STEVIE RAY FROMSTEIN

I don't like dating rednecks because you can't do anything cultural with them. Take them to an art gallery, and they'll say, "This is crap." "That's a Picasso," I reply. "What about this bunch of damn squiggles?" "That's a Kandinsky." "All right, well, like in this one the guy's got a pencil neck, his nose is upside down, and his eyes are on the same side of his head." "That's a mirror."

PAM STONE

Did you ever have one of those nights where you didn't want to go out . . . but your hair looked too good to stay home?

JACK SIMMONS

You wouldn't want to meet the person of your dreams in a bar. 'Cause when you get married and your little boy says, "Dad, what was it like when you first met Mom?" you've got to go, "Well, son, I woke up and there she was."

JONATHAN SOLOMON

It's slim pickings out there. When you're first single, you're so optimistic. At the beginning, you're like: I want to meet a guy who's really smart, really sweet, really good-looking, has a really great career . . . Six months later, you're like: Lord, any mammal with a day job.

CAROL LEIFER

I honestly believe there is absolutely nothing like going to bed with a good book. Or a friend who's read one.

PHYLLIS DILLER

Bisexuality immediately doubles your chances for a date on Saturday night.

WOODY ALLEN

Death

My Uncle Pat, he reads the death column every morning in the paper. And he can't understand how people always die in alphabetical order.

HAL ROACH

I had written to Aunt Maud,
Who was on a trip abroad,
When I heard she'd died of cramp
Just too late to save the stamp.

HARRY GRAHAM

In the drinking well
    Which the plumber built her,
Aunt Eliza fell—
    We must buy a filter

HARRY GRAHAM

Don't you think the important thing when you're freezing to death is to keep your cool?

PETER DE VRIES

If Shaw and Einstein couldn't beat death, what chance have I got? Practically none.

MEL BROOKS

I'm not afraid to die. I just don't want to be there when it happens.

WOODY ALLEN

Definitions

Advertising: The science of arresting the human intelligence long enough to get money from it.

STEPHEN LEACOCK

Aerobics: Gay folk dancing.

BRUCE SMIRNOFF

Bagel: A pretzel that got its head together.

RON SMITH

Baker's Dozen: Twelve of to-day's doughnuts and one of yesterday's.

JOHNNY HART ("BC")

Bargain: Something you can't use at a price you can't resist.

FRANKLIN P. ADAMS

Bigamist: An Italian's description of his last visit to London.

JOHNNY HART ("BC")

Butler: A solemn procession of one.

P. G. WODEHOUSE

Cardiac: Obsessed poker player.

RAY HAND

Culture: What your butcher would have if he were a surgeon.

MARY PETTIBONE POOLE

Education: Something you get so you can work for guys with no education.

MOREY AMSTERDAM

Egotist: A man who thinks that if he hadn't been born, people would have wondered why.

DAN POST

Epitaph: A belated advertisement for a line of goods that has been permanently discontinued.

IRVIN S. COBB

Extravagance: Anything you buy that is of no earthly use to your wife.

FRANKLIN P. ADAMS

Fan Club: A group of people who tell an actor he's not alone in the way he feels about himself.

JACK CARSON

Glossary: Shoeshine stand.

RAY HAND

Hypocrite: A hypocrite is a person who—but who isn't?

DON MARQUIS

Ignorance: When you don't know something and somebody finds it out.

JETHRO BURNS

Immorality: The morality of those who are having a better time.

H. L. MENCKEN

Impeccable: Unable to be eaten by a chicken.

RAY HAND

Infinity: Time on an ego trip.

JANE WAGNER

Kleptomaniac: A person who helps himself because he can't help himself.

HENRY MORGAN

Lavatory: Volcano

RAY HAND

Limbo: Place where arms and legs go when they die.

RAY HAND

Locomotive: An insane reason to commit a crime.

JOHNNY HART ("BC")

Macramé: That's like bondage for driftwood.

BILL ENGVALL

Mistress: Something between a mister and a mattress.

THE DUKE OF PADUCAH

(WHITEY FORD)

Modesty: The gentle art of enhancing your charm by pretending not to be aware of it.

OLIVER HERFORD

Pessimist: A person who has had to listen to too many optimists.

DON MARQUIS

Pillage: To Plunder a pharmacy.

JOHNNY HART ("BC")

Plagiarism: The only "ism" Hollywood believes in.

DOROTHY PARKER

Preamble: Warm-up before a walk.

RAY HAND

Stalagmites: Miniature German prison guards.

SPIKE MILLIGAN

Universe: All-purpose poem.

RAY HAND

Dentists

Some tortures are physical and some are mental, but the one that is both is dental.

OGDEN NASH

I don't like going to the dentist. I don't like having any part of a man in my mouth for that long.

MARTIN MULL

A dentist's waiting room is a smartly furnished chamber of horrors.

SHELLEY BERMAN

Dieting

I've been on the Valium diet for eight and a half years now. If you take enough Valium it'll help you lose weight. It doesn't really curb your appetite, but most of your food falls on the floor.

GEORGE MILLER

I can talk about Weight Watchers with affection—even though I was on their casualty list. The thing I remember most about Weight Watchers was the weekly meetings . . . Every week three hundred of the fattest people in the area would gather in one room and discuss their common problems—how to get out of the room.

TOTIE FIELDS

I was on the grapefruit diet. I kind of goofed on that. For breakfast I ate fifteen grapefruits. Now when I go to the bathroom I keep squirting myself in the eye.

MAX ALEXANDER

I saw a product in the market —Mr. Salty Pretzels. Isn't that nerve? Everything nowadays is low-salt or salt-free. Here's a guy—the hell with you— Mr. Salty Pretzels . . . like Mr. Tar-and-Nicotine Cigarettes, Mr. Gristle-and-Hard-Artery Beefsteak . . .

BILL MAHER

I have a great diet. You're allowed to eat anything you want, but you must eat it with naked fat people.

ED BLUESTONE

The second day of a diet is always easier than the first. By the second day you're off it.

JACKIE GLEASON

This summer I'm starting my "six-week pizza diet." I only eat six-week-old pizza.

MIKE PETERS

Divorce

Divorce is painful. There's an easy way to save yourself a lot of trouble. Just find a woman you hate and buy her a house.

PAT PAULSEN

It is a sad fact that 50 percent of marriages in this country end in divorce. But hey, the other half end in death. You could be one of the lucky ones!

RICHARD JENI

Divorce comes from the old Latin word "divorcerum," meaning "having your genitals torn out through your wallet." And the judge said, *"All* the *money*—and we'll just shorten it to *alimony!"*

ROBIN WILLIAMS

Open marriage is nature's way of telling you you need a divorce.

MARSHALL BRICKMAN

I know a couple that got remarried. He missed two alimony payments and she repossessed him.

BILL BARNER

My first wife divorced me on grounds of incompatibility. And besides, I think she hated me.

OSCAR LEVANT

I recently saw this among other graffiti in my neighborhood laundromat: "Better to have loved and lost than to do thirty pounds of wash each week."

HAL LINDEN

All of a sudden I noticed she was saying *my* daughter, *my* son, *my* silver, *my* furniture, *my* house, and *your* friends, *your* troubles, *your* worries, *your* problems, and *your* fault.

H. MARTIN

Nowadays when a man makes a mistake, he has to take care of that mistake until it's 18 years old. A mother the other day was talking to her little mistake. She said to her daughter, "It's that time of the month. I think you better run over to your daddy's house and get the monthly payment." She said, "Okay, Momma." So she skipped over to her daddy's house and knocked on the door. Her daddy opened the door and said, "Come in, little girl."

He said, "Isn't this your eighteenth birthday?"

She said, "Yes, it is."

He said, "Ha-ha, here, you take your momma this money and tell her that's the last payment she'll ever get, and watch the expression on her face."

The girl ran home and said, "Momma, the man told me to give you this money and tell you it was the last payment you was gonna get, and watch the expression on your face."

Her momma said, "You go back and tell that man he ain't your daddy, and watch the expression on *his* face!"

DAVE TURNER

Love, the quest; marriage, the conquest; divorce, the inquest.

HELEN ROWLAND

Many a man owes his success to his first wife. And his second wife to his success.

JIM BACKUS

Doctors

One night my mother sent me to fetch the doctor. "What's the matter with me? I'm sick from top to bottom. My head pounds, my eyes flicker, my heart jumps, my stomach gurgles, my knees crack, my ankles swell, my feet burn, and I myself don't feel so good. If I weren't, thank God, so healthy I couldn't stand the pain . . ."

SAM LEVENSON

Be suspicious of any doctor who tries to take your temperature with his finger.

DAVID LETTERMAN

I went to the doctor. I said, "Doc, my foot! I can't walk!" He said, "You'll be walking before the day is over." He took my car.

BUDDY HACKETT

Casey came home from seeing the doctor looking very worried. His wife said, "What's the problem?" He said, "The doctor told me I have to take a pill every day for the rest of my life."

She said, "So what, lots of people have to take a pill every day for the rest of their lives." He said, "I know, but he only gave me four."

HAL ROACH

There's no such thing as an unsuccessful operation. It's the recovery that gets 'em.

LEE TULLY

I'm a little upset. I just found out I have to have this little procedure done. Nothing complicated, but they tell me it *is* going to improve my vision about 70 percent. But I'm a little nervous. I hate getting my bangs cut.

ANITA WISE

I went to the doctor last week. He told me to take all my clothes off. Then he said, "You'll have to diet." I said, "What color?"

KEN DODD

Once I was sick, and I had to go to an ear, nose, and throat man to get well. There are ear doctors, nose doctors, throat

doctors, gynecologists, proctologists—any place you got a hole there's a guy who specializes in your hole. They make an entire career out of that hole. And if the ear doctor, nose doctor, throat doctor, gynecologist, or proctologist can't help you, he sends you to a surgeon. Why? So he can make a new hole!

ALAN PROPHET

How come every time you go to the emergency room of a hospital they got foreign doctors from India there? I don't want to put my life in the hands of any doctor who believes in reincarnation. Give me a good old-fashioned American doc who'll make sure you live to pay that bill!

GLEN (MR. BULLHORN) SUPER

Dogs

Dogs are animals that poop in public and you're supposed to pick it up. After a week of doing this, you've got to ask yourself: Who's the real master in this relationship?

ANTHONY GRIFFIN

My neighbor has two dogs. One of them says to the other, "Woof!" The other replies, "Moo!" The dog is perplexed. "Moo? Why did you say, 'Moo'?" The other dog says, "I'm trying to learn a foreign language."

MOREY AMSTERDAM

This woman took her dog to Israel. When she got off the plane, she said, "Where's my dog? Where's the case?" They finally find the case in the baggage room. They open it up—and the dog is dead.

They're all upset—they know the woman will kill them. They go and get the manager, and they tell him the dog is dead and the woman is carrying on waiting for her dog. She's shrieking, she's complaining, she wants to sue us.

The manager says, "Look, it's a cocker spaniel. Next door there's a pet shop. Go buy a cocker spaniel the same size and she'll never know the difference."

They run and buy a cocker

spaniel and put it in the case. They yell, "Lady! Lady! We found it."

She says, "It's about time!"

She looks at the dog and says, "That's not my dog!"

The manager says, "How do you know that's not your dog, lady?"

She says, "My dog died. I was taking it to Israel to bury it."

JAN MURRAY

I went to an exclusive kennel club. It was very exclusive. There was a sign out front: "No Dogs Allowed."

PHIL FOSTER

I have a dachshund. It curses when it barks! Why? You would too if you were draggin' your balls on the sidewalk.

BILLY CONNOLLY

Did you ever notice when you blow in a dog's face he gets mad at you? But when you take him in a car he sticks his head out the window.

STEVE BLUESTEIN

I just bought a Chihuahua. It's the dog for lazy people. You don't have to walk it. Just hold it out the window and squeeze.

ANTHONY CLARK

The other day I saw two dogs walk over to a parking meter. One of them says to the other, "How do you like that. Pay toilets!"

DAVE STARR

They say the dog is man's best friend. I don't believe that. How many of your friends have you neutered?

LARRY REEB

I have a great dog. She's half Lab, half pit bull. A good combination. Sure, she might bite off my leg, but she'll bring it back to me.

JIMI CELESTE

Dog owners are out in all kinds of weather. They tell you it's small payment for the love their dogs bear them. Some love. If that dog weren't on a leash, he'd be off like a flash after another dog, a cat, or any stranger walking along the street with a wet bag of meat.

If dog owners walked around in all kinds of weather for the Postal Service they'd really

know love. A retirement plan. Social security. Medical insurance. Pension.

SELMA DIAMOND

We used to have a dog. He begged for scraps from the table, and by God, we fed him! Now we have a Spotless kitchen.

PHYLLIS DILLER

Ever notice how a dog likes to bark at a drunk? And vice versa?

PAT BUTTRAM

Oh, that dog! Ever hear of a German shepherd that bites its nails? Barks with a lisp? You say, "Attack!" And he has one. All he does is piddle. He's nothing but a fur-covered kidney that barks.

PHYLLIS DILLER

From the very beginning dogs set out to please their masters, not the other way around . . . They were put to work to perform a wide variety of chores. And so today's canine community is broken up into such groups as hunting dogs, shepherd dogs, military dogs, racing dogs, watchdogs . . . Not so with cats. All go under the banner of "pet," a word the dictionary defines as "any loved and cherished creature," an excellent choice of words from the cat's point of view . . . Dogs travel hundreds of miles during their lifetime responding to such commands as "come" and "fetch." Cats approach people only when there is a reason, and not always even then.

STEPHEN BAKER

Dachshunds are ideal dogs for small children, as they are already stretched and pulled to such a length that the child cannot do much harm one way or the other.

ROBERT BENCHLEY

They have dog food for constipated dogs. If your dog is constipated, why screw up a good thing? Stay indoors and let 'im bloat!

DAVID LETTERMAN

My kid said, "I want a dog." Well, I went to the kennel. The first dog I saw had legs four inches long in front, two feet long in back. I said, "That's a strange-looking dog." The salesman says, "That's true,

but he's the fastest animal in the world going downhill." I got something more normal. A Chihuahua. They're good. If you lose one, just empty out your purse.

JEAN CARROLL

I bought my grandmother a Seeing Eye dog. But he's a little sadistic. He does impressions of cars screeching to a halt.

LARRY AMOROS

Aristocrats have heirs, the poor have children, the rest keep dogs . . . There was a time when the forebears of our contemporary dogs ran free in packs . . . It's hard to believe that the lump of hairy fat slobbed out in front of a Belgravia fire is a direct descendant of those once-noble creatures. Since 1945, a bundle of yapping nerves with hair on, called a poodle, has become the status symbol of the top OK people . . .

You can see the whole lunatic menagerie any morning after ten-thirty in the vicinity of the Round Pond, Kensington. While little children are being strapped down in prams, incarcerated in reins, sat on, hit, shouted at, and generally terrorized, dogs are allowed to bite, chew, leap at old ladies, terrify, eat wild ducks, copulate and urinate at will, and sometimes on him (I spelled his name with a small *w* as he wishes to remain anonymous).

SPIKE MILLIGAN

There is no way to get a grip on a dog so that you can give it a legitimate hug. You wind up hugging it around some delicate reproductive organ . . . Puppies smell fine. Old dogs don't smell that terrific. But when it comes to dogs in their middle period, it's not that clear-cut. One of the toughest and most exhausting things to figure out is if a middle-aged dog smells all right or if it's a little off.

BRUCE JAY FRIEDMAN

Driving

There are no liberals behind steering wheels.

RUSSELL BAKER

If your wife wants to learn to drive, don't stand in her way.

SAM LEVENSON

I like driving around with my two dogs, especially on the freeways. I make them wear little hats so I can use the carpool lanes.

MONICA PIPER

The gas-station attendant looks at the car and says, "You got a flat tire." I said, "No, the other three just swelled up."

BILL ENGVALL

Everything is drive-through. In California they even have a burial service called Jump-in-the-Box.

WIL SHRINER

Have you noticed? Anybody going slower than you is an idiot, and anyone going faster than you is a moron.

GEORGE CARLIN

I was stopped once for going 53 in a 35-mile zone, but I told 'em I had dyslexia.

SPANKY (STEVE McFARLIN)

One time we were driving through a construction zone

and the sign said, "Speed Limit 35 Ahead." And there were four of us. We were through there in no time.

GEECHY GUY

If you ever have an accident, I hope you have on clean underwear. You're driving a truck—right into another truck. Now comes your mother to the hospital: "Did he have clean underwear?" "Yes, we found it in the glove compartment."

BILL COSBY

The highway cop said, "Walk a straight line." I said, "Well, Officer Pythagoras, the closest you could ever come to achieving a straight line would be making an electroencephalogram of your own brain waves." I said, "Officer, I'm taking my mom to the hospital. She OD'd on reducing pills." He said, "I don't see any woman with you." I said, "I'm too late." He said, "You're under arrest. You have the right to remain silent. Do you wish to retain that right?" I thought: Oooooh! A paradox . . .

EMO PHILIPS

I think all cars should have car phones in 'em and their license plates should be their phone number. So you can call 'em up and tell 'em to get the hell out of the way. Old people would have 800 numbers.

JOHN MENDOZA

#

It's not called cocaine anymore. It's now referred to as "Crack Classic."

BILLIAM CORONEL

Now MTV is running that "Rock Against Drugs" campaign. Right. That's an awful lot like "Whores Against Sex."

BOB HARRIS

What would happen if the President, the Supreme Court, and all members of both houses of Congress were stoned out of their gourds twenty-four hours a day? The chilling truth is, it might be an improvement.

ALLAN SHERMAN

The problem of narcotics is dreadfully serious. You'd be surprised at the people you see in your everyday life who use drugs. I knew a fellow who had a habit. Very bad habit. In fact, his habit got so bad I stopped selling to him.

FLIP WILSON

I could recommend mescaline to everyone. Listen, there's a lot of people in this room. If one of you fell off a roof someday, if you did that in your normal state of mind—forget it. But if you took mescaline and fell off that same roof, you'd be saying, "So far, so good."

"UNCLE DIRTY" (BOB ALTMAN)

I smoked pot at a drive-in movie theater. But the screen was this tiny. It was itsy-bitsy thumb and forefinger tiny. Till I realized I was so stoned I'd backed in and I was watching it from my rearview mirror.

SANDY BARON

You should just say no to drugs. That will drive the prices down.

GEECHY GUY

I liked morphine from the start. It made me graciously tolerant of every form of human imbecility, including my own.

ALEXANDER KING

I took Benzedrine—I got clairvoyance. With Benzedrine you can have a very wide view of the world—like you can decide the destiny of man and other pressing problems, such as which is the left sock?

MORT SAHL

I've asked, "What is it about cocaine that makes it so wonderful?" And they say, "Well, it intensifies your personality." Yes. But what if you're an asshole?

BILL COSBY

"A nod"—that's like a very hip nap.

DEL CLOSE

There's always one guy who tries to impress you with how big a joint he can roll. The guy takes the Sunday *Times*, drops a kilo brick in with the strings on it . . . we roll it up and pass it around . . . have to use fireplace tongs for the roach. And all of a sudden I realize—I've oversmoked. Oh yeah. You can tell when you've oversmoked—when you try and brush something off your shoulder and it's the floor.

CHRIS RUSH

My wife doesn't give me any trouble anymore. She died. I had her cremated. I mixed in a little marijuana and smoked her. It was the best she ever made me feel.

JACKIE VERNON

How can a kid 10 years old find a dope pusher and the FBI can't?

RED SKELTON

Drunks

There are two groups of people in the world now. Those that get pathetically drunk in public —and the rest of us poor bastards who are expected to drive these pinheads home.

DENNIS MILLER

This drunk in the movie theater was lying across the seat, going, "Uhh, uhh." And the usher says, "Cut the racket, will ya? Sit up in your seat." And the drunk just goes, "Uhh, uhh." And the manager can't move him. So they get a policeman. Cop says, "All right, sit up in your seat there or leave the theater. Stop making all this noise. What do you mean behaving like this? What kind of behavior do you call this? Where are you from, anyway?" Drunk says, "I'm from the balcony. Uhhhh. Uhhhhh. Uhh-hhh . . ."

ADAM KEEFE

A drunkard is like a whiskey bottle; all neck and belly and no head.

AUSTIN O'MALLEY

I've never been drunk, but often I've been overserved.

GEORGE GOBEL

I must say that I have a very good reason for bein' loaded tonight. I been drinkin' all day!

FOSTER BROOKS

You shouldn't drink and drive. If you get drunk, don't call a cab. That could cost you twenty dollars or forty dollars or fifty dollars. Do what I do. Call a tow truck. It might cost a little more, but your car will be there when you wake up.

JEFFREY JENA

My uncle staggered in the other night, loaded. His wife said, "Where have you been?" He said, "I bought something for the house." She said, "What did you buy for the house?" He said, "A round of drinks."

JIMMY JOYCE

The gentleman was very inebriated. His white shirtfront was smudged and his high silk hat hung on one ear. He seemed unhappy and had a look of utter frustration.

"Pardon me, shir," he said to a passerby, "what timesh it?"

"Eleven o'clock," the man answered.

"I must be losin' my mind," the drunk muttered. "Asked everybody the same question and all evenin' long gettin' different answers!"

BENNY RUBIN

A habitual slot-machine gambler, also a drunk, staggered into the Automat. He walked up to the sandwich section and deposited some nickels. A ham sandwich popped out. He deposited more coins, collecting more and more sandwiches. The manager walked over to him and said, "Pardon me, sir, but why don't you stop? Haven't you got enough?" The drunk turned on him and said, "What? Quit when I'm on a winning streak?"

JOE E. BROWN

I'm not a big drinker. I just put away a lotta little ones. I mean to say I'm not a steady drinker —'cause I shake too much. My doctor tells me if I keep drinkin' I'll never see a ripe old age. But I don't believe the dear doctor. 'Cause every night I see more old drunkards than I see old doctors.

JOE E. LEWIS

Did you ever get up in the morning: the hell with the Visine, get out the Liquid Paper!

DR. GONZO (JOHN MEANS)

A drunk manages to arrive in time to catch the last bus home. He flops down in the first seat he comes to. Just be-

83

fore the bus starts, a lady gets in. With great difficulty, he gets up out of his seat and he says, "Pardon me, madam, would you care for my seat?" She said, "Thanks very much," and she sat down.

So, he strap-hanged three quarters of an hour for the five-mile trip, thrown all over the bus, till finally the conductor shouted, "Terminus, everybody out here." He gets out, gets on the platform, and says to the conductor, "Did you see me give my seat to that lady?" The conductor said, "Yes, I did." "You did? That's just to point out to you that chivalry is not yet dead in this country!" And the conductor said, "Oh, that's what it was. I was wondering what it was, 'cause there was only you and her on the bus!"

ROBB WILTON

Folks, buy Guzzler's gin, a nice smooth drink! With Guzzler's, you don't need a chaser. Nothing can catch you!

RED SKELTON

A man who overindulges lives in a dream. He becomes conceited. He thinks the whole world revolves around him—and it usually does.

W. C. FIELDS

A guy walked into a bar and said to the bartender, "Since when did you have sawdust on the floor?" "That's not sawdust," the bartender said. "It's last night's furniture."

JOEY ADAMS

Fellow lived next door to me, he drank all the time, I never seen a man drink like that. I went home the other night, he was so drunk, walkin' all around, he was staggering up on the porch and he put his key in the door and when he turned the key the door came open.

He said, "Yeah, I know I'm in the right house, 'cause this key I got jus' opened this door." And he walked around a little bit further in the house and said, "I know I'm in the right house now, 'cause there's that great big ol' beautiful dresser I bought for my old lady."

And he ended up in the bedroom. "I told you I was in the right house, 'cause there's my old lady lyin' over in the bed.

Look at that, I know I'm in the right house now, 'cause there I am layin' over there in the bed with her. Now I gotta figure out who the devil is this standin' up talkin'!"

LEROY "SLOPPY" DANIELS

Why, you barfly, I'll stick a wick in your mouth and use you for an alcohol lamp!

CHARLIE McCARTHY (EDGAR BERGEN)

A drunk tried several times to navigate a revolving door, but finally gave up in disgust. He wandered over to lean against a nearby lamppost. A man came along the street and walked into the door. As it revolved, the other side revealed a pretty girl stepping out. The drunk looked intently at her and remarked, "It's a good trick, but I still don't see what the guy did with his clothes!"

VICTOR BORGE

Callahan was one of these fellas who was Irish through and through. Well, mostly. About seven parts Irish and one part vodka . . . This one day he was really lugging a load . . . and he was blind. He couldn't see the dashboard. He got into his car and he started to drive.

He drove in a short circle far and through the night. He was lost. Somebody moved the town. Finally he saw a taillight and he began following the taillight. He followed the taillight for quite some time. Finally, the taillight came to a stop.

But not Callahan.

He smashed his car into the other fella's car and he gets out of his car very, very indignant. He says, "What's the matter with you, wiseguy? Don't you know you're supposed to put your arm out when you come to a stop?"

The fella says, "What? In my own garage?"

DANNY THOMAS

I'm sitting in a bar, having a drink. Over here is a man having a drink. He falls down three times. I pick him up each time. I said, "Bartender, where does this guy live? I'll give him a lift home."

He tells me where he lives. I grab the guy, pull him down to the car, open the back door, put him in the back seat. He falls down. I get to the address they gave me. I pull him out, he falls down three more times. I pick him up each time. I knock on the door. "Mrs. Phillips, I brought your husband home." She says, "Where's his wheelchair?"

HENNY YOUNGMAN

Economy

I went into the grocery store today. I said, "Give me a dollar's worth of potatoes." He said, "We don't slice 'em." I said, "Give me fifty cents' worth of Swiss cheese." He wrapped up six holes.

JIMMY EDMONDSON
  (PROFESSOR BACKWARDS)

England

The English think incompetence is the same thing as sincerity.

QUENTIN CRISP

A lot of my countrymen say rude things about England because it has the lowest standard of living in the world, and I don't think that's fair. I think that's mean and horrid. Because I know England will rise again. It will—say, to the level of Sicily or Ethiopia.

DAME EDNA EVERAGE
  (BARRY HUMPHRIES)

I say help the British! If it wasn't for them, we'd be talking some language we couldn't understand.

BO BROWN

I'm married to an English guy. He's a typical English guy. He's very reserved. In fact, it wasn't until after we were married that I actually knew he wanted to go out with me.

KIT HOLLERBACH

When I meet an Englishman and he speaks with that funny accent, I'd never say, "You're a liar." But . . . I believe that if you wake an Englishman in the middle of the night, he'll speak just like us.

MILT KAMEN

It's spring in England. I missed it last year. I was in the bathroom.

MICHAEL FLANDERS

I think the Europeans are hostile toward the English because the English have some irritating habits—the habit, for instance, of ending sentences with questions that sound like reprimands: "You say it's difficult for you to tell because you haven't read the survey? Well, you'll have to read it, then, won't you?" See how snotty that sounds?

Why do the English talk so funny? For one thing, they're all hard of hearing. All Englishmen are hard of hearing. That's why they end a lot of sentences with questions—just to check and make sure the other fellow heard what they were saying . . . That's why they're always saying, "I say!"

CALVIN TRILLIN

The state of England . . . The drain on Britain's gold reserves has finally stopped. They've all gone . . . We would all have had our backs to the wall—but we're so far behind with the building program that the wall isn't ready. Parliament is opened by Her Majesty the Queen, who would be well advised to take one quick look and shut it again.

DAVID FROST

They's an old saw to the effect that the sun never sets on the British Empire. While we was there, it never even rose.

RING LARDNER

After lovemaking, a German woman is practical. She will say, "Ach, dat vas goot!" A French woman is solicitous. She will say, "Ah, *mon chéri*, did I please you?" And an English woman will say . . . "Feeling better?"

GODFREY CAMBRIDGE

Epitaphs (Self-Written)

This lot for sale.
CHIC SALE

Here lies Nunnally Johnson. If I don't come back, go right ahead without me.
NUNNALLY JOHNSON

I had a hunch something like this would happen.
FONTAINE FOX

Dear God: Enclosed please find Rube Goldberg. Now that you've got him, what are you going to do with him?
RUBE GOLDBERG

Here lies Irvin S. Cobb, not that it makes any difference.
IRVIN S. COBB

On the whole, I'd rather be in Philadelphia.
W. C. FIELDS

Here lies the body of Harry Hershfield. If not, notify Ginsberg & Company, Undertakers, at once.
HARRY HERSHFIELD

If you can read this, you're too close; get off my grave, idiot!
GLEN (MR. BULLHORN) SUPER

Here stands Tony Randall. I am not going to take this lying down.
TONY RANDALL

If this is a joke—I don't get it.
DAVID BRENNER

A nice part—only "four sides" —but good company and in for a long run.
EDWARD EVERETT HORTON

Excuse my dust.
DOROTHY PARKER

I told you I was ill.
SPIKE MILLIGAN

Over my dead body.
GEORGE S. KAUFMAN

Keep the line moving.
JACK PAAR

Esquire Magazine

Esquire is always on the cutting edge of twerpiness. It's a magazine read by men who actually worry about whether their socks are out of style.

P. J. O'ROURKE

Exercise and Fitness

I don't exercise. What's in it for me? You've got to offer me more than my life to get me on a Stairmaster grunting for two hours. I view my body as a way of getting my head from one place to another.

DAVE THOMAS

Physical fitness is in. I recently had a physical fit myself.

STEVE ALLEN

The best form of exercise is picnics. You can use up two thousand calories trying to keep the ants and flies away from the potato salad.

JACK E. LEONARD

You have to stay in shape. My grandmother, she started walking five miles a day when she was 60. She's 97 today and we don't know where the hell she is.

ELLEN DeGENERIS

I'm not into working out. My philosophy: No pain, no pain.

CAROL LEIFER

I tried Flintstones vitamins. I didn't feel any better but I could stop the car with my feet.

JOAN ST. ONGE

I bought an excrcise bicycle two years ago. It has an eighth of a mile on it. See, what happened is, I discovered that the handlebars fit my sport jacket perfectly. And there's a place for my beer and McDonald's right under it . . . the most expensive coat hanger in New York.

ROBERT KLEIN

Think about it. Do you want to be known as a girl who pedals it all over town? Of course not. There is a tremendous current revival of bicycling throughout the country. They say that it brings health and happiness. You know who this bicycle craze is making healthy and happy? The Schwinn Company. If you must ride a bike there's only one way to do it—sitting on the handlebars while somebody else pedals.

TOTIE FIELDS

We work out entirely too much. We waste time. A friend of mine runs marathons. He always talks about this "runner's high." But he has to go twenty-six miles for it. That's why I smoke and drink. I get the same feeling from a flight of stairs.

LARRY MILLER

Last year I entered the LA marathon. I finished last. It was embarrassing. And the guy who was in front of me, second to last, was making fun of me. He said, "Hey, Gerry, how does it feel to be last?" I said, "You want to know?" So I dropped out.

GERRY BEDNOB

They say the best exercise takes place in the bedroom. I believe it, because that's where I get the most resistance.

JEFF SHAW

What a foul smell, indeed, a gymnasium has! How it suggests a mixture of Salvation Army, elephant house, and county jail.

H. L. MENCKEN

The gym teacher's name was Mr. Caruso. Mr. Caruso did not speak English. He spoke "Gym." One day I was playing basketball and Mr. Caruso told me I would have to get an athletic supporter. He didn't express himself exactly that way, though. He said, "Hey, you, one day you're gonna go up for a rebound and the family jewels aren't gonna go with ya." I had no idea what he was talking about. Next day I showed up for practice without my watch and my mezuzah. He said, "Did ya take care of the family jewels?" I said, "I left 'em in my locker." Took us a half hour to revive Mr. Caruso.

GABE KAPLAN

talk to my wife. Say anything!" He flattered me so much I bought the tie, bought six shirts. I didn't have enough money. I said, "Will you accept my check?" He said, "Do you have any identification?"

TONY RANDALL

Fame

I can't imagine myself ever getting big enough to do two things: have a cartoon series about myself or wave from a float.

RICHARD LEWIS

I don't have a photograph, but you can have my footprints. They're upstairs in my socks.

GROUCHO MARX

I was walking down Madison Avenue and I saw a very good-looking tie in a shop window. So I went in. Before I could say anything the manager said, "Oh, Tony Randall! In my store! Please, just a minute, wait, wait, I gotta call my wife —she'll never believe me!"

He calls her up and says to me, "Here, say hello, anything,

Family

The reason grandparents and grandchildren get along so well is that they have a common enemy.

SAM LEVENSON

My family tree was chopped down and they made the lumber into toilet paper. We've never been closer.

BARRY STEIGER

Having a family is like having a bowling alley installed in your brain.

MARTIN MULL

Goldberg and Epstein, who hadn't seen each other for years, had a reunion. "Since I last saw you I got married," said Epstein. "I got a lovely wife and three kids and have a new apartment up in the Bronx. Come up and have dinner with us sometime."

"I would be very happy to," said Goldberg. "Where do you live?"

"Here's the address," said Epstein, "and when you get off the subway you walk two blocks and when you come to the apartment house just kick the front door open with your foot. Then you go to the elevator and you press the button with your left elbow. Then you go to the sixth floor and then you see my name there on the bell and you press the button with your right elbow and then I'll let you in and we'll have a good time."

"Just a minute," said Goldberg. "What is this kicking the front door open and pushing this button with the left elbow and that button with the right elbow? What's the idea?"

"You're not coming empty-handed, are you?" said Epstein.

JOE LAURIE, JR.

I left for college. Dad said, "I'm going to miss you." I said, "Well, now that I broke the sight off your rifle." Yeah. My parents threw quite a going-away party for me. According to the letter.

EMO PHILIPS

My youngest child is the funniest one of the group. I had just finished eating and my stomach was swollen from the food that went in it. And she patted me on the stomach and she said, "Dad, you have a big stomach."

And as a father I tried to give her wisdom. And I said, "Dad's stomach is full of food, that's why it looks that way."

And she said, "Yes. And you have a big nose because you don't pick it."

BILL COSBY

This is gross . . . My Aunt Velveeta lets that stupid dog of hers sit right next to her in the dining room. And when she gets done eating, she will take her plate and let that dog lick it clean right at the table! Then she'll put some Poli-Grip on it and slip it right back in her mouth.

HEYWOOD BANKS

If the kids are alive at the end of the day, I've done my job.

ROSEANNE BARR ARNOLD

I was out in the backyard one beautiful day. I said to my mother, "Mama, why don't I have no sister or no brother?"

She said, "Go away, go play, don't worry your mother, dear. As lazy as your father was, you're lucky that you got here."

NIPSEY RUSSELL

When I was a boy, my mother wore a mood ring. Whenever she was in a good mood, it turned blue. Whenever she was in a bad mood, it left a big red mark in the middle of my forehead.

JEFF SHAW

My wife and I—to our regret—took seriously the admonition that you should give children responsibility at an early age.

A while back the wife and I went to a movie, taking our daughter with us and leaving the three boys—David, 12, Scott, 10, and Lon, 8—to clean up the supper dishes.

On our return from the movie the boys were draped about the living room. "Well," my wife asked, "what did you boys do?"

Proudly, David said, "I washed the dishes."

Scott said, "And I dried them."

Turning to Lon, my wife asked, "What did *you* do, Lon?"

"I picked up the pieces."

CAL TINNEY

The trouble with the average family is it has too much month left over at the end of the money.

BILL VAUGHAN

Two businessmen were having lunch and they started talking about world problems, high taxes, the cost of living, their families.

And one of them says very proudly, "I have six boys."

So the other guy says, "That's a nice family. I wish to heaven I had six children."

And the proud father says with a touch of sympathy in his voice, "Don't you have any children?"

And the other guy says, "Yeah. Ten!"

SOUPY SALES

My parents used to send me to spend summers with my grandparents. I hate cemeteries!

CHRIS FONSECA

Farms and Farmers

I grew up on a big farm. Last time I was home visiting my folks I delivered a calf. I tell ya, I feel so much thinner now.

HENRIETTE MANTEL

A guy bought a farm. He didn't know anything about farms, but he bought one anyway. He decides he's going to plant something. Anything. "What are you going to plant?" his friend asks. "Razor blades and cabbages." His friend looks at him. "Razor blades and cabbages? What could you possibly get out of that?" "Cole-slaw."

BUDDY HACKETT

A small farmer on a kibbutz was talking to a big Texan. The Texan says, "How big is your farm?" Well, he says, it's 200 feet by 300 feet. He said to the Texan, "How big is your land?"

The Texan says, "I could get in my car and drive from sunrise to sunset and never reach the end of my land."

The Israeli said, "I once had a car like that too."

ALAN KING

I heard a noise in the barn the other day. I went down there. My brother bought a new mule and he was trying to get the mule through the barn door but he couldn't get the mule through the barn door because the mule's ears was too long.

So brother had a saw and he was sawing off the top of the barn door to get the mule in. I said, "It's a dirt floor, why don't you just dig a trench and take the mule in that way?"

And brother said, "It ain't his legs that's too long, it's his ears!"

MINNIE PEARL

Human milk is better than cow's milk. It's cheaper, keeps better over the weekend, and the cat can't get at it.

DONALD McGILL

He owned the biggest brussels sprout farm in East McKeesport. Well, he didn't start out to have the biggest brussels sprout farm. It's just that his cabbages never made it.

DONNA JEAN YOUNG

It's so cold . . . Father can't milk the cows by hand because he has to wear his wool mittens. This tickles the cows. They get hysterical and nothing comes out but cottage cheese.

CHARLEY WEAVER (CLIFF ARQUETTE)

It was so hot I seen a cow lying on her back giving herself a shower.

HOMER HAYNES

Two farmers were boasting about the strongest kind of wind they'd seen. "Out here in California," said one, "I've seen the fiercest wind in my life. You know these giant redwood trees? Well, the wind once got so strong, it bent them right down." "That's nothing," said the other. "Back on my farm in Iowa, we had a terrible wind one day that blew a hundred miles an hour. It was so bad one of my hens had her back turned to the wind and

she laid the same egg six times."

JOE LAURIE, JR.

Fashion

Never let a panty line show around your ankles.

JOAN RIVERS

Where lipstick is concerned, the important thing is not the color, but to accept God's final decision on where your lips end.

JERRY SEINFELD

Did you see that new bathing suit they have for women now? That thong bathing suit? It has that one thin strap up the middle in the middle in the back. Puh-leeze! I spend my whole life tryin' to keep my underwear outta there, some idiot goes and designs 'em that goes there on purpose.

DIANE FORD

A lot of women are getting tattoos. Don't do it, that's sick. That butterfly looks great on your breast when you're 20, 30.

When you get to be 70, 80, it stretches into a condor.

BILLY ELMER

What counts is not how many animals were killed to make the fur but how many animals the woman had to sleep with to get a fur.

ANGELA LaGRECA

I didn't pay a lot for this dress. I got it for a bargain. I heard somebody say I must've got this dress for a ridiculous figure.

MINNIE PEARL

I base my fashion taste on what doesn't itch.

GILDA RADNER

When spring comes around, I merely write my tailor, send him a small sample of dandruff, and tell him to match it exactly.

OLIVER HERFORD

I got some new underwear the other day. Well, new to me.

EMO PHILIPS

Fashion is what you adopt when you don't know who you are.

QUENTIN CRISP

My dad's pants kept creeping up on him. By 65 he was just a pair of pants and a head.

JEFF ALTMAN

Fat

I went out with this girl who was really fat. Did you ever hear the expression "as big as a house"? She was wearing aluminum siding. She had two pictures. "Before" and "Before That." And she was shaped like an egg. I said, "Hey, that's a really nice necklace you've got on." She said, "It's my belt."

STU TRIVAX

I won't tell you how much I weigh, but don't ever get in an elevator with me unless you're going down.

JACK E. LEONARD

I ate Hostess fruit pies all day —I got so fat my picture would fall off the wall.

BRUCE SMIRNOFF

You either have to lose weight or make more friends—six pall-bearers isn't going to cut it.

JOHNNY PARKER ("The Wizard of Id")

I got hit by a Volkswagen—and had to go to the hospital to have it removed.

PAT McCORMICK

I don't mind being . . . fat. I was in the Big Man's Shop and a salesman came up to me and said, "We have jogging suits in *your* size." *Why?* Last time I ran was in '82. I didn't hear the bells on the ice-cream truck the first time.

MAX ALEXANDER

You guys—you gain thirty pounds and we call you cuddly. We gain an ounce and you call us taxis. Then you don't call us at all.

CAROL SISKIND

You're getting so big I need double vision to take you in.

PETER DE VRIES

My wife's on a diet. She used to be so fat every time she got into a taxi the driver rushed her to the hospital. She went to the health club and one week she lost fifteen pounds. One of those machines tore her leg off.

DAVE BARRY (stand-up comic of the 1960s)

She was so big she could kick-start a 747.

GEORGE "GOOBER" LINDSEY

My ex-girlfriend was fat. How fat is she? She sweats gravy.

BEN CREED

Then there's my fat, obnoxious cousin, Roweena. When she walks through the living room, the radio skips. She says she just retains water, and I say, "So does the Hoover Dam."

JEFF FOXWORTHY

I got an aunt named Minnie. Weighs 264. When she sits on the chair there's so much of her there—most of her sits on the floor.

MOREY AMSTERDAM

A guy sees a fat lady carrying a duck. The guy says, "What are you doing with that pig?" The fat lady snorts, "That's not a pig, it's a duck." The guy says, "I'm not talking to you, I'm talking to the duck."

JACK CARTER

I was a test-tub baby. All the other kids were in test tubes. And I was in a three-liter Coke bottle.

BILLY ELMER

My thighs—five more pounds and they'll be eligible for state-hood.

AUDREY BUSLIK

When I dance, the band skips. I have a sunken bathtub—and a sunken toilet!

BOB ZANY

I won't say my wife is fat, but she's the only woman I know . . .

BENNY HILL

You're too fat in the first place, you know it's true. You're too fat in the second place too.

HOMER HAYNES

I've fallen down and not even known it.

PAT McCORMICK

When I was a child, I was so fat that I was the one chosen to play Bethlehem in the school Nativity play.

THE SEA MONSTER (JO BRAND)

It's time to go on a diet when the man from Prudential offers you group insurance. Or when you take a shower and you have to let out the shower curtain. Or when you're standing next to your car and get a ticket for double parking.

TOTIE FIELDS

She is so fat, he danced with her for half an hour before he realized she was still sitting down.

ED WYNN

You know you're getting fat when you can pinch an inch on your forehead.

JOHN MENDOZA

Father

I once asked my father if things were bad for him during the Depression. He said the first six months were bad, then he got used to me.

RODNEY DANGERFIELD

My son is 38 and he's still trying to "find himself." I told him when he does it won't be such a big discovery. He said, "I'll be a millionaire before I'm 40!" I said, "Yeah, if I drop dead when you're 39."

ALAN KING

What is it about American fathers as they grow older that makes them dress like flags from other countries?

CARY ODES

I never got along with my dad. Kids used to come up to me and say, "My dad can beat up your dad." I'd say yeah? When?

BILL HICKS

Oh yeah, my father would thrash me now and then. And he'd talk while he did it! He'd hit me and shout, "Have you had enough?" Had enough? What kind of question is that? "Why, Father, would another kick in the balls be out of the question?"

BILLY CONNOLLY

I was raised by just my mom. See, my father died when I was eight years old. At least, that's what he told us in the letter.

DREW CAREY

I never know what to get my father for his birthday. I gave him a hundred dollars and said, "Buy yourself something that will make your life easier." So he went out and bought a present for my mother.

RITA RUDNER

Feminine Hygiene

You walk into the market. Big signs: "Feminine Protection." What's in those boxes? Pink guns? And panty shields . . . what do they do, protect you from your own underwear?

ELAYNE BOOSLER

I've been sort of crabby lately. It's that time of the month again—the rent's due.

MARGARET SMITH

I went to a party given for Noël Coward, and at those parties everybody tries to act so Brit-

44444444

ish. There was one dame there riding a Kotex sidesaddle.

JACK BENNY

I got to readin' all those articles on PMS—premenstrual syndrome. I thought I had it. I went to the doctor. The doctor said, "I got some good news and I got some bad news. The good news is you don't have premenstrual syndrome." He said, "The bad news is—you're just a bitch."

RHONDA BATES

They've got a product called a disposable douche. Of course it's disposable. Who'd want to keep one of those things around?

LEWIS GRIZZARD

Women who insist upon having the same options as men would do well to consider the option of being the strong, silent type.

FRAN LEBOWITZ

Women go to work in those corporate Godzilla outfits: skirt suit, track shoes, shoulder pads. Those shoulder pads designed to "Knock men outta my way! I can do any job a man can do and I can give birth while doing it!"

ALLAN HAVEY

I treat women as my equal. Of course, most women don't like to be treated like a paranoid balding Jew with contact lenses.

DAVID FELDMAN

Feminists

I think your demands are outrageous—like that demand that they build a hole next to the Washington Monument equally as deep.

CHRIS RUSH

Flowers

I like to tease my plants. I water them with ice cubes.

STEVEN WRIGHT

Botany is not a science; it is the art of insulting flowers in Greek and Latin.

ALPHONSE KARR

Food

I live in a country where food is considered entertainment. So I suppose all those people in the Third World are not starving—they're bored.

JIMMY TINGLE

I visited an American supermarket. They have so many amazing products here. Like powder milk. You add water and you get milk. And powder orange juice. You add water and you get orange juice. Then I saw baby powder. And I said to myself, what a country! I'm making my family tonight!

YAKOV SMIRNOFF

French wine growers fear that this year's vintage may be entirely spoiled due to the grape treaders' sit-in.

RONNIE CORBETT

An hors d'oeuvre is an unfamiliar creature curled up on a cracker and stabbed with a toothpick to make sure it's dead.

PAT BUTTRAM

Canapés—a sandwich cut into twenty-four pieces.

BILLY ROSE

What is a croquette but hash that has come to a head?

IRVIN S. COBB

I was in a convenience store. Somebody had blown a hole through every one of the Cheerios. It wasn't hard to figure who it was—a cereal killer.

TOMMY SLEDGE

Bananas are a waste of time. After you skin them and throw the bone away, there's nothing left to eat.

CHARLEY WEAVER (CLIFF ARQUETTE)

Why is a birthday cake the only food you can blow on and spit on and everybody rushes to get a piece?

BOBBY KELTON

Some of the stuff that stares out of gumbo should not be al-

lowed out except for Halloween . . . Ugly makes Cajuns
hungry. The Elephant Man
wouldn't last ten minutes in
Louisiana . . . These people
eat anything that moves. They
don't even bother selling Raid
in Louisiana except as a sea-
soning.

STEVE EPSTEIN

I don't want to panic, but my
alphabet soup says, "Forget
about me . . . just try to save
yourself."

TOM WILSON ("Ziggy")

Licorice is the liver of candy.

MICHAEL O'DONOGHUE

A woman went to the butcher's
to buy some meat. So she
bought some steak, a few
pounds of hamburger, a few
pounds of ribs, and a big roast,
and then she says to the
butcher, "Deliver it!"

The butcher says, "I can't
deliver it, lady."

She says, "What's the matter with you? You've gotta deliver it. Your delivery wagon's
parked right out front."

The butcher says, "I know

that, lady, but you got most of
the horse!"

JIMMY DURANTE

We've got a name for sushi in
Georgia . . . bait.

BLAKE CLARK

A Catskill manhattan: a glass
of beet soup with inside floating a small boiled potato.

MRS. NUSSBAUM (MINERVA PIOUS)

Luther Burbank crossed a potato with a sponge. He got
something that tastes awful
but it holds a lot of gravy.

DOODLES WEAVER

I got food poisoning today. I
don't know when I'm gonna
use it.

STEPHEN WRIGHT

It has been said that fish is a
good brain food. That's a fal-
lacy. But brains are a good fish
food!

MEL BROOKS

Do you think anyone's ever bit-
ten their tongue and then decided to eat the rest?

DRAKE SATHER

Chitlins? That's pig intestines!
That includes the lower tract.

Ain't no food down in that area. Chitlins—I think somebody misspelled that word.

BILL COSBY

Most cheeses need work. I don't want to be in the same country as goat cheese. It always tastes the way a yak looks in one of those National Geographic specials.

ERMA BOMBECK

Tofu—what is that stuff? It's like spackling compound. It's like chickpeas and grout. Food should not caulk windows.

BILLIAM CORONEL

I stopped my subscription to *Consumer Reports* . . . I don't want to know about the "acceptable amount" of rodent hair in wholesale tuna fish. I'm a very weird guy. I have *no* acceptable amount of rodent hair. Some people, 300, 400 hairs in a can. Some, seven or eight. For me, even two is too many for me!

ROBERT KLEIN

Why is it that Swiss cheese has the holes when it's Gorgonzola that needs the ventilation?

DAVID FROST

The worst gift is a fruitcake. There is only one fruitcake in the entire world, and people keep sending it to each other.

JOHNNY CARSON

Finish your vegetables! There are children in Beverly Hills with eating disorders.

JOHN CALLAHAN

Tell me, why do they keep saying, "This cereal is shot out of a cannon." Who cares? So are cannonballs, but they don't taste good with cream and sugar. In fact, so is the man in the circus shot out of a cannon, but he just lands in a net. And what's so good about a cereal that makes a loud cracking noise? So would the man in the circus if you took away the net.

HENRY MORGAN

Who invented cottage cheese? And how did they know when they were done? It looks like it's already been eaten.

Never buy anything you have to order by the size of its curd.

Of *course* it's a perfect diet

food. Look at it. Do you have an appetite now?

CAROL SISKIND

Cured ham? No, thanks, pal. Cured of what? What if it has a relapse on my plate?

TOMMY SLEDGE

They have this stuff in the supermarket—*imitation* crab-meat. You know there aren't fish at the bottom of the ocean going, "Wait—I do a *great* crab!"

RICK CORSO

Despite the fact that meat is made from dead animals . . . almost all varieties of meat are good enough to be better than vegetables, except veal. Veal is very young beef and, like a very young girlfriend, it's cute but boring and expensive . . .

Poultry is like meat, except when you cook it rare. Then it's like bird-flavored Jell-O.

Fish—you have to wonder about a food that everybody agrees is great except that sometimes it tastes like what it is . . .

Most vegetables are something God invented to let women get even with their children. A fruit is a vegetable with looks and money. Plus, if you let fruit rot, it turns into wine, something brussels sprouts never do.

P. J. O'ROURKE

Lunchtime. My momma used to pack those tongue sand-wiches. And I couldn't eat them tongue sandwiches. I couldn't eat tongue. I couldn't eat nothing that came out of an animal's mouth. I had too much class. My favorite was egg sandwiches.

LARRY STORCH

If a Real Man doesn't eat quiche, just what does his diet consist of? Essentially, Real Men are meat and potatoes eaters. Real Men eat beef. They eat frozen peas. And wa-termelon. Plus French fries and apple pie (two important diet staples). As a general rule, Real Men won't eat anything that is poached, sautéed, minced, blended, glazed, cur-ried, flambéed, stir-fried, or *en brochette* . . . and above ev-erything else—all trends aside —Real Men refuse to refer to spaghetti as pasta.

BRUCE FEIRSTEIN

I had fried mozzarella cheese. Deep-fried cheese. Oh, there's a cardiovascular dream come true. The cheese doesn't have enough fat—let's give it a cholesterol Jacuzzi!

RICK CORSO

According to statistics, a man eats a prune every twenty seconds. I don't know who this fella is, but I know where to find him.

MOREY AMSTERDAM

Everything tastes so much better at a picnic—the ants, the sand, *everything!*

STAN HUNT

I hate skinny women, especially when they say things like "Sometimes I forget to eat." Now, I've forgotten my mother's maiden name, and my keys, but you've got to be a special kind of stupid to forget to eat!

MARSHA WARFIELD

Football

Across this pretty little green cow pasture, somebody had drawn white lines all over it, and drove posts in it and I looked down and I saw five or six convicts running up and down and blowing whistles . . . I seen thirty or forty men come runnin' out of one end of a great big outhouse. And everybody where I was a sittin' got up and hollered. And about that time thirty or forty come runnin' out of the other end of the outhouse . . . Both bunches full of them men wanted this funny-lookin' little punkin to play with. And I know, friends, that they couldn't a eat it because they kicked it the whole evening and it never busted. Both bunches full wanted that thing, and one bunch got it and it made the other bunch just as mad as they could be, and, friends, I seen the awfullest fight that I have ever seen in my life. They would run at one another, and kick one another and throw one another down, and stomp on one another, and grind their feet in one another, and just as fast as one of 'em would get hurt they'd tote him off and run another on!

Well, they done that as long as I sat there . . . I got up and left. And I don't know, friends, to this day, what it was they was a doin' down there, but I have studied about it. I think it's some kind of a contest where they see which bunch full of them men can take that punkin and run from one end of that cow pasture to the other, without either gettin' knocked down or steppin' in something.

ANDY GRIFFITH

They call it football, but the object of the game is to bash the other guy so hard that he's eventually carried off the field on a stretcher. I can't watch football anymore. My psychiatrist said it's better that way. I used to watch a game, see the players in a huddle—and think they were talking about me.

JACKIE MASON

I would let all forty-five guys play at the same time . . . Get in there and hurt some-body! And never mind lining up. Just grab the ball and run . . . Leave the injured on the field! They always say it's like a war. Fine, let the Red Cross come and pick these assholes up!

GEORGE CARLIN

I love football . . . Football's a fair sport for my people. Only sport in the world a Negro can chase a white man and 40,000 people stand up and cheer him.

DICK GREGORY

America's favorite sport is talking. Football is really just talk. You only get about four and a half seconds of action and then everybody talks. The commentators talk, the spectators talk, even the players get together and talk. Then they go back, sadly silent, play for another four and a half seconds, and then they get together and talk again!

JOHN CLEESE

Halftime shows really stink. The announcers don't even want to watch. "Now, the Phillips High School band pays a tribute . . . to mayonnaise!" They form a gigantic mayon-

naise jar on the field. One kid missed practice, doesn't know where to go. He's running around. From the stands it looks like a fly in the mayonnaise jar. And they announce it: "There's a fly in the mayonnaise jar! Very clever . . ."
ROBERT KLEIN

Foreign Languages

I would love to speak a foreign language but I can't. So I grew hair under my arms instead.
SUE KOLINSKY

Boy, those French, they have a different word for everything.
STEVE MARTIN

Fourth of July

We have killed more people celebrating Independence Day than we lost fighting for it.
WILL ROGERS

French Translations

Coup de grâce: Lawn mower
Chateaubriand: Your hat is on fire
Pas de tout: Father of twins
Entrechat: Let the cat in
Marseillaise: Ma says okay
F. S. PEARSON 2d

La Belle Dame Sans Merci: The beautiful lady who never says thank you.
MICHAEL FLANDERS

Apéritif: a set of dentures.
SPIKE MILLIGAN

"*Mal de mer* is merely a Frenchman's way of saying, "You can't take it with you."
MAURICE CHEVALIER

Freedom

Don't ever tell anyone they ain't free, 'cos they're gonna get real busy killin' and maimin' just to prove they are.
TERRY SOUTHERN (script for *Easy Rider*)

107

Frigidity

She looked as though butter wouldn't melt in her mouth— or anywhere else.

ELSA LANCHESTER

My wife and I made love on a water bed. Her side froze! My wife was so frigid that when she opened her mouth, a light would come on.

RIP TAYLOR

Funerals

I'd started making up this revenge list, like people I'd like to get sooner or later. And the hang-up about doing this is that you're worried about them dying and you won't get the chance. So I started to get different ways to be offensive at the funerals:

Shake the widow's hand with an electric buzzer. Stand around the cemetery saying, "At least he'll no longer be tormented over being impotent."

Tell the clergyman that the deceased was a vampire and ask if you can drive a stake through his heart . . . On the way home from the cemetery, tell the widow that you're not sure, but you think that you saw the body move.

ED BLUESTONE

A funeral eulogy is a belated plea for the defense delivered after the evidence is all in.

IRVIN S. COBB

My uncle's funeral cost five thousand dollars so far. We buried him in a rented tuxedo.

DAVE MADDEN

Forest Lawn is like a Disneyland for shut-ins.

JACK PAAR

I hope you'll think this is funny. A man calls an undertaker and says, "You better make arrangements for a funeral. My wife passed away." The undertaker says, "You must be drunk. I buried your wife two years ago." He says, "I got married again." The undertaker says, "Oh! Congratulations!"

What else do you say?

Speaking of undertakers, an undertaker calls a son-in-law: "About your mother-in-law, should we embalm her, cremate her, or bury her?" He says, "Do all three. Don't take chances."

MYRON COHEN

There's nothing funny about a funeral. Except in the South . . . Southerners are naturally humorous. The funeral procession started by and everybody got quiet, put their hand over their heart, and I whispered to this ol' boy, "Who died?" He said, "The one in the first car."

JERRY CLOWER

Martin Levine has passed away at the age of 75. Mr. Levine had owned a movie theater chain here in New York. The funeral will be held on Thursday, at 2:15, 4:20, 6:30, 8:40, and 10:50.

DAVID LETTERMAN

I think the easiest job in the world has to be coroner. Surgery on dead people. What's the worst thing that could happen? If everything went wrong, maybe you'd get a pulse.

DENNIS MILLER

Joe and Willie were partners in the fur business, and they agreed that whichever one died first, the other would place one thousand dollars in the coffin of the deceased to cover whatever expenses came up in the next world.

Some time after the agreement was made, Willie passed away. When Joe returned from the funeral, the wife said, "I bet you were too cheap to put one thousand dollars in the coffin like you promised." Joe swore that he did. "I tell you, I put one thousand dollars in the coffin. Here, look at the checkbook.

EDDIE CANTOR

I'm not afraid of death. It's the make-over at the undertaker's that scares me . . . They try to make you look as lifelike as possible, which defeats the whole purpose. It's hard to feel bad for somebody who looks better than you do.

ANITA WISE

The mere thought of cremation turned him ashen.

PETER DE VRIES

Questioning an undertaker: Can a person furnish his own casket? Would a large radio cabinet be acceptable for burial if hollowed out and made into a child's casket? My uncle, a midget, is dying; can I get a special rate for him? Can I bury a dog in his own doghouse? Is it permitted to plant tomatoes atop the grave? If I own a funeral plot, am I allowed to dig there for fishing worms after a rain? Is there any way the deceased can signal after interment if he's still alive? How do I know you're not going to dig up the casket after a funeral and resell it?

W. C. FIELDS (anecdote recalled by

CARLOTTA MONTI)

The $1.98 funeral—naturally that's not an elaborate ceremony. In fact, they don't bury you for that. They put you in a plain brown envelope and mail you out of town. For an extra fifty cents they'll have the postal clerks hum a hymn as you go through the cancellation.

PAT BUTTRAM

Funeral services were held this week for 82-year-old chewing-gum magnate Philip K. Wrigley. In keeping with his last request, Wrigley's remains will be stuck to the bottom of a luncheonette counter.

JANE CURTIN

Gambling

You should never challenge "worse." Don't ever say, "Things couldn't get worse." Worse is rough . . . I was down to my last two hundred dollars. I mean, not to my name, but I lost all I could sign for. And I said, "I'm gonna win something! It can't get worse!"

I went over to the roulette wheel. And got two hundred dollars' worth of quarter chips. Covered the table—I mean, covered the table! Red and black, even up. I'm going to win something before I go to sleep. And the guy spun the ball and it fell on the floor.

BILL COSBY

I used to be a heavy gambler. But now I just make mental bets. That's how I lost my mind.

STEVE ALLEN

My wife and I were in Las Vegas. My wife called down and asked for room service—and a half hour later they send up a table and a dealer. Of course, my wife doesn't gamble, so she sent the table back. And then just before I left the apartment, I sent the dealer back. I don't gamble either.

VICTOR BORGE

Mr. Goldfarb couldn't resist temptation. He got into a dice game one night. As everyone watched, the loser turned into a winner. His luck kept holding, and he was up by three thousand dollars. He decided to make one last bet—and lost everything. The shock was so great he had a heart attack and dropped dead. The other men around the table had to figure out how to tell Mrs. Goldfarb the news.

One of them went to tell Mrs. Goldfarb. He knocked on the door and said, "Mrs. Goldfarb, your husband was shooting dice with me and my friends tonight."

"That bum!" she said. "I told him never to gamble!"

"Well, he did—and he won three thousand dollars."

"My goodness!"

"Then he bet it all on the next roll of the dice and he lost."

"What? He lost all the money?"

"That's right!"

"That bum! He should drop dead!"

"He did."

BENNY RUBIN

Gambling is a way of getting nothing for something.

WILSON MIZNER

Bookie: A pickpocket who lets you use your own hands.

HENRY MORGAN

Germans

My husband is German. Last night I dressed up as Poland and he invaded me.

BETTE MIDLER

Germany is a little sullen. It's gray, unhappy. I think the big hope for Germany is if Ted Turner would buy it and color it.

BILLY CRYSTAL

I eat at this German-Chinese restaurant and the food is delicious. The only problem is that an hour later you're hungry for power.

DICK CAVETT

I'm half Jewish—and my wife is half German. At the wedding my wife was so nervous her monocle kept falling off. And then after the wedding my side of the family signed the wedding book—and her side of the family burned it . . . Not the wedding book . . . They burned my side of the family. The reception was great. Her father was a lot of laughs once

we got him away from the machine gun . . . His idea of a good time is a forced march to Milwaukee.

DON ADAMS

Gloom

My grandfather used to make home movies and edit out the joy.

RICHARD LEWIS

I say stay away from the miserable people, because misery does love company. Just look at a fly strip. You never see a fly stuck there saying, "Go around! Go around!"

MARGARET SMITH

The meek shall inherit the earth. They won't have the nerve to refuse it.

JACKIE VERNON

I made quite a name for myself back home. I left when I found out what it was.

HERB SHRINER

My friend thought he was not gonna make it. Then he started

thinking positive. Now he's positive he's not gonna make it.

BROTHER SAMMY SHORE

I took up a collection for a man in our office. But I didn't get enough money to buy one.

RUTH BUZZI

Happiness isn't something you experience. It's something you remember.

OSCAR LEVANT

In high school my parents told me I ran with the wrong crowd. I was a loner.

JEFF SHAW

I'm going to start living within my means. Even if I have to get a loan to do it.

TOM WILSON ("Ziggy")

The chief obstacle to the progress of the human race is the human race.

DON MARQUIS

Life wasn't too bad. The trouble with man was, even while he was having a good time, he didn't appreciate it. Why, thought Milligan, this very mo-

ment might be the happiest in my life. The very thought of it made him miserable.

SPIKE MILLIGAN

Creator: A comedian whose audience is afraid to laugh.

H. L. MENCKEN

And God looked down and saw that the land and the people were bad. If he didn't look down so much, maybe things would pick up.

DAVID STEINBERG

It is the final proof of God's omnipotence that he need not exist in order to save us.

PETER DE VRIES

God is in my mind and the devil's in my pants.

JONATHAN WINTERS

God gave us these bodies because he has better ones at home.

B. KLIBAN

Golf

While playing golf today I hit two good balls. I stepped on a rake.

HENNY YOUNGMAN

I'm convinced the reason most people play golf is to wear clothes they would not be caught dead in otherwise.

ROGER SIMON

A Scot was playing golf. He'd never tried it before, so he went to the clubhouse for some equipment. He bought a half dozen golf clubs—and one golf ball. He came back after being out on the links for a few hours, and he told the man in the clubhouse, "I want to buy another half dozen clubs." The man said, "And would you want to buy another ball, sir?" He said, "Another ball? Why, I have not hit the first one yet!"

HARRY LAUDER

A guy is standing in front of his locker at the country club admiring a golf ball he has in his hand. One of his golfing buddies says to him, "What'd you do, get some new golf balls?"

And the guy says, "Would you believe that this is the greatest golf ball ever made. You can't lose it. You hit it into the rough and it whistles. You hit it into the woods and a bell inside goes off. If you drive it into a lake, a big burst of steam shoots up six feet in the air for two minutes."

And his friend says, "That's great. Where did you get it?"

And the guy says, "I found it."

SOUPY SALES

I had a wonderful experience on the golf course today. I had a hole in nothing. Missed the ball and sank the divot.

DON ADAMS

Let me get this straight: The less I hit the ball, the better I am doing . . . Then why do it at all?

JOHNNY HART ("BC")

You got the ball. You had it right there. Then . . . you hit it away! And then . . . you go and walk after it again! It's a dumb game!

BILL COSBY

I play in the low 80s. If it's any hotter than that, I won't play.

JOE E. LEWIS

I like the story about the two drunks who went out to play golf. The first drunk didn't even tee the ball up, he just threw it down on the ground. He said, "By golly, Fred, it looks like I got a half dozen golf balls down there." The second drunk said, "Then you shouldn't have any trouble hittin' 'em with all the clubs you have in your hand."

Half an hour later the same two drunks are stumbling up the 3rd fairway. This one drunk turned to the other and said, "Fred, I'm going up and tell those two women up there to either get the devil off this golf course or let us play through . . ." So he ran up, got almost up to 'em, and ran back saying, "Good heavens, Fred, I almost got trapped. One of those girls is my wife and the other's my mistress. Boy, what a close call."

Second one says, "I'm new around here. I'll go tell 'em." Well, the second one races up, he gets almost up too, turns around and runs back and says,

"By God, John, it's a small world, isn't it?"

WOODY WOODBURY

Golf, there's a thing that torments you and won't let you enjoy yourself. You've got to relax. I got out of this country's worst sand trap with just one stroke. Of course, the doctor said if I had another stroke like that it would be all over.

DAVE ASTOR

You drink at a bar in the daytime, people call you a drunkard. You drink at the golf course, you're a sportsman! So I get drunk like a sportsman. And it's convenient. You fall down, you land on grass, you never get hurt. If somebody hollers "Fore!" that means two doubles.

JACKIE MILES

If you watch a game, it's fun. If you play it, it's recreation. If you work at it, it's golf.

BOB HOPE

I was hitting some horrible shots one time. It wasn't unusual for me. I turned to the old guy who was caddying for me, and I said, "I suppose you've seen worse golfers in your time." He didn't say a word. So I repeated my question. Almost shouting this time, I said, "Hey! I suppose you've seen worse golfers in your time." He said, "I heard you the first time—I was just trying to remember when."

I wonder if it was the same old codger who caddied for my wife one day. She said, "I've never played this badly before." And he said, "You've played before?"

BOB KALIBAN

Guns

Ditsey Baummortal went duck shooting with old Uncle George Terwilliger. A flock of ducks flew overhead and Uncle George took a potshot at them and one fell down on the beach —dead. Ditsey walked over and looked at it. "Hey, Uncle George," he said. "That was a waste of ammunition to shoot that duck. The fall alone would have killed it."

"SENATOR" ED FORD

But why do I need a gun license? It's only for use around the house.

CHARLES ADDAMS

The NRA is attempting to lift the ban on machine-gun sales. Well, as an avid hunting enthusiast, I've been hoping to buy a fully automatic Uzi in time for duck-hunting season! One thing about a machine gun, it really takes the guesswork out of duck hunting.

MARK RUSSELL

He is running for Congress . . . Do you know why he will be elected? Because all the gun owners will vote for him. Why will they vote for him? Because he is against any new law which will require registration of firearms. He claims that if there is a war, we might be invaded by Communists. And we will all need guns. With nuts like that in Congress, it could happen.

LARRY SIEGEL

The most violent sport of all has to be hunting—if you consider it a sport. After all, a hunter sneaks up on his prey. That's not very sporting. Between rounds a boxer doesn't tiptoe around the apron of the ring and smack his opponent in the back of the head! Hunters are cowards—if they weren't, they'd hunt each other. Now, that would be a sport: "Look at the big fat one I got over by the tavern. He was wearing an orange hat, I couldn't miss him . . ."

JEFF STILSON

Without guns, how are we gonna shoot anybody? We need guns. You never can tell when you're walking down the street you'll spot a moose. Suppose a man comes home early and finds another man with his wife? What's he supposed to do? Poison him? How about suicide? Can you imagine trying to beat yourself to death with a stick?

But let's be objective about this. Guns are not the real problem. The real problem is bullets.

PAT PAULSEN

The fascination of shooting as a sport depends on whether you are at the right or the wrong end of the gun.

P. G. WODEHOUSE

Gynecology

The gynecologist says, "Relax, relax, I can't get my hand out, relax." I wonder why I'm not relaxed. My feet are in the stirrups, my knees are in my face, and the door is open facing me . . . Can we talk here? Men don't understand . . . For a woman to lie in those stirrups, is that the worst? And my gynecologist does jokes! "Dr. Schwartz at your cervix!" "I'm dilated to meet you!" "Say ahhh." "There's Jimmy Hoffa!" There's no way you can get back at that son of a bitch unless you learn to throw your voice.

JOAN RIVERS

I'd like to be an obstetrician. Look at all the guys you have working for you all the time.

BERT HENRY

In what other business could a guy tell a girl to get undressed —and send the bill to her husband?

JACKIE MASON

Hollywood

Hollywood is a place where people from Iowa mistake each other for movie stars.

FRED ALLEN

You ought to go to Hollywood. The walk would do you good.

ARCHIE CAMPBELL

On Hollywood Boulevard, not far from where we are, we have the stars' names lying on the sidewalk. In the old days the stars themselves were lying on the sidewalk.

STEVE ALLEN

Hollywood is a place where you spend more than you make, on things you don't need, to impress people you don't like.

KEN MURRAY

Homeless

They say the homeless are homeless by choice. That's true. I was walking down Bleecker Street at two in the morning, and I just had that burning desire to go to sleep right there.

SCOTT BLAKEMAN

I'm dating a homeless woman. It was easier to talk her into staying over.

GARRY SHANDLING

I was walking down 126th Street on my way to work. Met a fella. He said, "Moms, I *hate this*, I really *hate this*, but, Moms, gimme some money! I ain't got *no home*. I ain't got *no family, no children, no wife!* My mother, my father are dead! Moms, gimme some money! I ain't got *nowhere to eat*, I ain't got *nowhere to sleep*. I ain't got *nothin'*, Moms. But this gun.

MOMS MABLEY

I saw this old woman digging for food through a garbage can. I don't know about you folks. I have a lot of love for old women going through garbage cans. They saved my life so many times as a baby.

EMO PHILIPS

Homes

I can't believe I actually own my own house. I'm looking at a house and it's two hundred grand. The realtor says, "It's got a great view." For two hundred grand I better open up the curtains and see breasts against the window.

GARRY SHANDLING

I'm leaving the apartment. But first I'm getting a thousand roaches. 'Cause it said in the rent book, "Leave the place as you found it."

DOLLY ALLEN

I'm living on a one-way dead-end street. I don't know how I got there.

STEVEN WRIGHT

The shower is the greatest invention. I don't like to take a bath. I don't like to wash my face in the water I've been sitting in.

LEWIS GRIZZARD

This morning there was ice on the pipes in my apartment. But the landlord fixed it. He put antifreeze in the radiator.

HERB SHRINER

My bathroom has a digital sink. When I want to stop the water running, I put my finger in the faucet.

RON SMITH

The fellow that owns his own home is always just coming out of a hardware store.

KIN HUBBARD

In our apartment house we have a very scientific plumbing system. Every apartment has three pipes running through it. One for hot water, one for cold water, and one to bang on when there is no hot or cold water.

ED WYNN

We are in the process of buying a home. When you buy a home you deal with realtors. Realtors are people who did not make it as used-car salesmen.

BOB NEWHART

Mr. Rivera was the landlord in the apartment building I grew up in. He was the kind of landlord who never wanted to fix anything in the apartment. But wanted a key anyway. In case of emergency. Like he was broke.

FREDDIE PRINZE

I just bought a new house. It has no plumbing. It's uncanny.

MOREY AMSTERDAM

In-window air conditioners don't actually cool the air. The noise takes your mind off the heat.

RICK DUCOMMON

They got some new apartments down on Riverside Drive, so I went down to get me an apartment. I said, "I'd like to have five rooms," and the man said, "Sorry, Mr. White, but we've got to put you on the waiting list. It'll be about two years before we can get you in this apartment house."

I said, "Two years? Okay, get me in as soon as you can." I ran my hand in my pocket, dropped a thousand dollars in the trash can. I said, "If you find anything, let me know. Here's my phone number."

I go on home. About a half hour later the phone rang. "Mr. White, we do have one apartment left." So I go back down and sign a five-year lease. About four days later I get a phone call from the same guy. He said, "Mr. White, that money in the trash can—it was counterfeit. It was no good."

I said, "I know, that's why I threw it away!"

SLAPPY WHITE

Homosexuals

"The strange thing about Dirk —we happened to go down to the Army induction center the same day . . . Everybody was very uptight. Now, you can't fool doctors, and the doctor said, "Dirk, be honest, do you really think you can kill a man?" And Dirk said, "Yes— but it would take weeks!"

SANDY BARON

My brother is gay and my parents don't care as long as he marries a doctor.

ELAYNE BOOSLER

In San Francisco, Halloween is redundant.

WILL DURST

Some men think that they can convert gay women, make them straight. I couldn't do that. I could make a straight woman gay, though.

JEFF STILSON

The Supreme Court ruled that homosexuality is a crime . . . Now, we don't know how our founding forepersons felt about this subject. Did Patrick Henry once say, "I know not the course others may take, but as for me, give me liberty or give me Fred"? We don't know. I don't think we ever had a President who was gay. A couple of 'em bordered on the jovial. But the criminality in question, defined by the Court, is sodomy, taken from the ancient city of Sodom. You can still commit Gomorrah—as long as it's practiced between two consenting Philistines.

MARK RUSSELL

I went to see the Gay Parade. Now, gay is a sexual preference. I don't know why they have their own parade. There's not a Missionary-Position Parade or a Woman-Superior Parade. How about a Doggie-Style Parade? I'd be on the float. I'd be leading that parade. Well, I'd be second . . . But I would rather know fifty gays than one Jehovah's Witness. You won't ever see a gay at your front door trying to convert you.

JEFFREY JENA

They go on so much about San Francisco and homosexuality when you tell people you're going there. When I got there I was quite relieved to find out it wasn't compulsory.

JASPER CARROTT

What do you call a man who marries another man? A vicar!

BENNY HILL

I've just been to New York, and when I went through Immigration they asked me if I was gay. I said, "No, but I've slept with a lot of guys who are."

SIMON FANSHAWE

I get even with my parents. I told them I was gay. 'Cause I'm going out with this guy I know they'll hate. Now when they meet him they'll love him.

MARGARET SMITH

My doctor said "I have some bad news and some good news for you." I said, "Okay, give me the bad news." He said, "Well, it's all how you regard something like this, but you show very definite signs of homosexuality." I said, "Oh, come on. What in the world is the good news?" He said, "The good news is I think you're cute."

FOSTER BROOKS

Horoscopes

Jupiter's passed through Orion and come into conjunction with Mars.
Saturn is wheeling through infinite space to its preordained place in the stars.
And I gaze at the planets in wonder—at the time and trouble they expend.

All to warn me to be careful in dealings involving a friend.

DONALD SWANN

Horoscopes: The book says people born in January are gentle. February people are honest. March people are sincere. April people are trustworthy and so on and so on. Now, what I don't understand is: Where the hell do all the rotten people come from?

LOU ALEXANDER

I read my horoscope. The first line said, "Ignore bad advice." Fine. I stopped reading my horoscope.

DAN SPENCER

Hospitals

I was real calm about the operation. Till I realized what I was doing. I'm lying there naked. On a table in front of people I don't know. And they have knives. What's wrong with this picture?

TOM PARKS

I had a general anesthetic. That's so weird. You go to sleep in one room, then you wake up four hours later in a totally different room. Just like college.

ROSS SHAFER

There's nothing wrong with you that an expensive operation can't prolong.

GRAHAM CHAPMAN

A bunch of guys were playing cards in the hospital. They figured out a method of playing poker using the diagnosis chart at the foot of the bed. First guy said, "I got a pair of hernias." Second guy says, "I have three ruptures." Third guy says, "Well, I have four enemas." Well, they gave him the pot.

DAVY BOLD

They try to humiliate you in the hospital. They make you pee in a bottle. I hate that. I was in the hospital. The nurse said, "You have to pee in a bottle." When she left I poured Mountain Dew in there. She came back and I chugged it. She was puking for days. It's a sick world and I'm a happy guy!

LARRY REEB

A little woman called Mount Sinai Hospital. She said, "Mount Sinai Hospital? Hello. Darling, I'd like to talk with the person who gives the information about the patients. But I don't want to know if the patient is better or doing like expected, or worse, I want all the information from top to bottom, from A to B."

The voice on the other end of the line said, "Would you hold the line, please, that's a very unusual request."

Then a very authoritative voice came on and said, "Are you the lady who is calling about one of the patients?"

She said, "Yes, darling! I'd like to know the information about Sarah Finkel, in Room 302."

He said, "Finkel. Finkel. Let me see. Feinberg, Farber—Finkel. Oh yes. Mrs. Finkel is doing very well. In fact, she's had two full meals, her blood pressure is fine, and if she continues this way, her doctor is going to send her home Tuesday at twelve o'clock."

The woman said, "Thank God! That's wonderful! She's going home at twelve o'clock!

I'm so happy to hear that, that's wonderful news."

The guy on the other end said, "From your enthusiasm, I take it you must be one of the close family."

She said, "What close family? I'm Sarah Finkel! My doctor don't tell me nothing!"

PHIL STONE

If I am ever stuck on a respirator or a life-support system, I definitely want to be unplugged—but not till I get down to a size 8.

HENRIETTE MANTEL

Hotels and Motels

Why is it that they have Bibles in every motel room? Why should a man want to read the Bible when he's with a woman alone in a motel room? Why would he be interested? Whatever he's praying for, he's already got!

JACKIE MASON

My hotel room is so small that when I die they won't have to put me in a casket. They'll just put handles on the room.

HERB SHRINER

I'm staying in a strange hotel. I called room service for a sandwich and they sent up two hookers.

BILL MAHER

My friend and his wife stayed in a hotel and got a bill for ninety dollars. He screamed, "For what, ninety dollars?" The desk clerk said, "For room and board, sir."

My friend said, "Room and board? We didn't eat here." The clerk said, "It was there for you. If you didn't get it it's your fault." My friend said, "You take forty dollars—I'm charging you fifty dollars for fooling around with my wife!"

The clerk said, "I never touched your wife." My friend said, "It was there for you."

NORM CROSBY

A hotel is a place where you get out of a taxi with two suitcases and an attaché case and the doorman says, "Are you checking in, sir?"

A hotel is a place that keeps

the manufacturers of 25-watt bulbs in business.

A hotel is a place where the minute your shower temperature is adjusted somebody signals the guy next door to flush his toilet and scald you to death.

A hotel is a place where you can keep in condition by leaping the trays of dirty dishes in the corridor.

A hotel is a place where you come out of the entrance with two suitcases and an attaché case and the doorman says, "Leaving us, sir?"

SHELLEY BERMAN

Housework

I haven't cleaned in a while. I've got a messy house—a milk carton with a picture of the Lindbergh baby on it.

GREG RAY

If you want to get rid of stinking odors in the kitchen, stop cooking.

ERMA BOMBECK

Sheets can be kept clean by getting drunk and falling asleep with your clothes on.

P. J. O'ROURKE

Supposing you're a housewife and you've goofed. Let's put it this way. It's 4:30 and you're still in bed—and that's pretty close to Ogre Time. Try the following: Put a little O'Cedar wax behind each ear. It makes you smell tired. Splash cold water on your face. If you pant a little, it looks exactly like beads of sweat. Rouge your knees. It will look like you have been scrubbing the floors.

PHYLLIS DILLER

There's the commercial on TV where the woman is smelling her clothes. She says, "They smell as fresh as all outdoors!" Is that ridiculous? Do you realize what all outdoors smells like? If she lived in New York, she'd cough for twenty-two minutes.

LARRY WILDE

Humor

A humorist is a man who feels bad but who feels good about it.

DON HEROLD

Husbands

A husband is what's left of a man after the nerve is extracted.

HELEN ROWLAND

There is a vast difference between the savage and the civilized man, but it is never apparent to their wives until after breakfast.

HELEN ROWLAND

I saw a woman walking in the street, crying. I felt such compassion, I went up and asked, "What's the matter?"

She said, "What's the matter? Oh! My husband! How I'm gonna miss him! Oh, gosh! I'll miss him! True, he was bad, he used to drink and smoke and gamble, and he'd bring women to the house, and he had lipstick on all his shirts—but OH! I'm gonna miss him!"

I said, "When did he die?"

She said, "He starts tomorrow."

JACK CARTER

The other day he woke up with a headache. I felt sorry for him. I would like to help him but I can't. I told him so many times; when he jumps out of bed—feet first.

JEAN CARROLL

My husband forgot my birthday and my anniversary. I didn't feel bad. On the contrary. Give me a guilty husband any day. Some of my best outfits come from his guilt!

BETTY WALKER

He can recall the score of the Army-Navy game of '54, the electoral votes the Republicans won in the last election, and the gas mileage of the first car he ever owned. But he can't remember what size socks he wears, the ages of his children, or the name of that old Cole

Porter number that his wife refers to as "our" song.

JANE GOODSELL

Translations from the Husband:

"There's not one clean shirt."

He's looking in the underwear drawer.

"I don't know what you're talking about."

He knows what you're talking about, but he doesn't know what you're saying about what you're talking about.

"Me? Angry?"

He. Angry.

"I don't want to talk about it."

He doesn't want you to talk about it anymore. Please.

"The subject is closed."

He'll bring you some flowers.

"Let's just forget all about it."

He'll bring you some flowers, and you remember it and he'll forget all about it.

ROBERT PAUL SMITH

I like a man that wears a wedding ring. 'Cause without it, they're like a shark without a fin. You pretty much got to know they're out there.

BRETT BUTLER

My wife thinks I'm too nosy. At least that's what she keeps scribbling in her diary.

DRAKE SATHER

He wrecked his car, he lost his job
And yet throughout his life,
He took his troubles like a man:
He blamed them on his wife

FRANK CONNORS

My wife and I were happy for twenty years. Then we met.

RODNEY DANGERFIELD

Hygiene

Deodorants are dangerous, man. Ever read on deodorant cans: "Caution, Contents Highly Inflammable. May Explode." I don't know about you people, but I don't want nothin' under my arm that's gonna explode!

RICHARD PRYOR

Hypochondria

The best cure for hypochondria is to forget about your body and get interested in somebody else's.

GOODMAN ACE

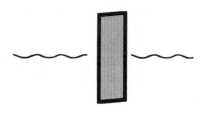

Ideas

Don't spend two dollars to dry-clean a shirt. Donate it to the Salvation Army instead. They'll clean it and put it on a hanger. Next morning buy it back for seventy-five cents.

BILLIAM CORONEL

My father invented the burglar alarm—which unfortunately was stolen from him.

VICTOR BORGE

I have invented rubber food for old people with time to kill.

PAT McCORMICK

I've invented salt that looks like pepper, and pepper that looks like salt, so if anyone takes the wrong one by mistake, it's all right.

COLONEL LEMUEL STOOPNAGLE

(FREDERICK TAYLOR)

I make stained-glass contact lenses—for people who want to sleep in church.

LONDON LEE

My uncle invented the solar-powered funeral home. He's got basic solar technology, big panels on the roof, the sun beats down, it heats up the panels. Trouble is, he can't cremate, he can only poach.

HEYWOOD BANKS

In the studio later we'll be showing you the latest thing in digital watches. When you press the button, a little finger comes out and points to the nearest person with the right time.

RONNIE BARKER

Illness

My aunt's had a terrible time. First off, she got tonsillitis, followed by appendicitis and pneumonia. After that she got rheumatism, and to top it off they gave her hypodermics and inoculations. I thought she never would get through that there spellin' bee.

JUDY CANOVA

I was lying in the street moaning and groaning from an attack of asthma when the driver of a library truck stuck his head out of the window and said, "Shh! Shh!"

STANLEY MYRON HANDELMAN

You have a cough? Go home tonight, eat a whole box of Ex-Lax, tomorrow you'll be *afraid* to cough.

PEARL WILLIAMS

My sister's asthmatic. In the middle of an asthma attack she got an obscene phone call. The guy said, "Did I call you or did you call me?"

JOHN MENDOZA

When you can't breathe through your nose, tomorrow seems strangely like the day before yesterday.

E. B. WHITE

As I said to the man with acromegaly, "Why the long face?"

STEVE ALLEN

Incest

The trouble with incest is that it gets you involved with relatives.

GEORGE S. KAUFMAN

Insanity

Insanity is hereditary; you can get it from your children.

SAM LEVENSON

Insults and Threats

You are excess baggage in the airport of life.

JUDY TENUTA

When you go to a mind reader, do you get half price?

BEN CREED

Cut yourself a slice of throat.

CURLY HOWARD

How are you holding up during the lithium shortage?

DAVID LETTERMAN

What do you use for birth control? Your personality?

RICHARD BELZER

Why don't you walk into a parking meter and violate yourself?

DICK CAVETT (written by Cavett for
   JACK E. LEONARD)

Your husband tells me you have a great mind. Too bad it hasn't reached your head.

JACK E. LEONARD

Why don't you put your face in dough and make jackass cookies?

SOUPY SALES

Don't think too hard . . . you might hurt yourself.

VICTOR MOORE

She's like a rose to me. They smell and so does she.

HOMER HAYNES

Why don't you bore a hole in yourself and let the sap run out?

GROUCHO MARX (in *Horse Feathers*)

I've got a good mind to join a club and beat you over the head with it.

GROUCHO MARX (in *Duck Soup*)

Do you mind if I jump up on your head? I feel like a walk around the block.

JACK KIRKWOOD

He's a self-made man . . . the living proof of the horrors of unskilled labor!

ED WYNN

He was the nearest thing I'd seen to a human being without actually being one.

SPIKE MILLIGAN

Save your breath, you may want it to clean your glasses later.

JULIUS TANNEN

If you ever become a mother, can I have one of the puppies?

CHARLES PIERCE

That corner over by the fireplace looks kind of bare. I'd like to see something hanging there —you.

LOU COSTELLO

I'll flip you like a cheese omelette, I'll lay you out like a wholesale carpet, buddy boy!

JEFF ALTMAN

The last time I saw a head like yours was in a bottle . . . I'll hit you on the top of your head so hard I'll drive your head down into your ribs. When you open your eyes you'll think you're in jail!

THE GREAT GILDERSLEEVE

(HAROLD PEARY)

Do you know the meaning of rigor mortis? Well, you will in a minute.

W. C. FIELDS

I just want to say, if you had lived, you would have been a very sick man.

JACK E. LEONARD

They say you shouldn't say nothin' about the dead unless it's good. He's dead. Good.

MOMS MABLEY

Elsie's awfully good to her mother—she never goes home.

CHARLEY WEAVER (CLIFF ARQUETTE)

You remind me of my brother Bosco—only he had a human head.

JUDY TENUTA

If my dog had your face, I'd shave his butt and teach him to walk backwards.

JAMIE FARR

He's got a wonderful head for money. There's this long slit on the top.

DAVID FROST

When you use your brain it's a violation of the child-labor law.

JOE E. LEWIS

You are a foul ball in the line drive of life.

CHARLES SCHULZ ("Peanuts")

131

It's a good thing you're wearing a mustache. It breaks up the monotony of your face.

RODNEY DANGERFIELD

The only reason you wear that mustache is because you're too cheap to buy scissors.

PAT COOPER

Ten million sperm and his had to win.

VALERIE LANDSBURG

I'll tear your esophagus out and shove it right in your eye . . . I'm gonna baste you in nitric acid . . . Remind me to tear out your Adam's apple . . . I'll tear your tonsils out and tie them around your neck for a bow tie . . . Remind me to kill you later.

MOE HOWARD

You're as goofy as a duck on ether.

DAVID LETTERMAN

What would you charge to haunt a house?

FRED ALLEN

When I get through making Benny eat his words he'll think he's been on a diet of dry alphabet soup.

FRED ALLEN

Intellectuals/ Intelligence

Intellectuals should never marry; they won't enjoy it, and besides, they should not reproduce themselves.

DON HEROLD

My father had silicone shots in his head to enlarge his brain. It worked. Now he has to wear a bra to keep his eyes in.

JACK GRAIMAN

If an animal does something, they call it instinct. If we do exactly the same thing for the same reason, they call it intelligence. Entomologists say that ants, for example, are guided entirely by instinct and not by intelligence. They say the ants do not know what they are doing. And do the entomologists know what *they* are doing? Besides watching ants, I mean. I'm only asking. I guess what they mean is that we all make mistakes, but intelligence enables us to do it on purpose.

WILL CUPPY

The dullard's envy of brilliant men is always assuaged by the suspicion that they will come to a bad end.

MAX BEERBOHM

|ntuition

Eva Goss was a woman given to uncanny intuitions. It was her contention, oft expressed to Mr. Goss, that the female of the species had an occult sixth sense which a mere male did not possess. Some of her intimations of disaster bordered on the supernatural, as witness the occasion, some years ago, when she had urged Mr. Goss to turn back to the house as they were setting out for a drive, because she had a premonition she left her cigarette burning somewhere. Mr. Goss could not find her cigarette, but while he was looking for it he had laid his lighted cigar on the hall table, and the house had burned to the ground. Mrs. Goss could not have been more pleased.

COREY FORD

|rish

My wife and I just celebrated our twelfth anniversary. I'm Catholic, so there's no real possibility of divorce. I'm Irish—so there is the possibility of murder.

J. J. WALL

My Uncle Tim met the parish priest and said, "Father, wasn't it a lovely bazaar we had two weeks ago?" "It was grand," said the priest. Tim said, "Incidentally, those automobiles that we had for prizes, who won the Cadillac?" And the priest said, "It so happens Father Duffy won the Cadillac. Wasn't he lucky?"

Uncle Tim said, "That he was. And the Oldsmobile we had there? Who won the Oldsmobile?" The priest said, "Well, Monsignor Fogarty won the Oldsmobile. Wasn't he lucky?"

He said, "Yes, that he was.

And the last car, the Plymouth, who won that?" The priest said, "Well, Bishop Donahue won that. Wasn't he lucky?" Then the priest said, "By the way, Timothy, how many chances did you take?"

He said, "I didn't take any. Wasn't I lucky!"

HAL McKAY

They were friendly enemies. Both were pub keepers. And they never missed a chance to put something over on one another.

Came election time and Mike was trying to get Pat to vote for him for alderman.

"I wouldn't vote for you if you were St. Peter himself," Pat announced.

Mike said, "If I were St. Peter you wouldn't be in my ward!"

LEW LEHR

A guy came into a nightclub and went up to the bar, pounded his fists on the bar, and yelled, "When Murphy drinks, everybody drinks!" So everybody got up—waiters, customers, hatcheck girls—everybody had a drink.

When the drink was fin-ished, Murphy again yelled, even louder and more emphatically, "When Murphy drinks, everybody drinks!" So everybody had a drink—the cop on the beat, the doorman—everybody had a drink.

When they finished that drink, Murphy slapped a dollar on the counter and yelled, "When Murphy pays—everybody pays!"

ROGER BOWER

The pubs close in Ireland at eleven o'clock at night. But we manage. Up in Donegal, this lovely part of Ireland, it is thirty minutes past closing time and some of the lads are still in the pub having a little drink. Father Murphy saw them as he went by, and he didn't like it, he was very annoyed. He walked in, he looked at them, and said, "Look at this! This is all we seem to think about, the demon rum has got us! For God's sake we must uplift ourselves and turn our backs on the evils of alcohol."

He said to Flynn, who was sitting at the bar, "Flynn, do you want to go to heaven?"

Flynn said, "God knows I do, Father, I do."

He said, "Right! Stand over there!"

He said to Hennessey, "What about you, Hennessey, do you want to go to heaven?" He said, "I do, Father, I do."

He said, "Right! Stand over there!"

Murphy is sitting at the bar with a pint of Guinness in each hand. That's his idea of a balanced diet. And the priest said, "Do you want to go to heaven?"

He said, "No, Father, not me, no, I don't, no."

The priest said, "You mean to stand there and tell me that when you die you don't want to go to heaven?"

He said, "Oh, when I die, yes! I thought you were going now!"

HAL ROACH

An Englishman thinks seated; a Frenchman, standing; an American, pacing; an Irishman, afterward.

AUSTIN O'MALLEY

This uncle of mine was on his way to a wake with a couple of fellas and they stopped in a saloon. One guy said to the bartender, "I'll have Three Feathers." The other guy said, "I'll have Four Roses." And the uncle said, "I'll have five martinis." They finally staggered out of there, and they were getting into the car, and one of them said to the uncle, "Dennis, are you gonna drive?" He said, "I'll have to. I can't walk." They got the car on a busy one-way street goin' in the wrong direction. And a cop stopped 'em. He said, "Where are you guys going? Didn't you see the arrows?" My uncle said, "I didn't even see the Indians." The cop said, "Where are you goin'?" The uncle said, "I don't know, but we must be late, 'cause everybody else is comin' back."

JIMMY JOYCE

Dugan and Finnegan were sitting around the cracker barrel in the village grocery store. "Ah, the spring," said Finnegan, "it's the best season of the year. When the April showers come and make everything come up out of the ground." "I hope not," said Dugan. "I got three wives down there."

"SENATOR" ED FORD

135

The ritual of the wake has not changed in a thousand years . . . They have the kitchen table, and they cover it with a white sheet and a silk pillow and they lay the remains out on the table and all the neighbors come in and pay their last respects.

Such a man lying there is Seamus O'Shaughnessy, passed on, deceased, gone over, demised, and he's stone dead as well.

Just then two of the legs on the table caved in and O'Shaughnessy slid onto the floor. And Muldoon said, "My God, what are we going to do?"

Murphy said, "Well, we'll have to level him up somehow. We'll put his head on a chair, we'll put a chair at his feet, we push a chair in underneath him, lift him up and level him out."

Muldoon said, "A good idea!"

Murphy said, "Leave it to me." Murphy looked at the people at the wake and said, "Can we have three chairs for the corpse?"

And they all went, "Hip hip hooray!"

HAL ROACH

The Irishman was crossing the street on a dark, cold, windy, miserable night. Oh, it was a horrible night, I tell you. Crossing the street and the rain was pouring and the wind was blowing, it was terrible. And in the darkness a car came along and gave an awful shot and down he went in the mud.

And he was lying there and a big crowd gathered and a policeman came along. He kneeled down alongside of him and said, "Can I do anything for you, sir?" And he said, "Yes." He said, "Would you mind calling me a rabbi?" And the policeman said, "You must be delirious, man. You must mean a priest, don't you?" He said, "No, no, call me a rabbi. I wouldn't get the good father out on a night like this."

HAL McKAY

A man walks into a bar and asks, "Is there a fella here called Rooney?" And this little fella like meself stood up and said, "I'm Rooney. What about it?" And the big fella nearly killed him! Broke his nose, broke six of his ribs, gave him two black eyes, and dashed out of the place. When he was gone, the little fella picked himself up and said, "I sure made a monkey out of him! Sure, I'm not Rooney at all!"

HAL ROACH

I come from an Irish family in Brooklyn, a few stockbrokers, a smattering of intellectuals . . . and 40 percent of the New York police force. My uncle the cop used to read me bedtime stories: "Humpty Dumpty sat on the wall, Humpty Dumpty fell—or was pushed—from the wall. The perpetrator has not been apprehended. Three male Hispanics were seen leaving the area."

COLIN QUINN

An Irishman was lying on his deathbed, and his wife was standing alongside of him. She whispered, "Is there anything I can do for you? Do you have a last dying wish?" He says, "Well, yes, I've been thinking about that. You know what I'd like, Maggie dear? I'd like some of that corned beef and cabbage I smell cooking in the kitchen." She said, "I'm sorry. I can't do that—I'm saving it for the wake."

HAL McKAY

Italian

I'm a defective Italian. I have absolutely no mechanical ability. You know when you go to the supermarket you step on that rubber part and the door opens? For years I thought that was a coincidence.

RICHARD JENI

I went to Palermo, that's a beautiful city. From the poorest peasants to the richest of nobility, they all understand and love opera deeply. Once a month they're graced with an opera star who performs for them. The month I was there they had a very bad experience. The opera star performing was terrible. He sang an aria but badly. Yet the people stood up and yelled, "Encore! Sing it again! Sing it again!" And he sang it again—worse than he sang it the first time. And the people stood up and said, "*Bravissimo!* Sing it again!"

He said, "You're a wonderful crowd, I'd love to sing for all of you, but I can't sing the same aria three times." And a little old man from the balcony stood up and yelled down, "You're gonna sing it till you learn it!"

CORBETT MONICA

A mother on my street walked into her son's room, four o'clock in the afternoon. He was asleep, a grown-up son, 42 years old. And she went right up to the bed in pointy shoes and she kicked him and said, "Look-a you. You 42 years old, you no work, sleep, ya big-a bum. You don't bring-a no money home, I cry-a my eyes out! Shame, shame on-a you, you bum."

And the fella stood up with tears in his eyes and said, "Mother, why do you talk like that? We're not Italian."

NORM CROSBY

Jail

Trouble at Dartmoor Prison today . . . A bomb destroyed the toilet block. Local residents have complained that, since then, at least twenty inmates have been seen going over the wall.

RONNIE BARKER

We will be talking to a man who was imprisoned in Wormwood Scrubs for his beliefs. He believed the night watchman was asleep.

RONNIE CORBETT

They have a big drive on now to rehabilitate prisoners. I think it's a great idea. They even bring in the wives of the prisoners to spend the weekend. In fact, the other day I read that a judge in Philadelphia suggested this, word for word: "Normal sexual relations should be provided in prison as long as they are properly supervised." What do you call this kind of a supervisor? A night watchman?

LOU ALEXANDER

The good thing about prison is that you never have to wonder what to wear.

CAROL SISKIND

My friend Larry's in jail now. He got twenty-five years for something he didn't do. He didn't run fast enough.

DAMON WAYANS

I think my mistake was yelling "Hi" to the eyewitnesses as they filed into court.

PHIL INTERLANDI

Jews

I belong to a Reform congregation—we're called Jews R Us.

DENNIS WOLFBERG

My mother is a typical Jewish mother. She was once on jury duty . . . They sent her home. She insisted *she* was guilty.

CATHY LADMAN

My mother is Jewish; my father, Catholic. I was brought up Catholic . . . with a Jewish mind. When we'd go to confession, I'd bring a lawyer in with me . . . "Bless me, Father, for I have sinned . . . I think you know Mr. Cohen?"

BILL MAHER

Moses marched and marched across the burning desert for forty days and forty nights. Then he turned left! If he had turned right, we would've owned the oil fields! We would've been rich people! They say that the Jews have all the money. It's true: Morgan, Mellon, Rockefeller, Du Pont, Getty, Hughes, Henry Ford, Queen Elizabeth. All these Jews got money . . . It's true the Jews had money. But you Christians borrowed it and never gave it back!

PROFESSOR IRWIN COREY

Reform Jews are so high-class they close the temple for the high holy holidays. I know a guy wanted to get in the temple on Yom Kippur. But without a ticket they don't let you in. He said, "Look, I just want to say something to someone." The guy at the door says, "You gotta have a ticket." He says, "Let me in for one second. I just have to say something to someone." The guy says, "Okay, I'll let you in. But if I catch you praying . . ."

PEARL WILLIAMS

There are only two things a Jewish mother needs to know about sex and marriage: (1) Who is having sex? (2) Why aren't they married?

DAN GREENBURG

I'm kind of a kinky guy. I'm into what they call Jewish bondage—that's having your money tied up in an IRA account.

"NOODLES" LEVENSTEIN

I'm Jewish but we're not religious. My mother had a menorah on a dimmer.

RICHARD LEWIS

I'm from a very liberal Jewish family. My parents believe in

the Ten Commandments but they believe you can pick five.

BILL SCHEFT

The little man was sitting on the subway next to a priest. He says to the priest, "I don't know who you are, young fella, but you dress something terrible." The priest says, "Why?" He says, "Your collar's turned around. Look, if I had a mirror, I'd show you. Your collar's backwards."

The priest says, "Well, I'm a father."

The man says, "I'm also a father, and a grandfather, and a great-grandfather. I wear a nice tie, and your collar's turned around. You look awful." The priest says, "You don't understand. I'm a father to many thousands." The little man says, "You're a father to many thousands? Better you should have your pants turned around!"

MICKEY KATZ

A Jewish friend of mine changed his name to C. D. Allen. I asked, "Where did you get a name like C. D. Allen?" He said, "Well, everybody around me was changing their name, I got disgusted. I was standing on the street corner, I look up at the sign, it said Allen Street, so I changed it to Allen." "Oh," I said. "Where did you get the C.D.?" He said, "Corner Delancey."

HERSCHEL BERNARDI

Why didn't you tell me your mother was Jewish? With a Protestant father you must have had the same kind of deal I had. I'm not upset that you're such a sly one, I'm upset over the missed opportunities. A million times I could have said, "Some of my best friend is Jewish."

CHARLES SIMMONS

A Jewish guy's idea of oral sex is talking about himself.

ABBY STEIN

A Jewish Princess is a girl who makes love with her eyes closed —because she can't bear to see another person's pleasure.

DAVID STEINBERG

Montgomery Epstein was taking an oral examination. He was asked to spell "cultivate" and did so correctly. "But do you know what the word means?" asked the teacher. "Can you use it in a sentence?"

For a moment Montgomery looked puzzled. Then he suddenly brightened up. "Last vinter on a very cold day," he said, "I vas vaiting for a streetcar. But it vas too cultivate, so I took the subway."

JOE LAURIE, JR.

Anybody here know what you call the man who performs the ritual of the bris? You know what it is? That's right. A moil. A moil. I want to tell you about a man who was walking along the street in New York. He passed by a jewelry shop, he walked inside, and he said to the owner, "Could you please repair my watch?" He said, "I'm sorry, I don't repair watches." "You don't repair watches? What do you do?" He said, "I'm a moil." "You're a moil? Then why do you put all those watches in the window?" He says, "Well, what do you *want* me to put in the window?"

DR. MURRAY BANKS

I come from a wealthy family. I was bar mitzvahed in the Vatican.

LONDON LEE

An old Jewish man is talking long-distance to California. All of a sudden he's cut off. He hollers, "Operator! Giff me beck de party!" She says, "I'm sorry, sir, you'll have to make the call all over again." He says, "What do you want from my life? I put de last money in de box . . . Giff me back de party." She says, "I'm sorry, sir, you'll have to make the call all over again." He says, "Operator, ya know vat? Take de telephone and shove it in you know vere!" And he hangs up.

Two days later he opens the door, two big strapping guys are standing there. "We came to take your telephone out." He says, "Vy?" They say, "Because you insulted operator 28 two days ago. But if you'd like to call up and apologize, we'll leave the telephone here." He says, "Vait a minute, vat's de rush! Vat's de hurry!"

He goes to the telephone and dials. "Hello? Get me operator 28. Hello, operator 28? Remember me? Two days ago I insulted you? I told you to take de telephone and shove it?" She says, "Yeah." He says, "Vell, get ready! Dey're bringin' it to ya!"

PEARL WILLIAMS

I knew a fellow named Otto Kahn. He was a very rich man, and his close friend was Marshall P. Wilder, who was a hunchback. They were walking down Fifth Avenue, and they passed a synagogue. Kahn stopped for a moment and said, "You know, I used to be a Jew." And Wilder says, "Really? I used to be a hunchback."

GROUCHO MARX

A rabbi went to a racetrack, the first time in his life. As he walked in he couldn't help but notice a Catholic priest there. He figured: If I stay close to him, I'll learn what to do.

The first race was about to start. He walked over and watched the priest. The priest looked over the horses, he came to Number 3 and made a few signs over it, and the first race came off and Number 3 came in and paid $27. The rabbi thought: This is really something. The second race was about to start and the Catholic priest went over, looked the horses over, picked out Number 7, made a few signs over it, and sure enough, Number 7 came in and paid $48. It was wonderful.

So when the third race was about to start, the rabbi said, "This is for me." And the priest went over, made a few signs over Number 9 that he had chosen, and the rabbi went and put all the money he had on Number 9.

Needless to say, Number 9 never showed up in the field. He must be still running. So after the race the rabbi went over to the good father and explained that he'd lost all his money, he saw him give a blessing, and he didn't know what happened and wanted to know what it was all about. And the priest said, "Sorry I am that you lost all your money. But it's a shame you don't know the difference between a blessing and the last rites."

HAL McKAY

This isn't about my mother, it's about Jackie Clark's mother. He got a job in a nightclub and he came home with a Kodachrome transparency of a beautiful girl. She was wearing dark blue leotards. From the waist up—nothing. He said, "Ma, when I work in nightclubs, that's the kind of girl I work with." She looks at the picture and says, "That's the color I want the drapes."

BILL DANA

Once a reader sent Alexander Woollcott a letter accusing him of being anti-Semitic. Alec was deeply hurt by the accusation, yet he didn't want to stir up a fuss over the matter. "Miss Dorothy Parker," he wrote back, "has seen fit to name my apartment 'Wit's End.' In light of the faith of most of my good friends who share with me its modest delights, I should see fit to rename it 'Jew Drop Inn.'"

HARPO MARX

Jobs

One of my first office jobs was cleaning the windows on the envelopes.

RITA RUDNER

I used to have a job in the Kotex factory. I thought I was makin' mattresses for mice.

RAY SCOTT

I used to sell life insurance. But life insurance is really strange. It's a weird concept. You really don't get anything for it. It works like this: You pay *me* money. And when you die, I'll pay *you* money.

BILL KIRCHENBAUER

The worst job I ever had was working in a Fotomat booth. I was the only one at the Christmas party.

MARK DOBRIENT

I got a job as a short-order cook. I was cooking a chicken on the rotisserie, I was turning the wheel and I was singing "Arrivederci, Roma," and a drunk came by and he said,

"You got a nice voice but your monkey's on fire."

LONDON LEE

Jogging

The only reason I would take up jogging is so that I could hear heavy breathing again.

ERMA BOMBECK

One of the wonderful things about running is what it does for your body . . . Running will give you sloping shoulders and a thin, haunted appearance which is irresistible to Finns. Don't be surprised if you develop a high adenoidal whine, like someone who was tortured in Algeria. Some of the fat that gets pared down may tend to collect in the form of high, billowing, steatopygic buttocks, common to Zulu warriors.

BRUCE JAY FRIEDMAN

My doctor recently told me that jogging could add years to my life. I think he was right. I feel ten years older already.

MILTON BERLE

Juggler

Some people think a juggler is talented. Could be a schizophrenic playing catch.

BOB DUBAC

Kamikaze Pilots

A loser is a stowaway on a kamikaze plane.

CHARLIE MANNA

Too bad about the kamikaze pilots. They had to do all their bragging ahead of time.

TOMMY SLEDGE

I'm desperately trying to figure out why kamikaze pilots wore helmets.

DAVE EDISON

Kissing

Kissing is a custom in France. We kiss a man we haven't seen in five years—or a woman we haven't seen in five minutes.

MAURICE CHEVALIER

People who throw kisses are hopelessly lazy.

BOB HOPE

A man snatches the first kiss, pleads for the second, demands the third, takes the fourth, accepts the fifth—and endures all the rest.

HELEN ROWLAND

A kiss is an operation, cunningly devised, for the mutual stoppage of speech at a moment when words are utterly superfluous.

OLIVER HERFORD

Lawyers

They get together all day long and say to each other, "What can we postpone next?" The only thing they don't postpone, of course, is their bill, which arrives regularly. You've heard about the man who got the bill from his lawyer which said, "For crossing the street to speak to you and discovering it was not you . . . twelve dollars."

GEORGE S. KAUFMAN

To save the state the expense of a trial, your honor, my client has escaped.

CHON DAY

Last week a mob attacked a white attorney because he was defending someone accused of killing a black man, and that's wrong. He should've been attacked because he's a lawyer.

A. WHITNEY BROWN

If you laid all our laws end to end, there would be no end.

ARTHUR "BUGS" BAER

What's the difference between a dead cat on the road and a dead lawyer on the road? A dead cat has skid marks around it.

ORSON BEAN

Four little boys had been arrested. The policeman had caught them in Mr. Blodgett's cherry tree.

The judge was a kindly man and he gave the boys a spiel on the evils of stealing and then asked 'em who their fathers were and what they were going to do to keep out of trouble in the future.

"My father is a doctor," the first boy said, "and I'm going to remember that eating stolen cherries can make me sick."

The second boy said, "My father is a banker and I'm going to remember that stealing cherries is as bad as stealing money."

"My father is a preacher,"

said the third boy, "and I am going to pray for strength to resist temptation."

"My father is a lawyer," said the fourth little boy, "and I'm going to sue Mr. Blodgett because I tore my pants on his tree!"

CAL TINNEY

My parents sent my brother through law school. He graduated. Now he's suing them for wasting seven years of his life.

MIKE BINDER

Here's an amazing story. A man in Orlando, Florida, was hit by eight cars in a row and only one stopped. The first seven drivers thought he was a lawyer. The eighth *was* a lawyer.

JAY LENO

If law school is so hard to get through, how come there are so many lawyers?

CALVIN TRILLIN

One day a gate breaks down between heaven and hell. So St. Peter arrives on the scene and calls out for the devil. And the devil saunters over and says, "What do you want?"

And St. Peter says, "Satan, it's your turn to fix it this time."

And the devil says, "I'm sorry. But my men are too busy to worry about fixing a mere gate."

And St. Peter says, "Well, then, I'll have to sue you for breaking our agreement."

And the devil says, "Oh yeah? Where are you going to get a lawyer?"

SOUPY SALES

A lawyer shows up at the pearly gates. St. Peter says, "Normally we don't let you people in here but you're in luck, we have a special this week. You go to hell for the length of time you were alive, then you get to come back up here for eternity."

The lawyer says, "I'll take the deal."

St. Peter says, "Good, I'll put you down for 212 years in hell . . ."

The lawyer says, "What are you talking about? I'm 65 years old!"

St. Peter says, "Up here we go by billing hours."

ORSON BEAN

Juries scare me. I don't want to put my fate in the hands of twelve people who weren't even smart enough to get out of jury duty."

MONICA PIPER

Laziness

My mother said, "You won't amount to anything because you procrastinate." I said, "Just wait."

JUDY TENUTA

Your husband is lazy if:

When he leaves the house, he finds out which way the wind is blowing and goes in that direction.

His idea of dressing for dinner is wearing a necktie over his pajamas.

Coffee doesn't keep him awake—even when it's hot and being spilled on him.

PHYLLIS DILLER

I'm kind of lazy. I'm dating a pregnant woman.

RON RICHARDS

It is better to have loafed and lost than never to have loafed at all.

JAMES THURBER

Liberals

Liberals feel unworthy of their possessions. Conservatives feel they deserve everything they've stolen.

MORT SAHL

Life

Life, you know, is rather like opening a tin of sardines. We are all of us looking for the key. And I wonder, how many of you here tonight have wasted years of your lives looking behind the kitchen dressers of this life for that key? I know I have. Others think they've found the key, don't they? They roll back the lid of the sardine tin of Life, they reveal the sardines, the riches of Life, therein, and they get them out,

they enjoy them. But, you know, there's always a little bit in the corner you can't get out. I wonder—I wonder, is there a little bit in the corner of your life? I know there is in mine.
ALAN BENNETT

I like life. It's something to do.
RONNIE SHAKES

Life's a tough proposition, and the first hundred years are the hardest.
WILSON MIZNER

Life is something to do when you can't get to sleep.
FRAN LEBOWITZ

Lisp

Lisp: To call a spade a thpade.
OLIVER HERFORD

Loser

A loser walks in Central Park with a German shepherd for protection—and meets a mug-

ger with a rhinoceros. A loser is a female impersonator who doesn't know it, a window washer who steps back to admire his work, and a health-nut submarine captain who sleeps with the windows open!
CHARLIE MANNA

He can remember the night he lost his innocence in the back seat of the family car. It would have been even more memorable if he hadn't been alone.
RED BUTTONS

I have no luck. I have a ten-dollar check and the only guy who would cash it for me was a guy I owed nine dollars to.
GENE BAYLOS

He is so unlucky that he runs into accidents which started out to happen to somebody else.
DON MARQUIS

I don't mind men who kiss and tell. I need all the publicity I can get.
RUTH BUZZI

You know it's going to be a bad day if you wake up with your water bed busted—and you know you ain't got a water bed.

JAN MURRAY

I was standing on the corner of the street, as quiet as quiet could be.
When a great big ugly man came up—and tied his horse to me.

BEA LILLIE

Dial-a-Prayer hung up on me.

JACKIE VERNON

The only thing he ever takes out on a moonlit night is his upper plate.

FRED ALLEN

I bought a cassette tape on how to be successful. It was one of those subliminal tapes, a motivational cassette. It was $19.95 and it kept saying, "Don't ask for your money back, don't ask for your money back." I exchanged it for one on how to be more assertive. Then I went back and threw it through the store window. The store owner came out. He had been listening to a motivational tape on how to commit murder. If he hadn't been lis-

tening at slow speed I would never have been able to dodge the bullets.

RON SMITH

I have bad luck with plants. I bought me a philodendron . . . and I put it in the kitchen and it drank my soup.

JOAN RIVERS

I asked my doctor if I should have a vasectomy. He said leave a sleeping dog lie. The last time I had sex my self-winding watch stopped.

LENNY RUSH

He was so lonely he couldn't eat Jell-O without fondling it first.

BOB HOPE

I don't get no respect. No respect at all. Every time I get into an elevator the operator says the same thing: "Basement?" No respect. When I was a kid we played hide-and-seek. They wouldn't even look for me. The other day I was standing in front of a big apartment house. The doorman asked me to get him a cab . . . I bought a used car—I found my wife's dress in the back seat.

RODNEY DANGERFIELD

L_ove_

Love is the same as like except you feel sexier.

JUDITH VIORST

Love is not the dying moan of a distant violin—it's the triumphant twang of a bedspring.

S. J. PERELMAN

Many a man has fallen in love with a girl in a light so dim he would not have chosen a suit by it.

MAURICE CHEVALIER

The difference between love and lust is that lust never costs over two hundred dollars.

JOHNNY CARSON

Dad taught me about love. When I was 14 he said, "Larry, someday you're gonna meet a girl that's gonna be so right and so wonderful and so per-fect that you're not even gonna haggle over price."

LARRY "BUBBLES" BROWN

Love is blind. I guess that's why it proceeds by the sense of touch.

MOREY AMSTERDAM

A lot of people wonder how you know if you're really in love. Just ask yourself this one question: "Would I mind being destroyed financially by this person?"

RONNIE SHAKES

Love is staying awake all night with a sick child. Or a very healthy adult.

DAVID FROST

Love is the only game that will never be postponed on account of rain.

HOMER HAYNES

Love is a feeling you feel when you're about to feel a feeling you never felt before.

FLIP WILSON

Teenagers don't know what love is. They have mixed-up ideas. They go for a drive, and the boy runs out of gas, and they smooch a little, and the girl says she loves him. That isn't love. Love is when you're married twenty-five years, smooching in your living room, and he runs out of gas and she still says she loves him. That's love!

NORM CROSBY

Macho

In the past, it was easy to be a Real Man. All you had to do was abuse women, steal land from Indians, and find some place to dump the toxic waste.

BRUCE FEIRSTEIN

My Uncle Murray said you're a man when you can make love for as long as it takes to cook a chicken.

DAVID STEINBERG

Guys are lucky because they get to grow mustaches. I wish I could. It's like having a little pet for your face.

ANITA WISE

One thing men can do better than women: read a map. Men read maps better. 'Cause only a male mind could conceive of one inch equaling 100 miles.

ROSEANNE BARR ARNOLD

You know, it's women like you who make men like me make women like you make men like me.

BOBBY CLARK

Mandalay

One gets used to the flying fishes, but that bloody dawn coming up like thunder is driving me crackers.

CHARLES ADDAMS

Manners and Etiquette

It's got so that if a man opens a door for a lady to go through first, he's the doorman.

MAE WEST

Etiquette means behaving yourself a little better than is absolutely essential.

WILL CUPPY

Marriage

Sex when you're married is like going to a 7-Eleven. There's not as much variety, but at three in the morning, it's always there.

CAROL LEIFER

I don't understand couples that break up and get back together —especially couples who divorce and remarry. That's like pouring milk on a bowl of cereal, tasting it, and saying, "This milk is sour. Well, I'll

put it back in the refrigerator— maybe it will be okay tomorrow."

LARRY MILLER

I was sitting with a little girl of eight one afternoon. She looked up from her Hans Andersen and said, "Does m-i-r-a-g-e spell marriage, Mr. Ade?" "Yes, my child," said I.

GEORGE ADE

When a man brings his wife flowers for no reason—there's a reason.

MOLLY McGEE (MARION JORDAN)

The bride wears white to symbolize purity. The groom wears black.

DAVID FROST

Sex in marriage is like medicine. Three times a day for the first week. Then once a day for another week. Then once every three or four days until the condition clears up.

PETER DE VRIES

I told someone I was getting married, and they said, "Have you picked a date yet?" I said, "Wow, you can bring a date to

153

your own wedding?" What a country!

YAKOV SMIRNOFF

Last week I told my wife a man is like wine, he gets better with age. She locked me in the cellar . . . My wife's an earth sign. I'm a water sign. Together we make mud.

RODNEY DANGERFIELD

Before marriage, a man declares he would lay down his life to serve you; after marriage, he won't even lay down his paper to talk to you.

HELEN ROWLAND

Marrying a man is like having your hair cut short. You won't know whether it suits you until it's too late to change your mind.

JANE GOODSELL

Marriages made in heaven are not exported.

SAMUEL HOFFENSTEIN

I read in the paper yesterday that a guy killed his wife after twenty years of marriage. I thought: Too bad. It was proba-

bly the first decision he'd made since the wedding.

JOHN WING

Marriage is not a man's idea. A woman must've thought of it. Years ago some guy said, "Let me get this straight, honey. I can't sleep with anyone else for the rest of my life, and if things don't work out, you get to keep half my stuff? What a great idea."

BOBBY SLAYTON

My parents want me to get married. They don't care who anymore, as long as he doesn't have a pierced ear, that's all they care about. I think men who have a pierced ear are better prepared for marriage. They've experienced pain and bought jewelry.

RITA RUDNER

The days just prior to marriage are like a snappy introduction to a tedious book.

WILSON MIZNER

I live just off Ventura Boulevard, where all the weirdos hang out, and I was on a corner the other day when a wild-looking sort of gypsy-looking lady with a dark veil over her face grabbed me right on Ventura Boulevard and said, "Karen Haber! You're never going to find happiness, and no one is ever going to marry you." I said, "Mom, leave me alone."

KAREN HABER

Marrying a man is like buying something you've been admiring for a long time in a shop window. You may love it when you get it home, but it doesn't always go with everything else in the house.

JEAN KERR

When you see what some girls marry, you realize how they must hate to work for a living.

HELEN ROWLAND

Marriage is a great institution, but I'm not ready for an institution.

MAE WEST

I belong to Bridegrooms Anonymous. Whenever I feel like getting married, they send over a lady in a housecoat and hair curlers to burn my toast for me.

DICK MARTIN

I can't understand why everyone nowadays has such a low opinion of marital sex. The marriage experts apparently believe that nine out of ten married couples find it easier to get the kids to bed than to lure each other there . . . Oddly enough, one never reads about an unmarried couple having any problems of sexual adjustment. Unlike Mr. and Mrs., who just can't seem to get the hang of it, the unmarried take to sex like ducks to water and unfailingly achieve perfect union in a star-spangled blaze of glory . . . They exist in a rarefied stratosphere, unmarred by the little domestic difficulties that plague marriage. You never read of an unmarried couple running out of cigarettes or losing the car keys. And they never, never, *never* disagree about what time is bedtime. It *always* is.

JANE GOODSELL

God made man. God made woman. And when God found that men could not get along with women, God invented Mexico.

LARRY STORCH

We would have broken up except for the children. Who were the children? Well, she and I were.

MORT SAHL

He tricked me into marrying him. He told me I was pregnant.

CAROL LEIFER

I've been married for forty-nine years and I'm still in love with the same woman. If my wife ever finds out she'll kill me. Now, take my wife. Please!

HENNY YOUNGMAN

I've had five years of happy marriage. Which isn't bad out of fifteen . . . She looked at me one night, said, "Do you think I'll lose my looks when I get old?" I said, "If you're lucky."

BUB THOMAS

Gettin' married's a lot like getting into a tub of hot water. After you get used to it, it ain't so hot.

MINNIE PEARL

They say I married my wife because her uncle left her a whole lot of money. That's not true. I would've married her no matter who left her the money.

SPANKY (STEVE McFARLIN)

An older couple are in bed one night, and the woman wakes up and says, "Sam, get up and close the window. It's cold outside." The fellow just keeps right on snoring. A little while later, she nudges him and says again, "Sam, get up and close the window! It's cold outside." He's about to go back to sleep, but she keeps shaking him, and so finally he gets up and shuts the window. He gets back into bed and says, "So now it's warm outside?"

MYRON COHEN

Marriage, as far as I'm concerned, is one of the most wonderful, heartwarming, satisfying experiences a human being can have. I've only been married seventeen years, so I haven't seen that side of it yet.

GEORGE GOBEL

The first year he talks and she listens. The second year she talks and he listens. The third year they both talk and the neighbors listen.

DONALD McGILL

Three fellas up in heaven. St. Peter's interviewing them. He says to the first guy, "How did you get up here in heaven?" He said, "Well, I live in this tall apartment building. I came home late one night, I accused my wife of cheating on me, she denied it, we got into a big fight, I got so mad I picked up the refrigerator, pushed it out the window, and it gave me a heart attack."

St. Peter said to the next guy, "How did you get up here in heaven?" He said, "I was in my convertible in front of this apartment building, and this refrigerator came down on my head."

St. Peter said to the third guy, "How did you get up here in heaven?" He said, "I don't know. I was sitting in this refrigerator . . ."

GEORGE "GOOBER" LINDSEY

A guy's laying in bed at two-thirty in the morning. His wife wakes him up and says, "Honey, I gotta ask you a question. If I die, would you remarry?"

"What kind of a question is that at two-thirty in the morning? I don't know. I never thought about it. I guess I would, I'm a young guy. I guess I'd remarry. Go to sleep, forget it."

She said, "Let me ask you another question. If I died, and you remarried, would you let her live in this house?"

"Honey, it's two-thirty in the morning. I guess so . . . I like the house. I suppose I would. Let's go to sleep."

"Let me ask you another question. If I died, and you remarried, and you let her live in this house, would you let her wear my clothes?"

"This is driving me crazy! I don't know. No reason to go out and buy a whole new wardrobe. I guess I would. Go to sleep."

"One more question. If I died, and you remarried, and you let her live in this house and let her wear my clothes, would you let her drive my sports car?"

He said, "Absolutely not. No way in the world."

She said, "Why not?"

He said, " 'Cause she can't drive no straight stick."

LEWIS GRIZZARD

I'm 33, single . . . Don't you think it's a generalization you should be married at 33? That's like looking at somebody who's 70 and saying, "Hey, when are you gonna break your hip? All your friends are breaking their hips—what are you waiting for?"

SUE KOLINSKY

Marriage is like a bank account. You put it in, you take it out, you lose interest.

PROFESSOR IRWIN COREY

I will not cheat on my wife. Because I love my house.

CHAS ELSTNER

It is better to have loved and lost than to have loved and married.

BROTHER SAMMY SHORE

My wife converted me to religion. I never believed in hell till I married her.

HAL ROACH

Married men live longer than single men. But married men are a lot more willing to die.

JOHNNY CARSON

She contradicts me even when I don't say anything!

BILL HOEST

When you're away, I'm restless, lonely,
Wretched, bored, dejected, only
Here's the rub, my darling dear,
I feel the same when you are here.

SAMUEL HOFFENSTEIN

I believe in tying the marriage knot, as long as it's around the woman's neck. Marriage is a two-way proposition, but never let the woman know she is one of the ways. In marriage a man must give up many of his old and pleasant habits, even if it means giving up the woman he married. Always have a woman sign a prenuptial agreement that if she leaves your bed and board, she takes off with as little as possible. Marry an outdoors woman. Then if you throw her out into the yard for the night, she can still survive. Marriage is better than leprosy because it's easier to get rid of. Never trust your wife behind your back, even if she claims she only wants to wash or scratch it. An ideal start for matrimony would be to have a drunken rabbi perform a Catholic ceremony in an Episcopalian church. Then it could be declared illegal in the courts.

W. C. FIELDS

The difference between wife and mistress is the difference between night and day.

HARRY HERSHFIELD

Masturbation

Recently when I'm alone I try to talk myself out of masturbation. I ask myself—why can't I just be *friends* with myself?

RICHARD LEWIS

The reason I feel guilty is, I'm so bad at it.

DAVID STEINBERG

If sex is so personal, why are we expected to share it with someone else?

LILY TOMLIN

Masturbation. A lot of people are turned off about masturbation jokes. Why? Some of the greatest people in the world . . . Example: Sir Edmund Hillary. Sir Edmund Hillary was the first man to climb Mount Everest. But when Sir Edmund was a precocious eleven, his mother came in the room, caught him in the act. She couldn't believe it. She said, "Sir Edmund! Why are you doing that?" He said, "Because it was there."

GABE KAPLAN

If God had intended us not to masturbate he would've made our arms shorter.

GEORGE CARLIN

My father said, "Mike, if you masturbate you'll go blind." I said, "Dad—I'm over *here*."

MIKE BINDER

Don't knock masturbation— it's sex with someone I love.

WOODY ALLEN

McDonald's Restaurants

We finally got a McDonald's in Bangladesh. They serve McNothings.

GERRY BEDNOB

I remember going into McDonald's when they had some promotional giveaway, and their sign read: "Offer available to McDonald's customers only." Now there's an exclusive group! I went into McDonald's yesterday and said, "I'd like some fries." The girl at the counter said, "Would you like some fries with that?" They're highly intelligent . . .

JAY LENO

The French fries are great. You can eat those or use them as dental floss. And the triple-thick milk shakes. Which you can drink or take home—pave the new driveway in front of your house . . . They have home delivery now. They'll bring those *big* juicy delicious hamburgers right to your house. And if you're not home, don't worry about it. 'Cause they'll slip 'em right under the door.

MIKE PREMINGER

Have you seen the fast-food version of a liquid? A triple-thick shake? You need an industrial suction pump to get it up the straw. There's people wandering around with bleeding ear holes because they've been sucking too hard. Everybody sucks together—the windows of the shop cave in! Big Macs. Fast food. Fast food? Why don't you just flush it straight down the toilet and cut out the middleman?

BEN ELTON

The Moscow McDonald's has lines two and a half hours long. That's fast food in Russia. But everyone loves McDonald's there. A man came out of McDonald's, he took the wrapper off his hamburger and he said, "They not only give you food—but free toilet paper with it!"

YAKOV SMIRNOFF

I started a grease fire at Mc-Donald's—threw a match in the cook's hair.

STEVE MARTIN

The first time I opened a Big Mac I thought: It's been eaten already.

JASPER CARROTT

I don't think I could take a mellow evening because I don't respond well to mellow. You know what I mean? I have a tendency to—if I get too mellow—I ripen and then rot.

WOODY ALLEN (in *Annie Hall*)

Men are very strange. When they wake up they want breakfast. They don't eat candy in the morning like we do. They want things like toast. I don't have these recipes.

ELAYNE BOOSLER

Men know that if a woman had to choose between catching a fly ball and saving an infant's life, she would probably save the infant's life, without even considering whether there were men on base.

DAVE BARRY

I don't believe in nagging at a man. You can accomplish so much more by hitting him with something.

NORMAN HOIFJELD

If you have trouble attracting men, try ordering pizza instead. This way you can get whatever you like—the right size, the right toppings, and once the delivery boy is in your house, he's yours.

HILARY DALTON

Men can read maps better than women. 'Cause only the male mind could conceive of one inch equaling a hundred miles.

ROSEANNE BARR ARNOLD

I asked this guy if he had the time. He said he'd love to give it to me, but he wasn't sure he could make the commitment.

CAROL SISKIND

I was talking to a businessman, and I said, "Don't you think most men are little boys?" And he said, "I'm no little boy! I make seventy-five thousand dollars a year." And I said, "Well, the way I look at it, you just have bigger toys."

JONATHAN WINTERS

Boys will be boys, and so will a lot of middle-aged men.

KIN HUBBARD

A woman is a woman until the day she dies. But a man's a man only as long as he can!

MOMS MABLEY

Guys will actually judge women based on the way they're built . . . A lot of guys think the larger a woman's breasts are, the less intelligent she is. I don't think it works like that. I think it's the opposite. I think the larger a woman's breasts are, the less intelligent the men become.

ANITA WISE

Milwaukee

I'll never forget the time I was flying over Milwaukee and the pilot said, "We're now approaching the great city; let's set our watches back one hundred years."

JACK E. LEONARD

Mimes

Street clowns—if you've got a white face, a red nose, and baggy trousers, you're supposed to be funny. It didn't work for Mussolini, did it?

ALEXEI SAYLE

In my youth I wanted to be a great pantomimist—but I found I had nothing to say.

VICTOR BORGE

I'm walking to work this morning and it's a lovely spring day, and I'm walking up Sixth Avenue and I see one of those mime performers. So the mime is doing that famous mime routine where he's pretending to be trapped in a box. So I stand there and watch the mime pretend to be trapped in a box. And he finishes up, and thank God, he wasn't really trapped in a box. And I see on the sidewalk there he's got a little hat for money—dollars, change, tips, donations, contributions. So I went over and I pretended to put a dollar bill in his hat.

DAVID LETTERMAN

My theory on mime: They've obviously waived their First Amendment rights by refusing to speak.

CALVIN TRILLIN

My uncle was thrown out of a mime show for having a seizure. They thought he was heckling.

JEFF SHAW

Misanthropy

I like long walks, especially when they are taken by people who annoy me.

FRED ALLEN

I've just learned about his illness; let's hope it's nothing trivial.

IRVIN S. COBB

It would be a swell world if everybody was as pleasant as the fellow who's trying to skin you.

KIN HUBBARD

"Be yourself" is about the worst advice you can give to some people.

TOM MASSON

A friend is a man who has the same enemies you have.

STEPHEN LEACOCK

One problem that recurs more and more frequently these days in books and plays and movies is the inability of people to communicate with the people they love. Husbands and wives who can't communicate, children who can't communicate with their parents, and so on. And the characters in these books and plays and so on, and real life, I might add, spend hours bemoaning the fact that they can't communicate. I feel that if a person can't communicate, the very least he can do is to shut up.

TOM LEHRER

The trouble with treating people as equals is that the first thing you know they may be doing the same thing to you.

PETER DE VRIES

All the problems we face in the United States today can be traced to an unenlightened immigration policy on the part of the American Indian.

PAT PAULSEN

If you had a penny and you were on top of the Empire State Building, and you took that penny and threw it off the Empire State Building and it hit somebody in the head, it would kill him. Talk about getting your money's worth.

HEYWOOD BANKS

You know how with some girls you feel sorry the next day? With Pamela you're sorry when it's going on.

ROGER PRICE

Nobody ever forgets where he buried the hatchet.

KIN HUBBARD

Money

Money: The only substance which can keep a cold world from nicknaming a citizen "Hey You!"

WILSON MIZNER

One good thing about inflation is that the fellow who forgets his change nowadays doesn't lose half as much as he used to.

KIN HUBBARD

America's best buy for a nickel is a telephone call to the right man.

ILKA CHASE

A study of economics usually reveals that the best time to buy anything is last year.

MARTY ALLEN

There's only one way to make money these days—with the pools. I know a young man, he's being doing the pools year in, year out, week after week. Eventually he won seventy-five thousand pounds. He went to his father and said, "Dad, I've done it at last! Seventy-five thousand pounds!" His father said, "What are you going to do with all that money?" He said, "I've been thinking it out. I'm going to give you a pound." So his father said, "You're going to give me a pound? What about the rest of it?"

His son said, "Oh, a cruise around the world, a Rolls Bentley, a yacht—I'm going to do everything I always wanted to do. What are you going to do with your pound?"

His father said, "I think I'll marry your mother."

So the son said, "You're going to marry my mother? Now you know what that makes me?"

His father said, "Yes, and a mean onc as well!"

SANDY POWELL

Government said Americans are all geographically illiterate and economically ignorant. It's true. How many times you said to yourself: "Where did all my money go?"

ALAN PROPHET

I carry a rabbit's foot in my pocket because it saves me lots of money . . . Every time my wife sticks her hand in she thinks it's a mouse.

"SENATOR" ED FORD

Money really isn't everything. If it was, what would we buy with it?

TOM WILSON ("Ziggy")

Morality

A conscience cannot prevent sin. It only prevents you from enjoying it.

HARRY HERSHFIELD

Sodom and Gomorrah! Wicked people destroyed by a tremendous conflagration, belching forth fire, hell, and brimstone from the heavens! Wicked people stooped to debaucheries, degeneracies, and perversion! All these wonderf—All these things could happen! Six hundred thousand souls snuffed out! Save for four good people: Lot, his wife, and his two daughters.

And Lot's wife looked around, and there were no men left in the vicinity save for her husband—who at the time was

138 years old! So in lieu of memory, Lot's wife turned around and gave one long last look at her long-lost lovers. And she turned into a pillar of salt. Therefore! The moral of that story is: All girls that cheat —taste salty!

PROFESSOR IRWIN COREY

Confession is good for the soul only in the sense that a tweed coat is good for dandruff.

PETER DE VRIES

Vice is its own reward.

QUENTIN CRISP

Christ died for our sins. Dare we make his martyrdom meaningless by not committing them?

JULES FEIFFER

If you're going to do something tonight you'll be sorry for tomorrow morning, sleep late.

HENNY YOUNGMAN

I know there are people in the world who do not love their fellow human beings and I hate people like that!

TOM LEHRER

"A big boob" is a clean. "Two big boobs" is a dirty . . . "A little wood sprite" is a clean. "A little fairy" is a dirty . . . "Desk" is a clean. "Drawers" is a dirty . . . "Lake Superior" is a clean. "Lake Titicaca" is a dirty . . . "Comma" is a clean. "Period" is a dirty . . . "No" is a clean. "Yes" is a dirty."

SHELLEY BERMAN

Be fair with others, but then keep after them until they're fair with you.

ALAN ALDA

Mother

Every time I find a girl who can cook like my mother—she looks like my father.

TONY RANDALL

Neither Papa nor Mama nor the schools taught me about sex, at least not officially. I wanted to know, but no one sat down to give me a sex organ recital. Mama certainly couldn't do it, in spite of the fact that she had given birth to ten children. When asked if she had ever heard of "sex appeal," she said, "I gave already."

SAM LEVENSON

The child had his mother's eyes, his mother's nose, and his mother's mouth. Which leaves his mother with a pretty blank expression.

ROBERT BENCHLEY

Mothers mold the children's minds. Some of you have done well. There are a lot of moldy-minded kids around.

NORM CROSBY

I was playing with my navel. My mother said, "All right, keep playin' with your navel, pretty soon you're gonna break it wide open, the air's gonna come right out of your body, you'll fly around the room backwards for thirty seconds, land and be flat as a piece of paper, nothin' but your little eyes buggin' out." I used to carry Band-Aids in case I had an accident.

BILL COSBY

I think I'd be a good mother—maybe a little overprotective.

Like I would never let the kid out—of my body.

WENDY LIEBMAN

My mother had a problem because she grew up during the Great Depression. And I had problems because I grew up during *her* great depression.

JANE STROLL

My mom was a little weird. When I was little my mom would make chocolate frosting. And she'd let me lick the beaters. And then she'd turn them off.

MARTY COHEN

There's not a lot of warmth between me and my mother. I asked her about it. I said, "Mrs. Stoller . . ."

FRED STOLLER

Mother-in-law

My mother-in-law broke up my marriage. My wife came home and found us in bed together.

LENNY BRUCE

Movies

You may recognize me from the movies . . . I go a few times a week.

WAYNE FEDERMAN

I was taking tickets at the movies when I got a phone call. This woman said, "How much is a ticket?" And I said, "Four dollars." She said, "How much is it for children?" And I said, "The same price. Four dollars." "Well," she said, "the airlines charge half fare for children." I said, "You go to the movie—put the kids on a plane."

ALAN GALE

I came to a movie theater. The marquee just read: "Dyslexia: Movie The."

TOMMY SLEDGE

Murder

You're not gonna believe this. I saw a murder. I got there five minutes after it happened. Apparently, from what I saw, the body fell onto a chalk line exactly the same shape.

HOWIE MANDEL

Granny used to say, the more ya know the less the better. She got mad reading the morning paper. She saw a piece about a murderer and she says, "Hangin's too good for 'im. A good kick up the ass is what he needs."

BILLY CONNOLLY

Music

The past few years have seen a steady increase in the number of people playing music in the streets. The past few years have also seen a steady increase in the number of malignant diseases? Are these two facts related? One wonders.

FRAN LEBOWITZ

The chief trouble with jazz is that there is not enough of it; some of it we have to listen to twice.

DON HEROLD

Modern music hasn't been around too long. And hopefully won't be.

VICTOR BORGE

Smetana mistakenly showed up at a theater across the street from the one in which his opera was playing. He didn't know which side his bride was bartered on.

HENRY MORGAN

Either heaven or hell will have continuous background music. Which one you think it will be tells a lot about you.

BILL VAUGHAN

A sobering thought: A century from now what we know as modern music will be considered old-fashioned. This thought almost makes one reconciled to the possibility that there may not be any twenty-first century.

FRANK SULLIVAN

To be a real folk-song singer you have to collect the songs straight from the horse's mouth. The way to do this is to go to a village and find the oldest inhabitant and ask him to sing you the songs his mother taught me. Him, I mean. Well, you'll probably find that he's deaf, and if he isn't deaf he can't sing, and if he can sing he doesn't want to, and by the time you've persuaded him and he does sing, you won't understand a word of what he's singing about. This is how folk songs have been passed down from generation to generation.

ANNA RUSSELL

Did you know that Mozart had no arms and no legs? I've seen statues of him on people's pianos.

VICTOR BORGE

When Beethoven went deaf, the mynah bird just used to mime.

GRAHAM CHAPMAN

Wallace Swine now has an orchestra in his restaurant, but the music is so bad that last night a waiter dropped a tray of dishes and everybody got up and started to dance.

CHARLEY WEAVER (CLIFF ARQUETTE)

Bop was based on a seventeen-note chromatic scale, which presented a problem as there are only twelve notes to an octave. They solved this problem by playing very rapidly.

ROGER PRICE

She was a town-and-country soprano of the kind often used for augmenting the grief at a funeral.

GEORGE ADE

Classical music is the kind that we keep hoping will turn into a tune.

KIN HUBBARD

Nebraska

Nebraska is proof that hell is full and the dead are walking the earth.

LIZZ WINSTEAD

Newlyweds

The newlyweds were married five days. He turns to her and says, "Honey, we're gonna make love a new way tonight. We're gonna lie back to back." She says, "How can that be any fun?" He says, "I've invited another couple."

WOODY WOODBURY

Honeymoon night was hot. She was moaning all night in ecstasy. Opening gifts: "An orange squeezer! Oh my God! A waffle maker!" Next morning the guy down the hall gave me the big thumbs-up. "Boy, you were using everything but the kitchen sink in there!"

MIKE BINDER

Let me tell you about a French mama who gives her daughter advice on the night of the marriage. She says to the daughter, "Listen well, Josette. When you marry your husband, if you want your marriage to be interesting all your life, never go to bed with your husband in the nude. Always wear something, to make the affair more mysterious. If you wear something over the body, it lends intrigue to the affair. Never just skin and bones."

Two weeks go by. One night the husband can contain himself no longer and he says to his wife, "Josette, come here. Can I ask you a question?" She says, "*Oui.*" He says, "Is there, somewhere along the line, insanity in your family?"

She says, "No, why do you ask?"

He says, "Well, we're married now for two weeks. And every night you go to bed with that damn hat on your head."

LARRY STORCH

Newspapers

USA Today—their slogan is: If you can't write, make a list.

BARRY CRIMMINS

I was reading the *Christian Science Monitor.* The news in that paper is just as terrible as it is in the other papers, only you *think* it's better.

GOODMAN ACE

New Year's Eve

I had a big New Year's Eve— they tell me. But New Year's Eve is a lot of fun. We had a big New Year's Eve party. We didn't like our furniture anyway. It was eighteenth-century Provincial. Now it's twentieth-century splinters. I invited Les Brown and the band over. We don't like our neighbors either. I invited the brass section too. We don't even like ourselves.

BOB HOPE

New Year's Eve, where auld acquaintance be forgot. Unless, of course, those tests come back positive.

JAY LENO

New York

New York is where you can get the best cheap meal and the lousiest expensive meal in the country.

ROBERT C. WEAVER

In yet another effort to clean up New York City the mayor urged the City Council to pass legislation that would require alternate side of the street urinating.

DENNIS MILLER

New York is a funny town. You can drown in whiskey and starve to death. Everybody says have a drink—nobody says have something to eat.

NIPSEY RUSSELL

New York: where everyone mutinies but no one deserts.

HARRY HERSHFIELD

New York: homes, homes everywhere, and not a place to live.

DON HEROLD

Let me give you a tourist tip. If you want to go to New York, bring your camera there, because you'll see things you'll never see again. The first thing you'll never see again is your camera.

MIKE REYNOLDS

Being a New Yorker is never having to say you're sorry.

LILY TOMLIN

I'll bet if George M. Cohan were alive today he wouldn't be telling all the gang at Forty-second Street he'd soon be there.

H. MARTIN

Anytime four New Yorkers get into a cab together without arguing, a bank robbery has just taken place.

JOHNNY CARSON

There was an item in the paper today. A lion got loose in the Central Park Zoo. And was severely mauled.

BOB NEWHART

It's a great city. It's very culturally enriching. I now understand English in seven foreign accents.

ANITA WISE

New York is like living inside Stephen King's brain during an aneurysm. It's the Land of Genetic Close Calls. There are a lot of people there who missed being another species by one chromosome. Look—that guy could've been a badger. There's Crab Man . . . And it's like a financial skeet shoot. Someone hollers "Pull!" and your wallet flies out.

KEVIN ROONEY

The National Council on Psychic Research have officially designated this to be true. If you are passing through New York City and you must even change planes here, that counts; that experience of changing planes in New York City now officially counts as a near-death experience.

DAVID LETTERMAN

Only real New Yorkers can find their way around in the subway. If just anybody could find his way around in the subway, there wouldn't be any distinction in being a real New Yorker except talking funny.

CALVIN TRILLIN

I used to live about an hour's drive outside of New York. Twenty minutes if you walked.

MIKE GUIDO

New York—in the event of a nuclear attack it'll look the same as it did before.

BILLY CONNOLLY

In New York crime is getting worse. I was there the other day. The Statue of Liberty had both hands up.

JAY LENO

My uncle got a job driving a cab. He had the cab parked right in front of Grand Central Station, and an Episcopal bishop got into my uncle's cab. He said, "Take me to Christ Church." So my uncle took him up to St. Patrick's Cathedral. And the bishop got mad. He said, "I said Christ Church." And my uncle said, "Look, if he's not here he's not in town!"

JIMMY JOYCE

New York's such a wonderful city, but at the library the guy was very rude. I said I'd like a card. He said, "You have to

173

prove you're a citizen of New York." So I stabbed him.

EMO PHILIPS

I went to the beach a couple of times in New York City. Tough summer out there, but I was pretty excited. I found what I thought at the time was a very rare seashell. And I took it to a friend of mine who works in a museum. And I was really disappointed. It turned out to be just a human ear. New York City's had kind of a tough summer. The people from *Roget's Thesaurus* announced that in their next edition New York City will be listed for the first time officially as a synonym for hell. If you're planning to travel to New York City, do yourself a favor—this is a lot of fun—check into a Times Square hotel. And take the Bible out of the nightstand there, if it hasn't already been stolen, of course. And open up to the Ten Commandments and go to the window, and on a good day you can check the commandments off as you see them being broken.

DAVID LETTERMAN

Now, folks, all I know is what little news I read every day in the paper. I see where another wife out on Long Island in New York shot her husband. Season opened a month earlier this year . . . Never a day passes in New York without some innocent bystander being shot. You just stand around this town long enough and be innocent and somebody's gonna shoot ya.

WILL ROGERS

When you leave New York you're camping out.

JACKIE GLEASON

Nose

It's hard having a big nose. All my pullover shirts have stretch marks. I go to the beach, my friends make me lie on my back facing north so they can tell time. I can't go in the ocean—I'll be doing the backstroke and someone'll shout, "Shark!"

RICK CORSO

You think it's a good idea to put a wet, drainy thing like that upside down over your mouth?

GALLAGHER

You oughta trim that little hair in your nose. You're gonna sneeze and flog yourself to death.

HERB EDEN

Nostalgia

Nostalgia is a longing for something you couldn't stand anymore.

FIBBER McGEE (JIM JORDAN)

The whole dating ritual was different when I was a kid. Girls got pinned—not nailed.

BILL MAHER

Nothing is more responsible for the good old days than a bad memory.

ROBERT BENCHLEY

Nudity

Down in Florida, there's a little hotel, four floors high. A girl used to take a sunbath there every day. Since there were no higher hotels near it, she would take off her bathing suit and be in the nude.

So she was in the nude and she was lying on her stomach, and she heard someone coming up the steps. She quickly grabbed the towel and put it around her. The man said, "I wish you wouldn't sunbathe in the nude up here."

She said, "You never protested before."

He said, "No, but I wish you would do it like you did before, in your bathing suit."

She said, "Why do you care? No one can see."

He said, "Madam, you happen to be lying on the skylight of a dining room."

JACK PAAR

Meanwhile, the search for the man who terrorizes nudist camps with a bacon slicer goes on. Inspector Lemuel Jones had a tip-off this morning but hopes to be back on duty tomorrow.

RONNIE BARKER

Every time a woman leaves off something she looks better, but every time a man leaves off something he looks worse.

WILL ROGERS

Exactly what Adam and Eve were ashamed of is never clearly explained, anywhere. And why did they cover their loins? Why not their noses or elbows or big toes? And what does God wear—a Pierre Cardin suit? (And why fig leaves? Fig leaves were intended to cover up figs.) The mind boggles: If I accept the anti-nude morality, I must be ashamed of my own body. But where can I go without it? Personally, I think God is losing a lot in translation. I can't imagine him being ashamed of anybody's nude body. On the contrary, he must think it's pretty peculiar when he sees us killing other animals and wearing *their* skins.

ALLAN SHERMAN

"Naked" means you ain't got no clothes on. "Nekkid" means you ain't got no clothes on and you up to somethin'!

GEORGE GRIZZARD

The only ones who seem to object to nudity are those who haven't tried it yet.

IRVIN S. COBB

In Sweden, where nudism is a general practice, the suicide rate is alarmingly high. Nudism may be a contributing factor. It's not unlikely that a potential suicide gets very depressed comparing himself with some of the others.

On the other hand, I'd expect nudists to be a happy group. There are some people I know who would be good for a laugh if you saw them with their clothes off.

SELMA DIAMOND

 Nurses

Nurses are easy . . . because they know where everything is.

PETE BARBUTTI

Men are so shallow. They like nurses! Single, vicious, good-looking girls . . . little short skirts, the top button undone, always leaning over in the operating room: "Let me help, let me help." While I was having my baby the woman in the next room died! Died, while a nurse was down the hall talking to a single man. That woman died! And she was a visitor.

JOAN RIVERS

An optimist is a man who has never had much experience.

DON MARQUIS

Give me a man that laughs all the time,
Though the rest of the world's in a rut.
Yes, show me a man that laughs all the time,
And, my friend, I'll show you a nut!

JACKIE KANNON

An optimist is a girl who mistakes a bulge for a curve.

RING LARDNER

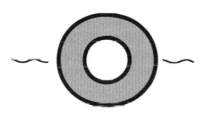

Optometry and Eye Care

Optimism

Hope is the feeling you have that the feeling you have isn't permanent.

JEAN KERR

I acquired my contact lenses a day or two later and they worked superbly. To insert them was but the work of a moment: all I had to do was pry open my eyes with a buttonhook, force the lenses in, and gulp as though swallowing a Chincoteague oyster.

S. J. PERELMAN

On this site I am going to build a forty-story building to house nothing but eye doctors and opticians. It will be a site for sore eyes.

COLONEL LEMUEL STOOPNAGLE

(FREDERICK TAYLOR)

Paranoia and Other Mental Illness

I'm paranoid about everything. Even at home, on my stationary exercise bike, I have a rearview mirror . . . This is rumor, but one of my uncles said that apparently at birth I snuck out. He said I turned around and looked over my shoulder as I came out of the womb. I was paranoid, I thought maybe someone was following me.

RICHARD LEWIS

It's hard to be nice to some paranoid schizophrenic *just because she lives in your body!*

JUDY TENUTA

I had to move to New York for health reasons. I'm extremely paranoid and New York is the only place my fears are justified.

ANITA WISE

Never get into an argument with a schizophrenic person and say, "Who do you think you are?"

RAY COMBS

He's so nervous that he wears a seat belt in a drive-in movie.

NEIL SIMON

Friday afternoon, I'm walking home from school and I'm watching some men building a new house. And the guy hammering on the roof calls me a paranoid little weirdo. In Morse code.

EMO PHILIPS

He was wearing a velvet shirt open to the navel. And he didn't have one. Which is either a show-business gimmick or the ultimate rejection of mother.

MORT SAHL

He was an angry man, Uncle Swanny. He had printed on his grave: "What are you lookin' at?"

MARGARET SMITH

I'm very insecure—I get depressed when I find out the people I hate don't like me. I'm kind of paranoid too. I often think the car in front of me is following me the long way around.

DENNIS MILLER

My first psychiatrist said I was paranoid, but I want a second opinion because I think he's out to get me.

TOM WILSON ("Ziggy")

Luposlipaphobia: The fear of being pursued by timber wolves around a kitchen table while wearing socks on a newly waxed floor.

GARY LARSON

My superiority complex turned out to be an inferiority complex. I said, "Great, that makes me the least of my problems."

SARA B. SIRIUS

I went to this conference for bulimics and anorexics. It was a nightmare. The bulimics ate the anorexics. It's okay—they were back ten minutes later.

MONICA PIPER

She's such a hypochondriac she cooks with penicillin.

BETTY WALKER

Anybody who acts normal nowadays, they're probably just not well. I'm telling you, I just don't understand. If I go too fast, I'll run into something. If I go too slow, something'll run into me.

MOMS MABLEY

I have an intense desire to return to the womb. Anybody's.

WOODY ALLEN

Instead of the Miss America Pageant I could enter the Miss Neurosis Pageant. Among my hobbies are stewing in my own juices and blowing things out of proportion.

CAROL SISKIND

I read this article, it said the typical symptoms of stress are eating too much, smoking too much, impulse buying, and driving too fast. Are they kidding? This is my idea of a great day!

MONICA PIPER

If you have a psychotic fixation and you go to the doctor and you want these two fingers amputated, he will not cut them off. But he *will* remove your genitals. I have more trouble getting a prescription for Valium than I do having my uterus lowered and made into a penis.

LILY TOMLIN

P*ets*

I got a friend who is not very kind to pets. He has a pet—he rubs its face in it, hits it with a belt—and that could *kill* a parakeet!

ANDY ANDREWS

This is a story about a guy who has a horny parrot. It's terrible. The guy reaches into the cage to change the paper, the bird is on his arm. He invites his elderly mother to tea, the bird is saying foul things in the cage . . . Finally he takes the parrot to a vet. The vet examines the bird extensively. Says, "Well, you have a horny parrot . . . For fifteen dollars, I have a sweet young female bird—your bird can go in the cage with my bird." The guy's parrot is in the cage listening . . . The parrot says, "Come on! Come on! What the hell!"

Finally the guy says all right. He gives the vet the fifteen. The vet takes the bird, puts him in the cage with the female bird, closes the curtain . . . Suddenly: *"Kwah! Kwah! Kwah!"* Feathers come flying over the top of the curtain. The vet says, "Holy gee!" Runs over, opens the curtain. The male bird has got the female bird down on the bottom of the cage with one claw. With the other claw he's pulling out

all her feathers. He is saying,
"For fifteen bucks I want you
naked! *Naked!*"

ORSON BEAN

My parakeet died. We were
playing badminton.

DANNY CURTIS

When I see the Ferris wheels
and swings and other toys on
sale in pet shops for birds, I
can't help feeling it's just a
waste of money.

We had two very happy birds
and we never thought of buying them anything to play with.
We figured, since one bird was
a boy and one bird was a girl,
they'll think of something.

SELMA DIAMOND

I bought an ant farm. I don't
know where I'm gonna find a
tractor that small.

STEVEN WRIGHT

My brother had a hamster. He
took it to the vet—it's like
bringing a disposable lighter in
for repair.

WAYNE COTTER

Ever let your parakeet out of its
cage? They fly across the room,
right into the mirror . . . He
would hit that mirror: *Bang!*
And he would fly off in some
other direction trying to get it
together. He's so stupid. Even
if he thought the mirror was
another room, you'd think he'd
try to avoid hitting the other
parakeet!

JERRY SEINFELD

Philadelphia

Philadelphia was a gay, light-
hearted town. Anyone found
smiling after the curfew rang
was liable to be arrested. If a
woman dropped her glove on a
street, she might be hauled before a judge for stripteasing.
The city had so many reform-
ers, they tried reforming each
other . . . Undertaking in Philadelphia—a mortician can
hardly tell if he's burying a
dead person or a live one.

W. C. FIELDS

Photography

Do you think you can manage a smile? It's only for a fiftieth of a second.

FRANK MODELL

Piano

An ambitious and aggressive mother conned pianist Arthur Rubinstein into listening to her 10-year-old son murder a nocturne by Chopin. At the conclusion of the massacre, Rubinstein announced, "Madam, that is undoubtedly the worst piano playing I ever heard." Whereupon the mother nodded happily and told her son, "You see, stupid? Now will you give up those expensive piano lessons and try out for the Little League baseball team?

ART BUCHWALD

The music teacher came twice each week to bridge the awful gap between Dorothy and Chopin.

GEORGE ADE

Plays

I saw the play at a disadvantage. The curtain was up.

GEORGE S. KAUFMAN

Poetry

Poetry is what Milton saw when he went blind.

DON MARQUIS

Politics

I am not a member of any organized party. I am a Democrat.

WILL ROGERS

We're getting a lot of government these days, but we'd probably be worse off if we were getting as much as we're paying for.

OLIN MILLER

State legislators are merely politicians whose darkest secret prohibits them from running for higher office.

DENNIS MILLER

I think the next four years we should try it with no President.

DANA FRADON

A statesman is any politician it's considered safe to name a school after.

BILL VAUGHAN

This week somebody sent a puppy to the President. The puppy was a Democrat. You could tell—he had his eyes open!

SENATOR CLAGHORN (KENNY DELMAR)

I would like to nominate a man who is honest and courageous. I'd like to, but this party doesn't have one of them kind of people. My candidate does not know the meaning of the word "compromise," does not know the meaning of the word "appeasement," does not know the meaning of the word "cow-

ardice"—and has done quite well despite this lousy vocabulary.

VAUGHN MEADER

I don't pick on politicians. They ain't done nothin'.

RED SKELTON

Our congressmen are the finest body of men money can buy.

MOREY AMSTERDAM

(written for WILL ROGERS)

This article says our congressman has taken money under the table. His name has been linked romantically with a lot of different ladies, and he enjoys a frequent nip. I'd say he's doing a terrific job representing my interests!

THAVES ("Frank and Ernest")

Diplomacy: Lying in state.

OLIVER HERFORD

Diplomacy is the art of saying "Nice doggie" until you can find a rock.

WILL ROGERS

Voting in this election is like trying to decide which street mime to stop and watch.

A. WHITNEY BROWN

We have a presidential election coming up. And I think the big problem, of course, is someone will win.

BARRY CRIMMINS

Congressional terms should be . . . ten to twenty with no possibility of parole.

WALT HANDELSMAN

Senate office hours are from twelve to one with an hour off for lunch.

GEORGE S. KAUFMAN

As far as the men who are running for President are concerned, they aren't even people I would date.

NORA EPHRON

Every politician we have, liberal or conservative, who gets caught drinking or chasing women is thrown out of office. It's backwards. It's more dangerous to have a clean-living President with his finger on the button. He thinks he's going right to heaven. You want to feel safe with a leader? Give me a guy who fights in bars and cheats on his wife. This is a man who wants to put off Judgment Day as long as possible.

LARRY MILLER

Politics has reached the level where we're goin' some if we can even get good, efficient people to vote, to say nothin' of runnin' for office.

KIN HUBBARD

I know a politician who believes that there are two sides to every question—and takes them both.

KEN MURRAY

Congress, our leaders, voted against a proposal to have a national seven-day waiting period to buy a gun. I don't want to sound like a Quaker, but when you think about it, is a week a *long* time to wait? To see if a former mental patient is qualified to own an Uzi? Come on, will ya, Congress? It takes *three* weeks to get a phone!

JIMMY TINGLE

If anybody comes up to you and says, "My kid is a conservative—why is that?" You say, "Remember in the '60s when we told you if you kept using drugs your kids would be mutants?"

MORT SAHL

The liberal says to you, "I'm so understanding, I can't understand anyone not understanding me, as understanding as I am."

LENNY BRUCE

Think of what would happen to us in America if there were no humorists; life would be one long *Congressional Record*.

TOM MASSON

I looked up the word "politics" in the dictionary and it's actually a combination of two words; "poli," which means many, and "tics," which means bloodsuckers.

JAY LENO

The only way to combat criminals is by not voting for them.

DAYTON ALLEN

Pollution and Ecology

The other day I bought a wastebasket and carried it home in a paper bag. And when I got home I put the paper bag in the wastebasket.

LILY TOMLIN

I remember when people used to step outside a moment for a breath of fresh air. Now sometimes you have to step outside for days before you get it.

VICTOR BORGE

Pollution is so bad that when I put air in my tires two of them died.

LEE TULLY

What about all those detergents that are going out into our rivers and the ocean? If this keeps up it's going to leave a ring around the country.

JOHN BYNER

The giant panda lives in bamboo thickets and feeds on bamboo shoots. There are only thirty-six giant pandas left. The reason there are only thirty-six giant pandas left is the shortage of bamboo shoots, which the natives eat in great quantities, especially with baked giant panda.

JACK DOUGLAS

A new report from the government says raw eggs may have salmonella and may be unsafe. In fact, the latest government theory says it wasn't the fall that killed Humpty Dumpty— he was dead before he hit the ground.

JAY LENO

Poor

We were so poor we used to use a substitute for margarine . . . In school I took algebra, history, and overcoats . . . We didn't have a TV set, we used to sit around and watch the mirror.

JACKIE VERNON

It's not hard to tell we was poor —when you saw the toilet paper dryin' on the clothesline.

GEORGE "GOOBER" LINDSEY

We were poor. If I wasn't a boy, I wouldn't have had nothing to play with.

REDD FOXX

We were very poor when I was a kid. I remember one winter, it snowed and I didn't have a sled. I used to go downhill on my cousin. And you know, she wasn't bad.

JOEY BISHOP

Times are hard, times are so hard right now people who don't intend to pay ain't buyin'.

SLAPPY WHITE

Population Explosion

We'll continue to have a population problem as long as screwing is more popular than dying.

ROWLAND P. WILSON

Pregnancy

They caution pregnant women not to drink alcohol. It may harm the baby. I think that's ironic. If it wasn't for alcohol most women wouldn't be that way.

RITA RUDNER

We noticed that the bride was pregnant. So at the wedding everyone threw puffed rice.

DICK CAVETT

When I found out I was pregnant, I was thrilled. It made me feel just like a high school girl again. Also, my condition really proved most eloquently the fact that I was loved—if only for a moment.

JOAN RIVERS

The idea with natural childbirth is to avoid drugs so the mother can share the first intimate moments after birth with the baby and the father and the obstetrician and the standby anesthesiologist and the nurses and the person who cleans the room.

DAVE BARRY

My next-door neighbor's little girl, 16 years old, pretty little girl—showed up just as pregnant as she could be. Her mama hit the ceiling.

She said, "Who done it? Who done this dastardly deed?"

The little girl said, "How do I know? You wouldn't let me go steady."

RALPH SMITH

My wife—God bless her—was in labor for thirty-two hours. And I was faithful to her the entire time.

JONATHAN KATZ

If pregnancy were a book, they would cut the last two chapters.

NORA EPHRON

Presidents

George Washington said to his father, "If I never tell a lie, how can I get to be President?"

RED BUTTONS

George Washington, father of our country. George Washington, when he was just a child, just a boy, honesty was his trademark. The classic story we all remember was when George Washington's father came up to George and said, "George Washington—father of our country—my son—I want to ask you a question. Someone cut down the cherry tree." And George Washington, though he was just a youth, said, "Father, I cannot tell a lie. It was I who cut down that cherry tree."

And his father punched him in the mouth.

Because George Washington cut down the cherry tree. And his father was in the cherry tree picking cherries!

TOM SMOTHERS

Do you believe the Washington Monument looks anything like George Washington?

BROTHER DAVE GARDNER

Abraham Lincoln always said you can't fool all the people all of the time. But Abraham Lincoln was fooling when he said that.

MARK RUSSELL

My father used to tell me, "When Abraham Lincoln was your age, Abraham Lincoln had a job. When Abraham Lincoln was your age, he walked twelve miles to get to school." I said, "Dad, when Abraham Lincoln was your age, he was President, okay?"

ANDY ANDREWS

Garfield was assassinated. Shot by a disappointed office seeker, right? Don't they always say that same sentence? It's crazy. Every time you read his name: James Abram Garfield: "Shot by a disappointed office seeker." That's all they can think of what he did in his short term of office. You look in the Encyclopaedia Britannica under Garfield, James Abram. It says, "See Office seeker, disappointed."

ROBERT KLEIN

Mr. Wilson's mind, as has been the custom, will be closed all day Sunday.

GEORGE S. KAUFMAN

Mr. Coolidge is the best Democrat we ever had in the White House. He didn't do nothin', but that's what we wanted done.

WILL ROGERS

On Presidents Day you stay home and you don't do anything. Sounds like *Vice* Presidents Day!

JAY LENO

Priests

When I was growing up, my mom wanted me to become a priest, which I think is a tough occupation. Can you imagine giving up your sex life and then once a week people come in to tell you all the highlights of theirs?

TOM DREESEN

In the Plaza Hotel once, when I was doing the quiz show, there was a priest in the elevator. I hope you're not offended by this—I'd tell a story about a rabbi but it doesn't fit, and neither did the rabbi and they finally threw him out of the synagogue. Anyhow, this priest says to me, "Aren't you Groucho Marx?" I said yes. He says, "Gee, my mother's crazy about you." And I said, "Really? I didn't know you fellas *had* mothers." I had a priest stop me in Montreal some years ago. He came up and said, "Aren't you Groucho Marx? May I shake your hand?" I said fine. I shook hands with him and he said, "I want to thank you for all the joy you've put in this world." And I said, "I want to thank you for the joy you've taken out of it."

GROUCHO MARX

A priest and a rabbi were enjoying the fights at Madison Square Garden. One of the fighters crossed himself before the opening gong sounded. "What does that mean?" the rabbi asked. The priest said, "Not a damn thing if he can't fight."

BELLE BARTH

Profanity

Swearing was invented as a compromise between running away and fighting.

FINLEY PETER DUNNE

I get broads come in here, they sit in front of me and they stare at me. Everything I do, they stare at me. Then they walk out saying, "She's so dirty!" They're so refined, how come they understand what I'm saying?

PEARL WILLIAMS

189

Progress

Progress might have been all right once but it has gone on too long.

OGDEN NASH

Prostitution

Prostitutes go to jail. Their customers go home and read the New York *Times*. In this country you're allowed to buy anything. If you need a shirt, you have a right to buy it. If you need sex, you don't. What's more important, sex or a shirt?

JACKIE MASON

You can lead a horticulture, but you can't make her think.

DOROTHY PARKER

An old man lost all his money. Seventy years old, hasn't got a dime. Who does he blame? His wife. He says, "If you were a good wife, you'd go out and work for me." She says, "What could I do?" He says, "You could be a whore!" "I could be a whore?" "You could try." She comes back the next morning all stooped over, dirty, disheveled. He says, "You made out?" She says, "Certainly I made out. I made twenty-four dollars and ten cents." He says, "Who gave you the ten cents?" She says, "Everybody."

BELLE BARTH

I wonder why prostitution is illegal. Why should it be illegal to sell something that's perfectly legal to give away?

GEORGE CARLIN

My sister claimed sexual harassment on the job, which was a little bit surprising, since she's a hooker.

GEORGE MILLER

A guy comes over here from Israel. He goes to a house of horizontal refreshment. He rings the bell, the madam comes to the door, she lets him in, and he says, "Who are you?" She says, "I'm Sarah." He says, "Oooh, Sarah! Darling! I want you! I want to go with you." She says, "Leave me alone, I'm old, I'm tired. Go pick out one of the girls." He says, "No, I want you! I want to go with you!" He says, "Sarah —for two hundred dollars?"

She says, "For two hundred dollars? All right, come upstairs." She takes him upstairs. He gives her the two hundred dollars, and he says, "I'll see you tomorrow." The second night, she takes him upstairs, he gives her another two hundred dollars, and he says, "I'll see you tomorrow." The third night, he comes back, gives her another two hundred dollars.

She says, "I'll see you tomorrow?"

He says, "No, I'm going back home to Israel."

She says, "Israel? You're from Israel! Oh, my mother lives in Israel! Maybe you know my mother in Israel?"

He says, "Do I know your mother in Israel? Your mother gave me six hundred dollars I should give you!"

PEARL WILLIAMS

A hooker picks up a Polish officer and takes him home. She feeds him and takes him to bed. The next morning, he rises first and puts on his uniform.

"Didn't you forget something?" the girl asks.

"What?" he asks.

"The money," the girl replies.

He says, "A Polish officer doesn't accept money!"

GROUCHO MARX

You know what I like about hookers? It doesn't matter what line you use on them, because they all work.

KIP ADDOTTA

The post office announced today that it is going to issue a stamp commemorating prostitution in the United States. It's a ten-cent stamp, but if you want to lick it, it's a quarter.

CHEVY CHASE

Proverbs

You can't be happy with a woman who pronounces both *d*'s in Wednesday.

PETER DE VRIES

The best way to make a fire with two sticks is to make sure one of them is a match.

WILL ROGERS

If a man's down, kick him! If he survives it, he has an opportunity to rise above it. I've always said it's more blessed to give than to receive.

BROTHER DAVE GARDNER

Never moon a werewolf.

MIKE BINDER

Remember, if you save nothing, you can't take it with you.

STAN LAUREL

You've buttered your bread—now sleep in it.

GRACIE ALLEN

Which came first, the chicken or the egg? Neither. It was the woman to cook them.

SHERRIE SHEPHERD

Things are going to get a lot worse before they get worse.

LILY TOMLIN

If you use a waffle iron for a pillow, be sure it is unplugged.

GARY OWENS

Early to bed and early to rise, and you'll meet very few of our best people.

GEORGE ADE

Tragedy is if I cut my finger. Comedy is if you walk into an open sewer and die.

MEL BROOKS

Build a better mousetrap and the world will beat a path to your door. Build a better door and the mice can't get in anyhow.

CAL TINNEY

Buy thermometers in the wintertime. They're much lower then.

SOUPY SALES

What's right is what's left if you do everything else wrong.

ROBIN WILLIAMS

If it wasn't for electricity we'd all be watching television by candlelight.

GEORGE GOBEL

Money can't buy love—but it certainly puts you in a wonderful bargaining position.

HARRISON BAKER

It is better to have loved and lost than to have paid for it and not liked it.

HIRAM KASTEN

If it wasn't for half the people in the world, the other half would be all of them.

COLONEL LEMUEL STOOPNAGLE

You show me a sculptor who works in the basement and I'll show you a low-down chiseler!

SOUPY SALES

If you can't laugh at yourself, make fun of other people.

BOBBY SLAYTON

Why should a worm turn? It's probably just the same on the other side.

IRVIN S. COBB

In spring, an old man's stomach turns.

LARRY SIEGEL

Be kind and considerate to others, depending somewhat upon who they are.

DON HEROLD

You cannot learn to swim until you get into the water and drown.

BROTHER THEODORE

Never use a big word when a little filthy one will do.

JOHNNY CARSON

It takes a heap of liver to make a dog a home.

FIBBER McGEE (JIM JORDAN)

No problem is so big or so complicated that it can't be run away from.

CHARLES SCHULZ (LINUS in "Peanuts")

Old friends are like old wine. They sour with age.

THE GREAT GILDERSLEEVE
   (HAROLD PEARY)

What is reality? Nothing but a collective hunch.

LILY TOMLIN

By Decoration Day all Easter chicks are chickens.

SELMA DIAMOND

We're all like the cleaning woman. We come to dust.

PETER DE VRIES

We're all cremated equal.

JANE ACE

Everything comes to him who waits. Except a loaned book.

KIN HUBBARD

193

The beaver is very industrious, but he is still a beaver.

WILL CUPPY

Don't worry about your heart. It will last you as long as you live.

W. C. FIELDS

The universe is like a safe to which there is a combination, but the combination is locked up in the safe.

PETER DE VRIES

Psychiatry

Remember when a couch was used for *making* love instead of *telling* about it?

JACK DOUGLAS

Psychoanalysis was a wonderful discovery; it makes quite simple people feel they are complex.

S. N. BEHRMAN

Psychiatrists tell us one out of every five people is completely disturbed. And the reason is the other four are nuts.

DAVE ASTOR

I asked him, "What will this cost me?" He told me seventy-five dollars a visit. I said, "For seventy-five dollars I don't visit, I move in." He said, "What's bothering you?" I said, "The seventy-five-dollar fee for the visit." He said, "We have to search for the real you!" I said to myself: If I don't know who I am, how would I know what I look like? And even if I find me, how would I know it's me? Besides, if I want to look for me, why do I need him? I could look myself, or I could call my friends. They know where I've been! Besides, what if I find the real me, and I find that he's even worse than I am? The psychiatrist said, "The search for the real you will continue at our next session. That will be seventy-five dollars." I said to myself: This is not the real me. Why should I give him seventy-five dollars? What if I find the real me and he doesn't think it's worth seventy-five dollars? For all I know the real me might be going to a different psychiatrist altogether. In fact, he might even be this psychiatrist himself! I said to him, "What if you're the real me? Then you owe me seventy-five dollars." He said, "If you promise never to come back we'll call it even."

JACKIE MASON

After twelve years of therapy my psychiatrist said something that brought tears to my eyes. He said, *"No hablo inglés."*

RONNIE SHAKES

How many psychiatrists does it take to change a light bulb? Only one, but the light bulb has to really *want* to be changed.

ANNE EVA RICKS

Two psychiatrists meet. One says to the other, "I went home for Easter and I made a terrible Freudian slip."

The other said, "What did you say?"

He said, "Well, I started to say to my mother, 'Pass the hot cross buns.' And I said, 'You've ruined my life, you bitch!' "

TONY RANDALL

Two psychiatrists were talking with each other, and one said, "You think you got problems? I've been doing some tests among my patients. I ask them three questions."

"What kind of questions?"

"Here's the first one. What would you say if I asked you what wears a skirt and employs the lips to give pleasure?"

"I'd say a Scottish bagpiper."

"Right! Here's the second question. What has stream-lined curves and arouses the most basic instincts in man?"

"A roller coaster."

"Right. Now here's the third one. What's warm and soft and a pleasure to share a bed with?"

"A hot-water bottle?"

"What else? But you should hear some of the crazy answers I get from my patients!"

EDDIE CANTOR

I had to go to analysis. They told me I had an unresolved Oedipus complex, which, according to them, meant I want to sleep with my mother. Which is preposterous. My father doesn't even want to sleep with my mother.

DENNIS WOLFBERG

Puberty

Have you noticed that your body is playing little tricks on you lately? If you are a boy, you may have noticed your legs, face, arms, and chest are becoming covered with thick, black hairs and your voice may be beginning to sound like a phonograph needle ruining your favorite stack of platters. If you are a girl, you may have noticed a painful swelling up here and some more funny business going on down there.

These dramatic changes can mean only one thing: cholera. If you are not among the lucky ones, then it simply means you are becoming a young man or a young woman, depending on how much fluoride they dumped in your parents' drinking water. I know that such changes can often be difficult for growing teens, but try to weather the storm and "grin and bear it." There is always impotence and menopause.

DOUG KENNEY

I had plenty of pimples as a kid. One day I fell asleep in the library. When I woke up, a blind man was reading my face.

RODNEY DANGERFIELD

A lot of schools around New York keep sending school reporters to interview me. So this girl comes over from a girls' college the other day and she says, "How old should a girl be before she goes to a prom in a strapless dress?" I said, "If it stays up, you're old enough."

SELMA DIAMOND

Puns

Demosthenes: Demosthenes can do is bend and hold the legs together.

ALEXANDER WOOLLCOTT

The waiter says, "The last man who was in the restaurant ate twenty-seven hotcakes right off the griddle." And the customer says, "How waffle!"

ED WYNN

Thomas Edison, who invented electric lights—he dedicated

his life to humanity. Edison went to remote Indian reservations and strung electric wire to the outhouses so that the older Indians could have illumination.

Don't ever forget. He was the first man in history to wire a head for a reservation.

NORM CROSBY

Fascinate: There were nine buttons on her nightgown, but she could only fascinate.

HOMER HAYNES

I loved him like a brothel.

S. J. PERELMAN

He fell into a vat of pudding mixture and was found battered to death.

KENNETH HORNE

One time a little parakeet flew in our window. My mom was making some hot chocolate, and she had a whole boiling pot of hot milk. And the parakeet flew right into that boiling milk. And I don't like cream of asparakeet.

TOM SMOTHERS

Two little mice went swimming. And one of the mice

started to drown. The other mouse dragged him out and tried to save him. How did he do it?

Mouse-to-mouse resuscitation!

FRANK FONTAINE

A rabbi on the West Coast was very discouraged. Half of his congregation had turned Quaker. Or as he put it, "Some of my best Jews are Friends."

MARK RUSSELL

Quandary

When you don't have any money, the problem is food. When you have money, it's sex. When you have both, it's health. If everything is simply jake, then you're frightened of death.

J. P. DONLEAVY

Did you ever feel like the whole world was a tuxedo and you were a pair of brown shoes?

GEORGE GOBEL

All the things I really like to do are either immoral, illegal, or fattening.

ALEXANDER WOOLLCOTT

I fear that one day I'll meet God, he'll sneeze, and I won't know what to say.

RONNIE SHAKES

What do we know about the beyond? Do we know what's behind the beyond? I'm afraid some of us hardly know what's beyond the behind.

BROTHER THEODORE

Questions

How come when you mix water and flour together you get glue . . . and then you add eggs and sugar and you get cake? Where does the glue go?

RITA RUDNER

Ever wonder if illiterate people get the full effect of alphabet soup?

JOHN MENDOZA

Why do we expect our Presidents to control destiny when they cannot even control the House of Representatives?

RUSSELL BAKER

The formula for water is H_2O. Is the formula for an ice cube H_2O squared?

LILY TOMLIN

Has any turtle ever outlived a shaker of turtle food?

JERRY SEINFELD

People in hell—where do they tell people to go?

RED SKELTON

Radio

The ideal voice for radio may be defined as having no substance, no sex, no owner, and a message of importance to every housewife.

HARRY V. WADE

Rain

I think God invented rain to give dead people something to complain about.

DAVID BRENNER

Rape

You can't joke about rape? I think it's hilarious! Picture Porky Pig raping Elmer Fudd.

GEORGE CARLIN

Reincarnation

I'd like to come back as an oyster. Then I'd only have to be good from September until April.

GRACIE ALLEN

I spend money with reckless abandon. Last month I blew five thousand dollars at a reincarnation seminar. I got to thinking, what the hell, you only live once.

RONNIE SHAKES

I believe in reincarnation. I've had other lives. I know. I have clues. First of all, I'm exhausted.

CAROL SISKIND

Relationships

Relationships give us a reason to live. Revenge.

RONNIE SHAKES

If you come home and he's using your diaphragm for an ashtray, it's over.

CAROL SISKIND

Guys are like dogs. They keep comin' back. Ladies are like cats. Yell at a cat one time, they're gone.

LENNY BRUCE

A man who was loved by three hundred women singled me out to live with him. Why? I was the only one without a cat.

ELAYNE BOOSLER

I can't get a relationship to last longer than it takes to tape their albums.

MARGARET SMITH

I met this girl very aggressively . . . I just walked up to her and I said, "Who are you? I have to know who you are!"

It's a good opener, but you can't sustain that level of excitement. Later on chicks start complaining the relationship doesn't have that much drive anymore. You have to remind them, "I'm the guy who ran up and said, 'Who are you?' "

And they always say, "Well, you never do that anymore."

And you have to say, "Yes, and I still don't know who you are."

MORT SAHL

I'm very loyal in relationships. Even when I go out with my mom I don't look at other moms.

GARRY SHANDLING

In talking to girls I could never remember the right sequence of things to say. I'd meet a girl and say, "Hi, was it good for you too?" If a girl spent the night, I'd wake up in the morning and then try to get her drunk . . .

STEVE MARTIN

I know there are no well-adjusted men in New York but I'd be happy to find one that's treatable.

AUDREY BUSLIK

When you're dating you're so insecure. My last relationship, I was always there for her and she dumped me. I told her about it.

I said, "Remember when your grandma died? I was there. Remember when you flunked out of school? I was there. Remember when you lost your job? I was there!"

She said, "I know—you're bad luck."

TOM ARNOLD

My girlfriend told me that she was seeing another man. I told her to rub her eyes.

EMO PHILIPS

Nobody liked me because I was too popular.

JACKIE VERNON

Religion

Born Again Christians . . . I'm a little indignant when they tell me I'm going to hell if I haven't been born again. Pardon me for getting it right the first time.

DENNIS MILLER

My brother joined a cult. We haven't seen him in two years. That's so scary 'cause they brainwash people, they all dress alike, talk alike, think alike. You might have heard of it—it's called IBM.

MIKE DUGAN

I'm a Catholic. I'm like most Catholics. When I grew up I quit. I can't quite understand some religions. They're all supposed to be right. But they all have one goal—to get to heaven. They all have their own way of getting there. So it seems to me you ought to be able to think this out. Like if you're Catholic and you want to get to heaven, you can't have sex unless you're married. If you're Jewish and you want to get to heaven, you can't eat pork. Come on, if you had to make a choice . . .

BOB DUBAC

I went to a convent in New York and was fired finally for my insistence that the Immaculate Conception was spontaneous combustion.

DOROTHY PARKER

The Hare Krishnas are a little strange. Guys, wake up and smell the decade, would you please? You're bald, you got a weed on your head, you look like an onion. What are you, Alfalfa on chemotherapy?

And what's the deal with incense? It smells like somebody set fire to a clothes hamper. Gym socks and jasmine. Do we need that smell? You know what incense smells like? If flowers could fart.

BILLIAM CORONEL

A church is a place in which gentlemen who have never been to heaven brag about it to persons who will never get there.

H. L. MENCKEN

A fella's talking to his priest. He said, "I gave up sex for Lent . . . Well, I tried to, but the last day of Lent my wife dropped a can of peaches and when she bent over to pick 'em up, I couldn't help it."

The priest said, "That's all right, son, a lot of people give in to temptation." He said, "You're not gonna throw us out of church?" The priest said no.

He said, "Well, thank goodness. They threw us out of the supermarket!"

GEORGE "GOOBER" LINDSEY

There was a very strict order of monks, and they had a rule that said speaking is permissible only one day a year, one monk at a time.

One day it was this monk's turn, and he stood up at the dinner table and said quietly, "I don't like the mashed potatoes here at all, they're too lumpy." And he sat down.

A year later it was another monk's turn and he stood up and said, "I rather like the mashed potatoes, I find them very tasty."

The third year came along and it was another monk's turn. He said, "I want to transfer to another monastery, I can't stand this constant bickering."

HAL McKAY

When I was a kid my mother switched religions from Catholic to Episcopalian. Which is what, Catholic Lite? One third less guilt than that regular religion! You could eat meat on

Friday but not a really good cut.

RICK CORSO

Following the Vatican declaration that women cannot become priests because they do not resemble Christ, sources report that Colonel Sanders has declared that he will not employ anyone who doesn't resemble a chicken.

JANE CURTIN

There was a big flood in Louisiana. This guy is standing in water up to his knees. They came by in a rowboat and said, "Get in." He said, "Oh no, the Lord will take care of me."

A few minutes later he's up on the porch, the water's up to his waist. Another rowboat comes by, they say, "Get in." He says, "Oh no, the Lord will take care of me."

Now he's on the roof. The water's up to his neck. A helicopter comes by. He says, "No, no, the Lord will take care of me."

Well, he drowned. He gets up to heaven, he meets the Lord, he says, "What happened?" The Lord says, "I don't know what happened—I

sent two rowboats and a helicopter for you!"

RED SKELTON

Most people past college age are not atheists. It's too hard to be in society, for one thing. Because you don't get any days off. And if you're an agnostic you don't know whether you get them off or not.

MORT SAHL

Every day, people are straying away from the church and going back to God.

LENNY BRUCE

They have a Dial-a-Prayer for atheists now. You can call up and it rings and rings but nobody answers.

TOMMY BLAZE

I guess I began to doubt the existence of God after I had been married about three years.

BRIAN SAVAGE

Our church was so poor we didn't have an organ. We had an accordion. But I'll never forget Our Lady of Spain.

We were skeptical Catholics. We believed Jesus walked on

the water. We just figured it was probably winter.

I was recently born again. I must admit it's a glorious and wonderful experience. I can't say my mother enjoyed it a whole lot.

JOHN WING

They're now desecrating the Christian Science churches. Little kids are running around writing Rx.

JAMES KOMACK

This guy went to confession. I went with him, we were kids. And he confessed that he had sex with a girl in his parish.

And the priest said to him, "Was it Mary Angardi?" He said no.

The priest said, "Was it Felice Endreeni?" He said no.

The priest said, "Was it Elise Guini?" He said no.

Well, the priest said, "You're gonna do fifty Hail Marys and give me half your allowance in the plate for the next three weeks."

He came out and I said, "How'd you do?" He said, "Not too bad, and I got three good leads!"

BUDDY HACKETT

Why is it when we talk to God we're said to be praying, but when God talks to us we're schizophrenic?

LILY TOMLIN

Restaurants

I went into a Polish-Cajun restaurant. They served blackened toast.

RICH CEISLER

Them fancy Japanese steak houses—they make you take off your shoes before you even go in. That's because the food is so bad they're afraid you're gonna kick 'em.

BILLY HOLLIDAY

Never eat any place where they mark the rest-room doors in any fashion but "Men" and "Women" or "Ladies" and "Gentlemen." Especially do not eat in a restaurant that specializes in seafood and marks its rest-room doors "Buoys" and "Gulls," because they have been too busy thinking up cutesy names for the rest-room doors to really pay attention to the food.

LEWIS GRIZZARD

I've got a friend who is a boxer. Once he hung up his coat in a restaurant but he was afraid someone would run off with it. He hung a sign on it saying, "This coat belongs to the champion boxer of the world and I'll be back."

When he came back, he found another sign hanging where the coat had been. This sign said, "This coat was taken by the champion runner of the world, and I *won't* be back!"

ED WYNN

Never eat in a restaurant where you see a cockroach bench-pressing a burrito.

PAT McCORMICK

Those restaurants where they serve chicken croquettes! Leftovers I can eat at home.

SELMA DIAMOND

I like the old-timey diners with names like Eat. But be careful if they advertise a bottomless cup of coffee. You could end up with a scalded crotch.

TOMMY SLEDGE

One day Sam said to Moe, "Look, Moe, we got a lot of money. We are very wealthy. I think tonight we should celebrate. I'm tired of eating in these joints. Let's go to the finest restaurant in New York City."

"Okay, you're on," said Moe.

So they went to the finest restaurant they could find.

They ordered something that cost about thirty-five dollars and took two hours to prepare. While waiting they had a little appetizer. First, some gefilte fish and chopped liver. After they sat there for about an hour and a half, all of a sudden they saw four waiters come in with an enormous tray. On it was a whole roast pig with an apple in its mouth.

Sam said to Moe, "There you are, I told you. This is the classiest place in town. Look how they serve a baked apple."

LEW LEHR

I went to an authentic Mexican restaurant. The waiter poured the water and warned me not to drink it.

BRAD GARRETT

Have you ever been in a restaurant and there's a couple in the next booth being overly affectionate? They're necking and groping and you're trying to eat your eggs. I always want to go up to them and say, "Excuse me . . . would you mind if I join you?" How do these people think? Do they wake up in the morning: "Do you want to have sex, honey?" "No, let's wait till we get to Denny's!"

BOBBY KELTON

The murals in restaurants are on a par with the food in museums.

PETER DE VRIES

Rich People

God shows his contempt for wealth by the kind of person he selects to receive it.

AUSTIN O'MALLEY

Rich people in Beverly Hills have surrogate mothers for their children. Oh, they give birth . . . they just have someone come in to nurture and kiss them.

BRETT BUTLER

My father got my mother a telephone in the limousine. Big deal, every time it rings he has to run down to the garage and answer it.

LONDON LEE

You know you've really made it when:

The boss invites you to his club for a game of golf and you purposely try to beat his pants off.

When you visit London, Paris, and Rome and don't even bother to take a camera along.

When your toupee blows off at the office and no one dares to laugh.

FRANK RIDGEWAY

Riddles

What goes, "Wiff wiff leap, wiff wiff leap, wiff wiff leap"? A hurdler in corduroy shorts.

JOHNNY HART ("BC")

What's brown and sounds like a bell? Dung!

ERIC IDLE

Russia

The Soviet Union has soap operas like *One Day to Live* and *Search for All My Children.* And game shows like *Bowling for Food* and *Wheel of Torture.* My favorite show was about a guy who had the opportunity to leave Russia and didn't: *That's Incredible.*

YAKOV SMIRNOFF

Looking for ways to ease my mind about signs that the danger of nuclear war is increasing, I stumbled across one comforting thought: Maybe the Russian missiles won't work . . .

Why didn't I think of this years ago? I have certainly read enough about the shoddiness of goods produced by Soviet industry—overcoats whose sleeves fall off now and then, television sets permanently tuned to the all-snow channel, refrigerators destined to become the only thing in a Moscow apartment that is never cold. I have read about those Russian tractor factories where vodka-sodden workers fulfill their monthly quota in a frantic last-minute push that can succeed only if they attach the transmission with Scotch tape. Why have I always taken it for granted that those goofballs would be so good at annihilating continents?

CALVIN TRILLIN

When I got to America, I saw an ad in the paper: "We guarantee our furniture and stand behind it for six months." That's why I left the Soviet Union. I don't want any people standing behind my furniture!

YAKOV SMIRNOFF

The capitalist system is the best, 'cause we can go somewhere else. Communism is one big phone company.

LENNY BRUCE

Are Russian leaders overweight and out of shape? The new national symbol is the hammer and fudgesicle.

CARL WOLFSON

A Russian official came up to a factory worker and said, "If you drank a shot of vodka, could you still work?" The worker said, "I think I could." The official said, "If you drank two shots of vodka, could you work?" The worker said, "I think I could." Then the Russian official said, "If you drank five shots of vodka, could you work?" And the worker said, "Well, I'm here, aren't I?"

YAKOV SMIRNOFF

Satire

Here's a letter from Mrs. Jerome Whatsis from West Jesus, North Dakota. She says, "Dear Sir: I don't know what I would do without satire. When my husband is home sick in bed and my children are screaming for food and there's no money, I thank God there is such a thing as satire . . ." Well, this is only one of the influences of satire. We all know how much satire did to stop the rise of Hitler in Germany in 1931.

ANTHONY HOLLAND

School

My teacher told me that today was the first day of the rest of my life. That explains why I didn't do yesterday's homework.

LORNE ELLIOTT

When I finished school I took one of those career aptitude tests and, based on my verbal ability score, they suggested I become a mime.

TIM CAVANAGH

I took biology two years in a row just to eat the specimens.

PAT PAULSEN

I had the worst study habits . . . the lowest grades . . . then I found out what I was doing wrong. I had been highlighting with a black Magic Marker.

JEFF ALTMAN

I was terrible at history. I could never see the point of learning what people thought back when people were a lot stupider. For instance, the ancient Phoenicians believed that the sun was carried across the sky on the back of an enormous snake. So what? So they were idiots.

DAVE BARRY

There is nothing so stupid as the educated man if you get off the thing he was educated in.

WILL ROGERS

I went to correspondence school. They threw me out from there. I played hooky . . . I sent them an empty envelope.

BARON MUNCHAUSEN (JACK PEARL)

I had a terrible education. I attended a school for emotionally disturbed teachers.

WOODY ALLEN

A five-year-old kid raised his hand at school. The teacher declined to let him leave the room. Five minutes later she reversed herself. She said, "All right, Sonny, you may go now."

The little boy looked up and said, "I don't have to."

She said, "What do you mean you don't have to?"

He said, "I opened up my geography book and went in the ocean."

NORM CROSBY

Two Egg High School is so unfriendly and hostile, the school newspaper has an obituary page.

ROCKY RAY

In school I was never the class clown, but more of the class trapeze artist, as I was always being suspended . . . Once the teacher said, "Emo, what's five-nincteenths divided by four-fifteenths?" and my brain began to bleed. She said, "Take it easy. What's our common denominator?" I said, "A fondness for little girls?"

EMO PHILIPS

The teacher asked three boys to write an essay. She said,

"Write on what you would do if you had a million dollars, and bring it in tomorrow."

So the next day the three little boys came in. She said to the first boy, "Percy, this is a nice essay on what you'd do with a million dollars. You said you'd give your mother a new home, your father a new car, send your sister to college—I think that's wonderful." And she said to the second boy, "I'm proud of you, David. You wrote a nice essay on what you'd do with a million dollars. You'd buy your mother a Cadillac and a mink coat . . ."

She looked at the paper of the third boy. She said, "Donny, you're paper has nothing on it!" He said, "That's what I'd do with a million dollars. Nothing!"

MOMS MABLEY

I'm enjoying summer school. I believe it's been good for me. It saves a lot on sunscreen.

CHARLES SCHULZ
(Peppermint Patty in "Peanuts")

I heard that Evelyn Wood just lost a lawsuit. A guy sued her because his eyeball blew out at ten thousand words a minute.

JAY LENO

Self-Help

I have a new book coming out. It's one of those self-help deals; it's called *How to Get Along with Everyone*. I wrote it with this other asshole.

STEVE MARTIN

Two approaches: "Live fast, die young, and leave a good-looking corpse." "Go to the dry cleaner's, clean out the attic, and take out the garbage."

MICK STEVENS

Sex

Everybody has sex now. When I was a kid only women had sex and you had to get it from them. We got a battery-powered sexual aid. Actually, a flashlight. When I was performing she would wave it back and forth to create an illusion of motion.

TONY STONE

Anyone who calls it "sexual intercourse" can't possibly be interested in actually doing it. You might as well announce you're ready for lunch by proclaiming, "I'd like to do some masticating and enzyme secreting."

ALLAN SHERMAN

A guy goes to the doctor. The doctor says, "I've got some bad news for you. You've got a terminal illness."

He said, "How long have I got to live?"

The doctor says, "Six hours."

He rushes home and his wife says, "How did the physical go?"

He said, "Terrible. I ain't gonna live. All I got's six hours."

She said, "Whaddya want to do for six hours?"

He said, "I don't know. You want to make love?"

She said, "Sure."

They did. Two hours. They got through, and they're laying there, and she said, "Whaddya want to do now? How much time have you got?"

He said, "Four hours."

"Want to make some more love?"

He said sure. They made love for another three hours.

They got through and she said, "Honey, how much time have you got?"

He said, "I ain't got but an hour left. Whaddya want to do now? Want to make some more love?"

She said, "No."

He said, "Why not?"

She said, "I got to get up in the morning. You don't."

LEWIS GRIZZARD

My wife told me of a book about finding the G spot. I went to a bookstore. I couldn't even find the book . . . My wife bought it for me. There were no pictures, maps, or diagrams. It just said it was about two-thirds of the way in. Great. Compared to who?

ROBERT SCHIMMEL

People make a living donating to sperm banks. Last year I let five hundred dollars slip through my fingers.

ROBERT SCHIMMEL

Love is blind, but desire just doesn't give a good goddamn.

JAMES THURBER

When I was growing up, all my friends wanted to have sex with anything that moved. "Why limit yourself?" I told them.

EMO PHILIPS

I've been experimenting with some new sexual positions. Now I'm getting ready to try them on people.

JIM SAMUELS

I was in bed one night when my boyfriend Ernie said, "How come you never tell me when you're having an orgasm?" I said to him, "Ernie, you're never around."

BETTE MIDLER

If God intended that the genitals were more important than the brain, he would've put a skull over the genitals. What the hell do you care if someone comes over and fools around with you and your genitals? What is it, it's a momentary thing. But you don't want anybody coming over and stroking your brains. They'll scramble your brains, you'll write the

wrong check out, you'll lose money.

MEL BROOKS

People want to take sex education out of the schools. They believe sex education causes promiscuity—if you have the knowledge, you use it. Hey, I took algebra. I never do math.

ELAYNE BOOSLER

The last girl I made love to, it was not going well. Anytime you make love and have to give her the Heimlich maneuver at the same time, it's not a good thing.

GARRY SHANDLING

If I ever write a sex manual, I'd call it *Ow, You're on My Hair.*

RICHARD LEWIS

In the hotel there was a mirror over my bed! I was uneasy going to sleep. When I sleep I toss and turn, and when I woke up I thought I saw a naked sky diver coming at me . . . But I don't know what it's there for. I really don't. You gonna shave in bed? What the hell you gonna watch? All I know is, from the way I . . . umm . . . you get a broken neck tryin' to watch

. . . and Camille's a virgin Catholic, I know she ain't peekin'!

BILL COSBY

My wife's been faking her orgasms—in front of my friends.

TONY DARO

The secret of a good sex life is to have a good sex life . . . In other words, kid, don't let yer meat loaf.

R. CRUMB

I worry about kids today. Because of the sexual revolution they're going to grow up and never know what "dirty" means.

LILY TOMLIN

One score and seven years ago, your fathers brought forth Incontinence, a new notion, conceived by Libertines and dedicated to the Proposition: All men, when procreating, are equal. But in a practical sense, we could not dissipate, we could not copulate, we could not wallow on this ground. It wasn't yet altogether fitting and proper that we should do this.

We did then slyly resolve that this nation should have no dearth of lewd freedom, and that any covering of the peephole, by the peephole, or for the peephole must perish from the earth.

ALLAN SHERMAN

I love the lines the men use to get us into bed. Please, I'll only put it in for a minute. What am I, a microwave?

BEVERLY MICKINS

This man wants to make love to his wife, but every time he tries he gets no response from his wife. He goes to the doctor and the doctor says, "You try these pills in hot coffee in the morning. If this don't get it, this broad is stone cold dead in the market."

So the next morning she has on a negligee, they're sitting up there drinking coffee. He sneaks a pill in her coffee. Then he thinks he better try one himself, so he drops a pill in his coffee. Then he says, "Baby, let's have a second cup of coffee." In the second cup of coffee, he drops a second pill. And in his second cup of coffee, he also drops a second pill. He says, "Let's have a third cup of coffee!" In her third cup of coffee, he drops a third pill. And in his third cup of coffee, he drops a third pill.

Then she said, "Oh, baby, I feel wonderful, I feel like having a man." And he says, "So do I, baby, so do I!"

NORMA MILLER

Sometimes men yell, "I'm coming, I'm coming."

I'm not going anywhere.

I think maybe they think I don't know what's going on. Then I think I'm not in bed with them as a partner. I'm there as a witness.

EMILY LEVINE

Sexual therapists think the whole problem is we don't communicate enough. Dr. Ruth says as women we should *tell* our lovers how to make love to us. *My* boyfriend goes nuts if I tell him how to *Drive!*

PAM STONE

Last week I got badly beaten up fighting for a woman's honor. Next time I'll pick a smaller woman.

HENRY GIBSON

Premature ejaculation was invented by the Scots, largely as a means for a quicker (and thereby cheaper) evening out.

ERIC IDLE

I object to all this sex on the television. I mean, I keep falling off.

GRAHAM CHAPMAN

This morning I caught my wife in a lie . . . I'm sitting there in the kitchen, having some coffee, biscuits, some jelly. About eleven-thirty my old lady came in, and her wig was amuss. All mussed up. Her blouse was torn to shreds, you could see the imprint of fingers . . . This really threw me off. So I asked her, "Where the hell have you been?" And she said she spent the night with her sister. You dig it? I knew she was lyin' because *I* had spent the night with her sister.

FLIP WILSON

Girls now say what they think. I was with one the other night. Two in the morning she told me to go to a sex clinic. Said I should ask for the emergency room.

MIKE PREMINGER

I actually learned about sex watching neighborhood dogs. And it was good. Go ahead and laugh. No, go ahead. I think the most important thing I learned was: Never let go of the girl's leg no matter how hard she tries to shake you off.
STEVE MARTIN

There's a double standard about sex. A father or mother becomes a father or mother. Beautiful. The arrival of a child is celebrated. But how that child was created and arrived is something that is cloaked in secrecy. They're ashamed of it. They thought it was pretty clever when they did it . . .
JACKIE MASON

Most guys'll tell you, if they had a choice of a way to die, they would want to die while in bed with a woman. Making whoopee. Which is great. For the guy.
For the woman, let's be honest, it's a drag. She has really two choices. Number one, she's totally mortified and she avoids sex for the rest of her life. Or number two, she's walkin' around with an inordinate amount of confidence! "Hey,

Denise, what's happening?" "Ohhhh, nothing . . . last night I killed a man . . ."
JEFF CESARIO

My wife insists on turning off the lights when we make love. That doesn't bother me. It's the hiding that seems so cruel.
JONATHAN KATZ

My sex life is very bad. If it wasn't for pickpockets I'd have no sex life at all.
RODNEY DANGERFIELD

He just kept rushing through the lovemaking. Which is the part I like, the beginning part. Most women are like that. We need time to warm up. Why is this hard for you guys to understand? You're the first people to tell us not to gun a cold engine. You want us to go from zero to sixty in 5.5. We're not built like that. We stall.
ANITA WISE

She was a very intelligent woman. I remember one time I thought she was cheating on me, but I couldn't prove it. So I followed her. She picked this guy up and they drove to a motel. They went inside; I could see them hugging and kissing and taking their clothes off, but just at that crucial moment, they turned the lights out, so I never knew for sure . . .

I think that's what we fought the most about—our sex life. I wanted one.

KIP ADDOTTA

Sex (Safe Sex)

Safe sex is very important. That's why I'm never doing it on a plywood scaffolding again.

JENNY JONES

In 1962 the expression "safe sex," all that meant then was you just move the bed from against the wall so you won't bang your head.

DAVID LETTERMAN

In the old days you didn't ask their sexual history, you'd just say, "Are you a mammal?" Now you take her home and you say, "Where do I set up the lab?"

JOHN RIGGI

You have to be very careful these days. If you get involved with somebody you have to know their health history. The best way to find out is to look through their medicine cabinet. It tells you what they have, what they don't have . . . With this girl—I opened up the medicine cabinet. It was empty. I said, "Jeez, I don't know what she's got, but whatever it is, there ain't no cure for it!"

JACK SIMMONS

I'm scared of sex now. You have to be. You can get something terminal, like a kid.

WENDY LIEBMAN

I'm finding it difficult at the moment, with AIDS and everything. That's changed my lifestyle a lot. I used to go out every night, and try and get laid, and fail, and I'd call that sexual frustration. Now I go out every night and try and get laid, and fail, but I can call it a "healthy lifestyle."

SIMON FANSHAWE

Remember when "safe sex" meant your parents had gone away for the weekend?

RHONDA HANSOME

Dating is hard on guys. Guys just got really good lying about how many women they have had; now they have to lie about how many women they haven't had.

DIANE FORD

I had an unusual case of crabs. Most people get that from someone else who has it already. I got it directly from a crabmeat cocktail.

ED BLUESTONE

You can't get AIDS from a toilet seat. Unless you sit down before the last guy got up.

HIRAM KASTEN

When I was in high school the worst thing you could ever get was VD. Talk about the sniffles! I just want to meet an old-fashioned girl with gonorrhea.

BILL MAHER

Sex (Sexual Perversions)

I'm really concerned about my wife since we moved to California. She's gotten kind of kinky. She likes to tie me up and then go out with someone else.

TOM DREESEN

If your sexual fantasies were truly of interest to others, they would no longer be fantasies.

FRAN LEBOWITZ

You're never disappointed in an x-rated movie. You don't say, "Gee, I never thought it would end *that* way."

RICHARD JENI

Breast feeding is popular now. It wasn't when I was growing up. In high school, my mom caught me with an inflatable sex doll. I told her, "Hey, you're the one who got me hooked with those plastic baby bottles."

XAVIER SKINNER

You go to jail for doin' something normal. Ain't no law

against peein' in public. They get you for indecent exposure. As long as you pee and don't zip your pants down, that's normal.

DICK GREGORY

There's a masochist who loves a cold shower every morning— so he has a warm one.

DAVID FROST

Two drunks sitting at the bar. One drunk says, "Hey, did you hear about the new ice cubes with the hole in the middle?" The other drunk says, "Whaddya mean hear about 'em? I married one!"

HAP HAPPY

"My father's great dread was going senile," said one aristocrat, apologizing for his father, who was happily exposing himself in the orangery. "But now he has, he's enjoying himself enormously."

JILLY COOPER

Fetishism, transvestism, and nasty foreign behavior: many people get a kick out of doing all sorts of apparently unpleasant things. Some like dressing up as the opposite sex—for ex-

ample, Joan of Arc and Commander Joan of the Ark Royal; others enjoy sexual acts with bits of string, fish, dead birds, bottles, hedgehogs, etc., etc. Never laugh at people like this. *They may be on to something.*

ERIC IDLE

Shakespeare

Hamlet is the tragedy of tackling a family problem too soon after college.

TOM MASSON

Shopping

I went into a general store. They wouldn't let me buy anything specifically.

STEVEN WRIGHT

When I walked into the supermarket the manager got a grocery cart for me. I said, "Why do you always give me a cart with a squeaky wheel?" He said, "We've only got one store detective, we can't watch everybody."

BOB HOPE

I was working in a cosmetics shop. A woman came in looking for something to bring out her bright blue eyes. I gave her meat skewers.

HATTIE HAYRIDGE

A woman, who weighed a bulging three hundred pounds, went into a store to buy some shoes. She tried on so many she almost drove the poor clerk crazy. Each pair was either too big, too small, too narrow, or the wrong color.

"Oh, this is the pair I like," she finally said to the startled clerk.

"But, lady," he replied, "you're wearing the boxes."

JOE LAURIE, JR.

It makes no difference what it is, a woman will buy anything she thinks a store is losing money on.

KIN HUBBARD

Harrods—what a snotty store! I mean, even the window dummies have attitudes.

KIT HOLLERBACH

I'm constantly on line behind some jerk with coupons! Oh good! I wanna *live* in this store! He's got a double-off two-cent coupon for some dehydrated non-edible product, and this guy has nothing but time on his hands! Get a *job!* You won't have to *save* the four cents!

RICK DUCOMMON

When I went in to buy the fur coat, the salesman told me, "You never in your life saw a coat this luxurious, this fine." And he takes the coat and throws it on the floor . . . You wanna try it on, you lay down and creep into it! I said, "Well, it looks very nice on the floor. How do you think it'll look on me?" He's a real diplomat. He says, "Even on you the coat'll look good." I always wondered why they throw the coat on the floor. I found out. It's so when they tell you the price you'll have something soft to faint on.

JEAN CARROLL

I went up to the salesgirl. I said, "I'd like to see something cheap in a man's suit." She said, "The mirror's on the left."

JIMMY EDMONDSON
   (PROFESSOR BACKWARDS)

Translations from the Saleslady:
"I'm afraid we really don't have anything quite like that."
You're a $19.95 girl prepared to spend $29.95 in an $89.95 store.
"Just look at the detailing."
The seams are sewed with thread.
"Just feel the body of that cloth."
It's thick material.
"Just see how that material drapes."
It's thin material.
"That material will wear like iron."
The store owner's mother is helping out for the day.
"I wouldn't lie. That's not for you."
The orange-and-green dress with the lavender bugle beads is too tight to get into.
"The new style? Styles aren't important, dear, it's what suits you."
They have some of last year's stock on hand.

"Madam, that dress (hat, coat, suit) is you!"
It fits and is not chartreuse or purple.

ROBERT PAUL SMITH

I used to eat while I was in the supermarket. I guess I didn't consider it stealing 'cause I took it out inside my body.

ARSENIO HALL

I hate discount stores. They're all deceptive. The way they advertise is misleading. I spotted a sign, three o'clock in the morning. This is what the sign said: "Stereo system, three-speaker, stereophonic record player, hi-fi tape recorder, $17, first come first served."
   Now, I spotted that sign at three o'clock in the morning—so I parked the car right in front of the store all night. The doors open at 10 A.M. I'm the first one in the store. I said, "Let me have that thing for seventeen dollars." The guy says, "We sold it." I said, "To who?" He said, "To the night watchman."

BOB MELVIN

My father was having a lot of security problems in his lingerie store because women were stealing underwear in the dressing rooms. He installed cameras in there. He's still getting ripped off but he makes it all back on the video sales.

DANNY KOCH

Short People

I was a tiny baby when I was born. Really tiny. I was breastfed intravenously. I had to have a special nurse 'cause I was so little. She didn't like to touch me. She used to put Q-tips in my ears and use them as handles . . .

My folks used to go out to shows, movies, go out to eat. I never had a babysitter. They used to sit me down on a piece of flypaper.

LENNY RUSH

I saw my friend Jill. Jill's about this big. She's one of these short people that are always making up excuses about how great it is to be short.

She actually said to me, "Short people live a lot longer than tall people."

I said, "No, they don't. They're just so irritating it seems like they're around longer."

MARGARET SMITH

Show Business

An associate producer is the only guy in Hollywood who will associate with a producer.

FRED ALLEN

A celebrity is one who is known to many persons he is glad he doesn't know.

H. L. MENCKEN

If a farmer fills his barn with grain, he gets mice; if he leaves it empty, he gets actors.

BILL VAUGHAN

In Hollywood a starlet is the name for any woman under thirty who is not actively employed in a brothel.

BEN HECHT

Sincerity

Son, always be sincere. Whether you mean it or not.

MICHAEL FLANDERS

He was as sincere as a tap dancer's smile.

MOREY AMSTERDAM

Sleep

I love sleep because it is both pleasant and safe to use. Pleasant because one is in the best possible company and safe because sleep is the consummate protection against the unseemliness that is the invariable consequence of being awake. What you don't know won't hurt you. Sleep is death without the responsibility.

FRAN LEBOWITZ

Do you wake up in the morning feeling sleepy and grumpy? Then you must be Snow White!

DAVID FROST

Small Towns

My hometown was so small the local Howard Johnson had only one flavor.

VAUGHN MEADER

Larchmont is so tiny there's a mirror at one end.

JOAN RIVERS

It was a small town: Ferguson, Ohio. When you entered there was a big sign and it said, "Welcome to Ferguson. Beware of the Dog." The all-night drugstore closed at noon.

JACKIE VERNON

The town was so small it had only one yellow page.

ORSON BEAN

A small town is one where there is no place to go where you shouldn't.

ALEXANDER WOOLLCOTT

It was such a small town we didn't even have a village idiot. We had to take turns.

BILLY HOLLIDAY

Our town was small but we got two things we're very proud of. Night and day. If you have a year to live, move there—it'll seem like a lifetime.

GEORGE "GOOBER" LINDSEY

It was a little town—when I was a kid we used to play Monopoly on it.

DONNA JEAN YOUNG

It's such a little town our radio station can't identify itself. It's off the air now. Somebody tripped over the tower.

DONNA JEAN YOUNG

I pulled into this town called Weedpatch. I check into the Weedpatch Hotel, they give me a *Key* magazine with all the events going on in town, I open it up—there's a picture of me checking into the Weedpatch Hotel.

MONICA PIPER

S*moking*

You know what bugs me? People who smoke cigars in restau-

rants. That's why I always carry a water pistol filled with gasoline.

PAUL PROVENZA

The last man in the tobacco industry with principle was Sir Walter Raleigh.

STEVE ALLEN

Of course I mind if you smoke. I don't want to smell *anything* that's coming out of your mouth!

CY KOTTICK

One morning, four years ago, something happened that I will never forget. I woke up, and I looked at myself in the mirror, because I happened to wake up in the bathroom, and I said to myself, "Dave, you have a wonderful wife, you have a newborn son, you have a good job, you have friends who care about you, you have a lawn mower that starts on the second or third pull—you have everything a man could possibly want, and a whole lifetime ahead of you to enjoy it in. Why not enjoy a cigarette right now?" And so I did.

DAVE BARRY

This guy was puffing his cigar in my petite flower face! So I said, "If I wanted to shorten my life—I'd date ya!"

JUDY TENUTA

Never expect a quick answer from a pipe smoker. He will always fiddle with his pipe first. That's the real reason he smokes a pipe.

ROGER SIMON

It seems to me the uses of tobacco aren't obvious right off the bat . . . You can shred it up and put it on a piece of paper and roll it up . . . and stick it between your lips . . . and then you set fire to it! Then what do you do? You inhale the smoke. It seems offhand you could stand in front of your fireplace and have the same thing going.

BOB NEWHART

The FCC came along and it said no more cigarette commercials on television . . . I'd much rather watch a pretty girl offer me a cigarette than an old lady ask if I'm constipated.

MARK RUSSELL

I have doubts about my health club. The locker room has a smoking and a non-smoking section.

ELLEN ORCHID

I quit smoking and it was a very, very disappointing experience. I found out my teeth are really brown.

BILL DANA

It's good to see people not smoking. You get dressed up, and you smoke, and it gets in your clothes. You go, "What should I wear tonight?" "I don't know, honey, how about something menthol?"

GEORGE LOPEZ

Anybody got a cigarette? Thanks very much, sir—I left mine in the machine.

LONDON LEE

I started smoking to lose weight. After I dropped that lung I felt pretty good.

MICHAEL MEEHAN

Buying cigarettes becomes an interview now. I said to the salesgirl in back of the counter, "I'd like a carton of cigarettes." She said, "There are so many brands, what would you like?" I said, "Give me a carton of Brand X, they're not doing too good." She said, "Soft pack or the crush-proof box?" "Soft pack." "King size or regular?" "King size." "Filter tip or plain?" "Filter tip." "Menthol or mint?" "Menthol." "Is this cash or credit?" I said, "Forget it, I broke the habit!"

BOB MELVIN

They say if you smoke you knock off ten years. But it's the last ten. What do you miss? The drooling years?

JOHN MENDOZA

The only thing that bothers me is if I'm in a restaurant and I'm eating and someone says, "Hey, mind if I smoke?" I always say, "No. Mind if I fart?"

STEVE MARTIN

Society People

I've come to the conclusion that café-society people must

work for hours in front of their mirrors to acquire that expression that sets in at sunset. They all look like they wished to spit but unfortunately had run out of saliva. The gentlemen usually look like they're smelling something and the ladies look like they've found it."

JACK DOUGLAS

Your grandparents did not endure the indignities of a steerage journey to Ellis Island so that you could stand outside a discotheque and beg a wallpaper designer to take you in with him.

FRAN LEBOWITZ

My sister's a Vassar graduate. Super-sophisticate. She used to drive with her legs crossed.

ED BLUESTONE

Never brag about your ancestors coming over on the *Mayflower*; the immigration laws weren't as strict in those days.

LEW LEHR

Song Titles

"She was Bred in Old Kentucky But She's Only a Crumb Up Here."

CURLY HOWARD

"Let's Get Out of the Wheat Field, Honey, We're Going Against the Grain."

RED SKELTON

"I'm So Miserable Without You It's Almost Like Having You Around."

KIP ADDOTTA

"You Threw Up on the Carpet of My Love."

LEWIS GRIZZARD

"I Was an Incubator Baby and She Was the Girl Next Door."

HARRY RUBY

"I'd Be a Red-Hot Mama If I Didn't Have These Varicose Veins."

ANNA RUSSELL

"The Shades of Night Were Falling Fast But I Got a Pretty Good Look Anyway."

JETHRO BURNS

"He Didn't Like Her Apartment, So He Knocked Her Flat."

HOMER HAYNES

"Your Eyes Match Garbo's, Baby, I Wish They Matched Each Other."

HENRY MORGAN

"You'll Never Get Away from Me, Darling, Because Even When You're Taking a Shower with Somebody Else, I'll Be the Soap on Your Rag."

LEWIS GRIZZARD

"You're Having My Baby, What a Lovely Way to Say That You Are Stupid."

JUDY TENUTA

The South

I was born in Alabama. I was raised in Georgia. I'm so Southern I'm related to myself. I have a 12-year-old daughter. She takes after my daddy. She ought to. She's his.

BRETT BUTLER

To be frank, I find these people anything but deep. I was in Birmingham, Alabama, working in a small comedy club called I Don't Get It.

DENNIS MILLER

Nice people down South. They take their guns seriously. We passed a pickup truck. It had a bumper sticker: "Guns Don't Kill People, I do!"

JON HAYMEN

For a black man, there's no difference between the North and the South. In the South they don't mind how close I get so long as I don't get too big; in the North they don't mind how big I get so long as I don't get too close.

DICK GREGORY

People down South are incredibly polite. Even their war was civil.

DUDLEY MOORE

In the South my grandmother used to tell me, "Hey, James Wesley, put down that wheelbarrow—you know you docsn't know anything about machinery."

JAMES WESLEY JACKSON

Have you ever been down South? I was in Troy, Alabama. I walk into a restaurant. I said, "Where do Jewish folks hang out?" They said, "See that tree?"

JACKIE GAYLE

Three men were talkin' about a new scheme, and one of them was an engraver. He said, "I can make a batch of money, and we'll pass it out and get rich."

He showed up with the money—all eighteen-dollar bills.

The other guys said, "You

must be nuts! Nobody'll take an eighteen-dollar bill." He said, "Don't get excited. I know where we can get rid of 'em—down in Tennessee." They said, "Well, come on, let's go get rid of 'em fast."

They drove down to the mountains of Tennessee and they pulled up to a filling station in front of a little country grocery store. The owner came out and said, "Y'all wanna get something?" They said, "Yeah, fill it up with Hi-Test, boy."

The guy filled it up and said, "Anything else?"

One of them got out an eighteen-dollar bill and popped it a few times and said, "You got change for that?" The country boy looked it over a few times, popped it a couple of times, and said, "Hell yes. Whaddya want, three sixes or two nines?"

THE DUKE OF PADUCAH

  (WHITEY FORD)

I love those slow-talking Southern girls. I was out with a Southern girl last night, took her so long to tell me she wasn't that kind of girl, she was.

WOODY WOODBURY

They talk about people "relating" to each other . . . Relating? Me being from Macon, Georgia, "relating" means dating your cousin.

BLAKE CLARK

I was in Tennessee and they hated me. They knew I came in from California. A guy stood up and said, "At least here in Tennessee we don't drive all over our freeways and shoot and kill people!" I said, "No, but you should."

PAM STONE

A hillbilly boy married a hillbilly girl and went on a honeymoon. They were supposed to stay two weeks, but they didn't stay two weeks, they stayed one night.

The next day the hillbilly boy came back up to his pappy's cabin. His pappy said, "Hey, boy, where's your woman?" He said, "I shot her, Paw." He said, "You shot her? What fer?" The boy said, "She were a virgin, Paw." He said, "I don't blame ya, boy, if she ain't good enough for her folks, she ain't good enough for us!"

DAVE TURNER

The hottest day I ever lived through—Monday, Memorial Day. When I was a boy in Kershaw, South Carolina, I remembered how good it was to swim in the creek. So I took my clothes off, hung 'em on a bush, and dived into the creek. I was really enjoying myself, but all of a sudden I heard a bunch of girls giggling. They grabbed my clothes and run with 'em!

I got to scramblin' around in the creek and my hand finally come across a big ol' dishpan. I just held it up in front of me, and I took off after 'em. I run eight blocks, right down the main street of Gatlinburg, and I finally caught up with 'em. And I run up to the ringleader and I said, "Young lady, do you know what I think? Do you know what I think?"

She said, "Yes, I know what you think. You think there's a bottom in that dishpan!"

RALPH SMITH

They laugh at us up North, they say we're ignorant. Of course, we realize it. They laugh at us. They say at nine, ten o'clock at night we're home in bed. That's all right, two o'clock in the morning they're still searchin' for it.

BROTHER DAVE GARDNER

You might be a redneck if:

You consider a six-pack of beer and a bug zapper quality entertainment.

If you honest to God think women are turned on by animal noises and seductive tongue gestures.

If your dad walks you to school because you're in the same grade.

If everybody you meet can tell what kind of underwear you're wearing.

If your wife's hairdo has ever been destroyed by a ceiling fan.

If your family tree does not fork.

JEFF FOXWORTHY

There are two kinds of guys in the South—good ol' boys and rednecks. The difference is, good ol' boys may raise livestock, rednecks get emotionally involved.

BLAKE CLARK

We was out visiting Uncle Ronnie Ledbetter, and my brother and I like to have had a heart attack. There was a hog

229

out there in a pen—with a wooden peg leg. And my brother said, "Uncle Ronnie, what in the world is that hog doin' with a wooden peg leg? Why has he got a peg leg?"

And the man said, "Sonny, that's the most wonderful hog in the world. My house was burning about a year ago, and that hog rescued the baby, got the baby out, saved its life. We love that hog, that hog's just like a member of our family. And a year before that, a little boy was drowning down at the baptizin' hole in the river, and that hog jumped in that river and grabbed him and rescued him. And that hog's like a member of my family. We love that hog!"

My brother said, "Yeah, but you still ain't told me why he's got a wooden peg leg."

And Uncle Ronnie said, "Sonny, you just don't eat a hog that wonderful but one ham at a time."

JERRY CLOWER

There were two nice-lookin' fellers standing next to me, and one of them said to the other, "You know, I believe I recognize her. That's that Minnie Pearl. She's been down there at the Grand Ol' Opry for 175 years." He said, "She carries on like she's from the country. I bet she's not from the country. I bet she don't know a goose from a gander." I turned around and I said, "Well, at Grinder's Switch we don't worry about that. We just put them all out there together and let 'em figure it out for themselves."

MINNIE PEARL

Speeches

If you haven't struck oil in the first three minutes, stop boring.

GEORGE JESSEL

No matter how much strong black coffee we drink, almost any after-dinner speech will counteract it.

KIN HUBBARD

$Sports$

Violent, televised hockey is the chief cause of prison riots in this country. Think about it: You're a convict sitting in your cell at the federal penitentiary watching a hockey player on TV get a two-minute penalty. You're serving seventeen years for the same offense.

JEFF CESARIO

At Crystal Palace this evening, Neville Stitch broke his own world record in the eight hundred meters. He was so pleased he went on to try the high hurdles, but, thinking they were the low hurdles, he shattered his personal best.

RONNIE CORBETT

Weight lifters are now taking steroids and the male hormone testosterone. One guy had so much male hormone in him he had to be classified as an East German woman!

CARL WOLFSON

In boxing they have the "undisputed heavyweight champion." Well, if it's undisputed what's all the fighting about? Undisputed means everybody agrees. Some guys are getting beat up pretty badly over something apparently we all agree on.

GEORGE CARLIN

I'm one of the few to ever throw a javelin two hundred yards . . . Well, actually I only threw it one hundred yards. The guy it hit crawled the other hundred.

JOSÉ JIMENEZ (BILL DANA)

Let me get this straight: The networks won't give gavel-to-gavel coverage of political conventions because they're too dull, but fight for the privilege of broadcasting all laps of the Indianapolis 500?

ROGER SIMON

Should women sports reporters be allowed in the men's locker rooms after the game? I say yes! Let 'em in! They're women, but they're sports reporters and they're doing their jobs, and they should be allowed in. They should be allowed to bring paper, pencils—no rulers.

MARC PRICE

I joined a health club. I was watching these jerks work out. This guy is working out with weights, and he's got a T-shirt on that says, "No Pain, No Gain." So I dropped a barbell on his foot. He started to yell and I said, "What are you complaining about? Now you're in pain! And you gained twenty pounds!"

CY KOTTICK

You just can't go to a public swimming pool and splash around anymore. Everyone's swimming laps now. Some guy jumped in behind me and said, "How long are you gonna be using this lane, dude?" "Until my bladder's empty, punk."

TOMMY SLEDGE

It's an old, seedy, run-down gymnasium on the lower West Side catering to young and old boxers. Amidst the yelling, the smell of fighters sweating, punching bags and each other, one of the boxers comes over to his corner following three rounds of heavy hitting and says to his manager, "I really want a shot at the kid, Kid Jackson. I know I'm getting old and a little punchy, but before I retire I just want one chance in the ring with him!"

And the manager, wiping the fighter's face with a towel, says, "Look, if I've told you once, I've told you a hundred times: *You're* Kid Jackson!"

SOUPY SALES

I like the one about the fella who swam the English Channel. It took him fifty-eight hours to swim there, twelve seconds to come back. His jockstrap got caught.

B. S. PULLY

Some sports I can't watch on TV. I don't mind the games—I don't like the interview after the game. Because the winning players always give credit to God while the losing players blame themselves. Just once I'd like to hear a player say, "Yeah, we were in the game—until Jesus made me fumble!"

JEFF STILSON

A fellow told me he was going to hang-glider school. He said, "I've been going for three months."

I said, "How many successful jumps do you need to make before you graduate?"

He said, "All of them."

RED SKELTON

We have fun—that's what I like about bowling. You can have fun even if you stink, unlike in, say, tennis. Every decade or so, I attempt to play tennis, and it always consists of thirty-seven seconds of actually hitting the ball and two hours of yelling, "Where did the ball go?" "Over that condominium!" Etc. With bowling, once you let go of the ball, it's no longer your legal responsibility. They have these wonderful machines that find it for you and send it right back.

DAVE BARRY

The women's uneven parallel bar event. I think I'm gonna be a little skeptical the next time a woman tells me I'm being too rough in bed. I'm watchin' these girls bang their cervix off a frozen theater rope at eighty miles per hour. You don't see men in that event, okay?

DENNIS MILLER

Stockbrokers

A stockbroker catches his wife in bed with another man. He says to her, "What's going on here?" She says, "Believe it or not, John, I've gone public!"

HENNY YOUNGMAN

Don't invest all your money in just one or two stocks. That's the danger. I know a man who put all his money in just two stocks, a paper-towel company and a revolving-door outfit. He was wiped out before he could turn around.

DAVE ASTOR

They're not calling it the stock market any longer. It's the stuck market. When a man walks into a hotel and requests a room on the ninth floor, the clerk asks, "For sleeping or for jumping?"

I shouldn't worry about my stocks. My stockbroker will carry me. He and three other pallbearers.

EDDIE CANTOR

233

Stupidity

I'm not saying this woman is stupid—but when the wind blows, her forehead buckles in . . . And my cousin, well, he wasn't too bright, I guess. Chickens teased him.

BRETT BUTLER

She saw a sign saying, "Wet Floor." So she did!

JOAN RIVERS

Subway

You can expose yourself on the subway and it doesn't cost you a dime. Unless you spit. Then it's a twenty-five-dollar fine. So if you're gonna spit, you might as well whip it out and have a little fun for the money . . . I was sitting on the subway. I was sitting on a newspaper and a man came over, he said, "Are you reading that paper?" I said, "Yes," stood up, turned the page, and sat down again.

DAVID BRENNER

I love New York City. I just got into town and I wanted to get on the subway. I asked a man, "I'd like to get on the subway. How do I get underground?" He said, "Drop dead."

CORBETT MONICA

I hate the subway. And these guys begging for spare change. They come around with their hand out yelling, "Spare a quarter!" They say they can't work, so they go, "Spare a quarter, spare a quarter." I've got the solution: Make 'em tollbooth clerks.

RON SMITH

We should be grateful for subways. At least they've taken crime off the street.

WILL JORDAN

Ask yourself why the New York subway system, alone among the mass transit systems of the world, has maps inside rather than outside the trains. It's to force you to get on the wrong train in order to find out where you're going . . . You decipher the map to discover that the first step in reaching your destination is to get off the wrong train at the next stop.

CALVIN TRILLIN

If it's so safe to fly, why do they give you an hour of instructions when you get on the plane? Have safety instructions where you know it's dangerous to travel—like the New York City subway system. Have the conductor come out and say, "Ay! Good evening, ladies and gentlemen, this is your conductor Angelo speakin'. Welcome to the D train. If the train should go aboveground through the Bronx, bulletproof vests can be located under your seat. If the vest don't inflate, duck. All weapons may be stored in the overhead compartments. And, please, no stabbing until the train has come to a complete stop in the terminal. You'll notice the conductor has turned off the 'No Urinating' sign. Just feel free to soil yourself. And now please return the homeless person to his original upright position. Should an unbathed bag lady walk on the train, a small mask will drop from the ceiling. Put it over your nose and mouth and breathe like your life depended on it."

GABE ABELSON

Success

If at first you don't succeed, keep on sucking till you do succeed!

CURLY HOWARD

Suicide

I was in analysis. I was suicidal. As a matter of fact, I would have killed myself but I was in analysis with a strict Freudian and if you kill yourself they make you pay for the sessions you miss.

WOODY ALLEN

I'd quit the job of being me, but I have accumulated so much seniority.

TOM WILSON ("Ziggy")

Not long ago, there was a little Cajun boy that brought himself in the house. And like all little boys, first thing he did, he yell, "Momma! Ho, Momma!" She say, "What it is, you yell like that?" He says, "Poppa done hung himself out there in the garage." She said, "What you said?" He said, "Poppa done hung himself in the garage, that what I said." She said, "Did you cut him down?" He said, "Hell no, he waddn't dead yet."

JUSTIN WILSON

The whole trouble with suicides today, as I see it, is that they are usually committed by the wrong people . . . I have known some perfectly dandy suicides, suicides who were simply cut out by nature to be suicides, ideal suicides, suicides who, the moment I first glimpsed their bright vapid smile, or felt their hearty slap upon my back, or heard them play three notes upon the piccolo, would make me clasp my hands ecstatically and murmur, "There goes the perfect suicide, so help me! So help me!"

And yet in every case these logical selections for self-destruction, far from being proud of their God-given qualifications for the perfect suicide, have proved the very first to resent any implication whatsoever of their vast natural fitness

for such a destiny . . . If the man who practices upon the cornet by an open window every morning at six-thirty would devote the same amount of effort and study to some practicable laboratory experiments with the subject of suicide, it would doubtless save his neighbor the necessity of terminating his career involuntarily with a sawed-off shotgun. In other words, if there were better and wiser suicides, there would be fewer murders.

COREY FORD

To a man on a ledge: "Thinking of jumping? Your first time, is it?"

BOB NEWHART

I never thought of killing myself, never, but if I did I'd want to be unique. Headline: "Sick comic succumbs, swallows 650 dexamine spansules. He was killed by his neighbors for talking too much."

LENNY BRUCE

I broke up with my psychiatrist. I told him I had suicidal tendences. He told me from now on I had to pay in advance.

RODNEY DANGERFIELD

Taxes

I wouldn't mind paying taxes—if I knew they were going to a friendly country.
DICK GREGORY

I would tax Raquel Welch . . . and I've a feeling she'd tax me.
MICHAEL PALIN

Of the two classic certainties, death and taxes, death is preferable. At least you're not called in six months later for an audit.
BILL VAUGHAN

Have you got your income tax papers yet? They've done away with all those silly questions now. There are only three questions on the form:

1. How much did you earn?
2. How much do you have left?
3. Send it in.
SANDY POWELL

I dislike letters from Inland Revenue that end "your obedient servant." And that space on every income tax form which says, "Do not write in this space." We suggest dropping a small blob of candle grease on it—on the very sound principle that if you can't write in that space . . .

The creed of the Inland Revenue is simple: "If we can bring one little smile to one little face today—then somebody's slipped up somewhere."
DAVID FROST

What gets me is that estimated tax return. You have to guess how much you're gonna make. You have to fill it out, fix it up, sign it, send it in. I sent mine in last week. I didn't sign it. If I have to guess how much I'm gonna make, let them guess who sent it.
JIMMY EDMONDSON
(PROFESSOR BACKWARDS)

You know what they're doing with your taxes? They're spending your money, hundreds of billions of dollars on defense. To defend us from the Russians, the Nicaraguans, the Libyans, the Iranians. When was the last time a Russian broke into your car and stole your stereo? I'm not worried about Russians, I'm worried about Americans! You're going to defend me, defend me from Americans! Get my butt back from Burger King alive!

BLAKE CLARK

Telephones

Well, if I called the wrong number, why did you answer the phone?

JAMES THURBER

The cellular-phone industry has greatly expanded, making complete local and long-distance service available to the homeless.

P. J. O'ROURKE

Cordless phones are great. If you can find them.

GLENN FOSTER

Two men were talking. One of them said, "The words 'aggravation' and 'irritation'—they're supposed to mean the same thing but they do not. He said, "I'll show you. Hand me that telephone book. I'll pick any name and any number at random and I'll call up. First I'll show you what irritation is."

He calls a number and a lady says, "Hello?" He says, "Hello, I'd like to speak to Herman." She says, "There's no Herman here, you must have the wrong number." He apologized and hung up. A minute later he dialed the same number. The same lady answered the phone. He said, "Hello, I'd like to speak to Herman." She said, "You must be the gentleman who called before. There's no Herman here. I'm sorry!" Another minute goes by, he dialed the same number again. He said, "I'd like to speak to Herman." By now she's mad. She says, "I told you three times there's no Herman living here! Leave me alone!" And she hung up.

The fellow turns to his friend and says, "Now that's irritation. Now I'll show you what aggravation is."

He dialed the same number. The same lady answered the phone. He said, "Hello, this is Herman, were there any messages for me?"

JACK BENNY

I call a wrong number. A guy on the other end says, "Well, what number did you dial?" "Well, did it ring at your house? Then I guess it's *yours*, Mr. Wizard!"

LARRY REEB

They've got so many of these Dial-a-Service numbers. They've got one that'll keep you occupied for hours, and it doesn't cost a cent. It's called a busy signal.

RON SMITH

Television

Ninety-eight percent of American homes have TV sets—which means the people in the other two percent of the households have to generate their own sex and violence.

FRANKLIN P. JONES

Our TV man had to take our set back to the store for an adjustment. It needed back payments.

GENE BAYLOS

If you read a lot of books, you're considered well read. But if you watch a lot of TV, you're not considered well viewed.

LILY TOMLIN

On cable TV they have a weather channel—twenty-four hours of weather. We had something like that where I grew up. We called it a window.

DAN SPENCER

Television is an invention that permits you to be entertained in your living room by people you wouldn't have in your home.

DAVID FROST

On commercial television the high quality of the entertainment is often spoiled by those annoying little interruptions, which we call programs.

KENNETH HORNE

Television—a medium, so called because it is neither rare nor well done.

ERNIE KOVACS

Thanksgiving

Thanksgiving is an emotional holiday. People travel thousands of miles to be with people they only see once a year. And then discover once a year is way too often.

JOHNNY CARSON

It was founded by the Puritans to give thanks for bein' preserved from the Indians, an' we keep it to give thanks we are preserved from the Puritans.

FINLEY PETER DUNNE

Time

We prefer the old-fashioned alarm clock to the kind that awakens you with soft music or a gentle whisper. If there's one thing we can't stand early in the morning, it's hypocrisy.

BILL VAUGHAN

Take Heraclitus. He went home to his wife Helen and he said, "Time is like a river which is flowing endlessly through the universe and you couldn't step in the same river twice, Helen."

And she says, "What do you mean by that, Heraclitus? Explain yourself." "That means you could go down to the Mississippi River, for example, and you could step in and you could step out, and then you could step in again, but that river that you stepped in has moved downstream, you see? It's here. And you would only be stepping in the Mississippi River because that's what it's called, you see? But if someone were on top of the water, for example a water bug, it would be downstream—unless, of course, it were swimming upstream. In which case it would be older and it would be a different bug."

And she said, "Don't be an ass, Heraclitus. You could step in the same river twice—if you walked downstream . . ."

He was amazed . . . They had a few drinks first and went down to the river and into the river they threw a piece of wood, just to test how fast the river was going. And so Heraclitus saw how fast the wood was going, so he stepped into the river and ran and stepped and ran and stepped and ran and finally he ran into the Aegean Sea and was drowned. So much for time.

SEVERN DARDEN

I don't mind going back to daylight saving time. With inflation, the hour will be the only thing I've saved this year.

VICTOR BORGE

How to tell time by children:

When they're very sleepy, it's time to go to school.

When they never felt more wide awake in their lives, it's time for the late late late late late movie.

When they have a slight fever and an unidentifiable rash, it's three o'clock Sunday morning.

When they break a collarbone, it's four o'clock Sunday morning during the doctor's vacation.

When they put on underwear and a flannel shirt, it's the middle of the first hot spell in July, and when they put on cotton socks, sneakers, and a mesh T-shirt, it's the day of the worst blizzard since '47.

ROBERT PAUL SMITH

Backwards thinking. I plan dates backwards: The movie's at ten, that means I pick her up at nine, that means I'm in the shower at eight, that means I'm running at seven, that means I leave work at six, that means I get to work at nine, that means I'm asleep the night before at midnight, that means . . . I'm late now. I can't make it.

LARRY MILLER

Time was discovered in the year called Who Knows by two brothers who stayed in their room all day trying to discover things . . . Frank and Dick Merriwell.

The daring brothers forged ahead . . . First they tried to measure time by burning candles. Frank started at one end, Dick at the other, and they invented the process of burning the candle at both ends. One day Frank and Dick accidentally sat on their candles. This was known as burning their ends at both candles. They cut notches in a candle. When the flame reached the first notch, it was lunchtime. When it reached the second notch, dinnertime, and at the third notch, it was night and bedtime. They called this process Burnas Notches . . .

Then Frank discovered that if he put a stick in the ground out in the sun, in the morning the shadow was long, then shorter, and when the sun was right overhead, no shadow. Dick said, "Incredible . . . I must have that stick!" Frank said, "It isn't the stick." Then he put twenty-four of them in the ground. "Egad," said Dick, "they *all* work. Those sticks are mine!" "No," said Frank. "They're mine!"

Finally after a long argument, Dick said, "I know what. We shall call them ours." And so the twenty-four ours were discovered. It was child's play to break the sticks into minutes and seconds. And since they had the minds of children, they did it. Time was discovered.

HENRY MORGAN

Toupees and Wigs

My hair is my own. I paid for it. I own it.
CARL REINER

His toupee makes him look twenty years sillier.
BILL DANA

Why don't you get a toupee with some brains in it?
MOE HOWARD

One old lady turns to another: "Oooh, who did your hair? Who did your hair? My God, your hair looks like a wig!"
She says, "It *is* a wig."
The first one says, "Is that so? You could never tell."
LARRY BEST

They say in an awkward or embarrassing situation don't freeze up. Pay a compliment. You will lessen the tension. I remembered that. I was talking to this guy, I didn't know him too well, and his toupee blew onto the sidewalk. Very embarrassing. So I said, "Gee, I like your hair like that."
GEORGE MILLER

Traffic

Signs on the freeway are funny. They have a sign that says, "Orange Cones Mean Men at Work." What else could orange cones mean? Psychedelic witches embedded in asphalt?

KARIN BABBITT

I've been having trouble waking up. I actually dozed off at a red light. It was so embarrassing. There I was, out cold, other pedestrians nudging me to cross the street.

ANITA WISE

Wouldn't it be great if cops gave you tickets—to a show? You're doing seventy in a forty-mile zone and they say, "All right, take this ticket—to a Wayne Newton show." Oh no!

RENO

Why do they call it rush hour when nothing moves?

ROBIN WILLIAMS

Trains

I came down from Jacksonville on a train that was the slowest train I'd ever been on. I said to the conductor, "Can't you run any faster?" He said, "Yeah, but I gotta stay on the train."

A woman ran up to the conductor and said, "Stop the train. I have to get to the maternity hospital." He said, "You had no business getting on the train in that condition." She said, "I didn't."

JIMMY EDMONDSON

(PROFESSOR BACKWARDS)

The maddest fella I ever heard of was riding the Illinois Central Railroad what runs from New Orleans to Chicago and back. He got on that train in Chicago, headed south. He told the porter, "I'm afraid to go to my roomette and go to sleep because I may not wake up in time to get off of this train in Wynona, Mississippi, in the morning. I'm hard to wake up, and if you call me and I don't answer you and you shake me, I have been known to come up a-fighting."

The porter said, "That's all right. I've had this job forty years. I fight somebody every morning. And I don't care how much resistance you give me, I don't care how much you fight, if you tell me to put you off the train, I'll put you off!"

Well, the man slept good. He woke up the next morning in McComb, Mississippi—two hours south of Wynona. He throwed a fit. He grabbed the porter and choked him. The police come aboard and calmed the fella down.

A man said to the porter, "You know, that's the maddest human being I ever seen in my life. Don't you agree?"

And the porter said, "He was a mad fella, but I seen one other man in my lifetime madder than him."

"Who in the world could that have been?"

He said, "The man I put off in Wynona this morning."

JERRY CLOWER

The most common of all antagonisms arises from a man's taking a seat beside you on the train, a seat to which he is completely entitled.

ROBERT BENCHLEY

Here's a piece of late news. Mr. Arthur Perkiss, the man who this week won five hundred thousand pounds on the pools, has announced that he will never work another day in his life. So he's staying on with British Rail.

RONNIE CORBETT

So much had been written about the Long Island Rail Road (Fred Allen called it "two strips of rust and a right-of-way") that I decided to take a ride on it a while back. What an experience!

It is not an exaggeration to say that it almost shook my teeth out. Then the jolts slackened a little, and I said to a passenger across the aisle, "It's a little smoother now, isn't it?"

"Yes," the regular rider said. "We're not on the tracks now."

CAL TINNEY

Travel

I went sightseeing in Windsor, Canada. As I was leaving, they asked me if I had anything to declare. I said, "Yeah, I'm glad I don't live here!"

JEFF SHAW

We were coming back into New York Harbor and we went under the Verrazano Bridge and I got a lump in my throat. We went under the Brooklyn Bridge and I started to cry . . . because we flew home.

TOTIE FIELDS

If you like to spend your vacation in out-of-the-way places where few people go, let your wife read the map.

JACK CARTER

When you look like your passport photo, it's time to go home.

ERMA BOMBECK

Africa is God's country, and he can have it. Well, sir, we left New York drunk and early on the morning of February 7. After fifteen days on the water

and six on the boat, we finally arrived on the shores of Africa. The first morning saw us up at six, breakfasted, and back in bed at seven. This was our routine for the first three months. We finally got so we were in bed at six-thirty . . . One morning I shot an elephant in my pajamas. How he got in my pajamas, I don't know. Then we tried to remove the tusks, but they were embedded in so firmly that we couldn't budge them. Of course, in Alabama, the Tuskaloosa. But that's entirely irrelephant to what I was talking about. We took some pictures of the native girls— but they weren't developed. But we're going back again in a couple of weeks.

GROUCHO MARX (in Animal Crackers)

I took the vacation I wanted all my life. I packed Alice and the kids and all the luggage in our station wagon and headed it right straight to Canada. Then I went to Las Vegas and had a ball.

GEORGE GOBEL

One of the main troubles about going to Europe is that no one wants to hear about ar trip when you get back ome. Your friends and rela- ives are rife with jealousy and are not only sorry you went to Europe but deeply regret that you came back.

ART BUCHWALD

When I feel like getting away from it all, I just turn the TV on to a Spanish soap opera and imagine I'm on vacation in a hotel in Mexico.

BRIAN McKIM

I was talking to an Englishman and I said, "It's absolutely re- markable. In this day and age, you could fly to New York in six hours." And you know what he said? "But why?"

JACK PAAR

I've got to hand it to the Vene- tians, though. I can't tell you how impressed I was with that city. Nowhere else in the world can you find a flood area bring- ing in so much tourist gold. Any other city in that condi- tion would've been declared a disaster area and the Red Cross would've been in there evacu- ating the residents.

I don't care what the travel folders say, this city was not planned to be on water.

All you have to do is take one look at what's floating around in those canals and you can see that the original city fa- thers goofed. Luckily for them, somebody on their Chamber of Commerce got the bright idea of making a tourist attraction out of a big sewage problem.

They even capitalized on their pigeon problem. Wait'll you see St. Mark's Square in Venice.

SELMA DIAMOND

If you are fond of hunting, there's no place that can com- pare— you may not bag a lion or a ti- ger or a bear— but if you want a jackass there are plenty of them there— Go West, young man!

HARRY RUBY

I brought my wife with me to Las Vegas. You know how you pack a lot of things you don't need.

DAVE BARRY (stand-up comic of the 1960s)

It's a thrill to be here in Russia . . . Surprisingly enough, I'm not having any trouble with the language. Nobody speaks to me.

BOB HOPE

Elsie is so ugly she's been turned down more times than a bedspread . . . Two weeks ago she won first prize in a beauty contest. It was for mules.

CHARLEY WEAVER (CLIFF ARQUETTE)

I had to take Dramamine just to keep eye contact with her.

JOHN RIGGI

I think the reason my parents didn't like me is I was not a good-looking kid. My whole family was embarrassed, they didn't want me to be seen . . .

They enrolled me in a school for the blind.

BILLY BRAVER

Two weeks after I was born my mother tried to have an abortion . . . When you're not wanted they never like you. All I heard when I grew up was: "Why can't you be like your cousin Sheila? Why can't you be like your cousin Sheila?" Cousin Sheila died at birth.

JOAN RIVERS

My best friend at home was a fellow named Sappo. He's my best friend in the world but he's ugly. When he was born the doctor slapped his mother. She used to have morning sickness after he was born. When he was a little baby his folks used to carry him everywhere they went so they wouldn't have to kiss him goodbye.

GEORGE "GOOBER" LINDSEY

On Halloween all the people in the neighborhood dress up like her.

SOUPY SALES

The Dean of Girls—not the most attractive woman the world has ever known. During the summer months she had a part-time job at Disneyland. She was one of the rides.

SANDY BARON

My Playtex living bra died—of starvation! I've turned many a head in my day, and a few stomachs. I never made Who's Who but I'm featured in What's That! I once went bra-less and wore a peekaboo blouse. It was embarrassing. First they'd peek, then they'd boo . . . Bob Hope has a joke on me, the most beautiful one I ever heard. He said, "A Peeping Tom threw up on her windowsill."

PHYLLIS DILLER

He paid me a compliment. He said I looked like a breath of spring. Well, he didn't use them words. He said I looked like the end of a hard winter.

MINNIE PEARL

My husband was so ugly, he used to stand outside the doctor's office and make people sick.

MOMS MABLEY

This woman on the train had an ugly baby. I know an ugly baby when I see one. And I only glimpsed it. This fellow enters the coach. He's half smashed. And he gets to the seat where the woman is with the baby . . .

She heard him when he said to himself, "Damn!"

She said, "What are you looking at?"

The guy said, "I'm lookin' at that ugly baby. That's a bad-lookin' baby, lady . . ."

The woman took this as an offense. She pulls the emergency cord, the train stops, and the conductor comes in. The lady says, "This man just insulted me . . ."

The conductor says, "Now calm down, lady. The railroad will go to any extent to avoid having differences with the passengers. Perhaps it would be to your convenience if we were to rearrange your seating. And as a small compensation from the railroad, if you'll accompany me to the dining car, we'll give you a free meal. And maybe we'll find a banana for your monkey."

FLIP WILSON

She was ugly! She was known as a two-bagger. That's a girl

who's so ugly, when you go out with her you put a bag over your head in case the bag over her head breaks. She was so ugly, you look in the dictionary under "ugly" and you see her picture. Me, I was a very ugly baby. When the doctor cut the cord, he hung himself. My old man, he didn't like my looks. He carried around a picture of the kid that came with the wallet. He made me sleep in the kitchen naked to get rid of the roaches.

RODNEY DANGERFIELD

When I was born my father spent three weeks trying to find a loophole in my birth certificate.

JACKIE VERNON

Vegetarianism

I won't eat anything that has intelligent life, but I'd gladly eat a network executive or a politician.

MARTY FELDMAN

I'm a Volvovegetarian. I'll eat an animal only if it was accidentally killed by a speeding car.

RON SMITH

Although I just can't take the plunge into bean sprouts or alfalfa, one day I did put a few carrot sticks and celery stalks into a bag and I took a healthful walk in the park. After a while, I sat down on a bench beside an old man who was both smoking and eating a chocolate bar, two serious violations of a longevity diet.

"Do you mind my asking how old you are?" I said. "Ninety-two," he replied. "Well, if you smoke and eat *that* stuff, you're gonna die." He took a hard look at my carrots and celery, and then he said, "You're dead *already*."

BILL COSBY

Tomorrow is "National Meat-Out Day." It's being sponsored by vegetarians. Not exhibitionists.

DAVID LETTERMAN

I thought I could do my own small part to save the planet by becoming a vegetarian. Actually, I did it not so much because I love animals but because I hate plants. I still like to hunt, though. In fact, I've found that plants are a lot easier than animals to sneak up on.

A. WHITNEY BROWN

I came from a poor family. We never had meat at our house. And whenever I would go by a butcher's window I thought there had been a terrible accident.

JACK PAAR

V*irginity*

I used to be a virgin. I gave it up because there was no money in it.

MARSHA WARFIELD

My friend Lance would call me up. He goes, "Bob . . . the first guy that gets your daughter—wouldn't that freak you out?" "No, Lance, that would not freak me out, Lance." "First guy who gets your daughter wouldn't bother you at all?" I said, "No, I hope my daughter experiences everything that there is in life." "First guy wouldn't bother you?" I said no. He said, "What would?" I said, "Number 200."

BOB GOLDTHWAIT

The only good woman I can recall in history was Betsy Ross, and all she ever made was a flag.

MAE WEST

In ancient times they sacrificed the virgins. Men were not about to sacrifice the sluts!

BILL MAHER

War

Do you know what's wrong with the world? England is in Palestine, Italy is in Ethiopia, Russia is in Spain, Germany is in Austria, Japan is in China—nobody stays home!

ED WYNN

At the age of four with paper hats and wooden swords we are all generals—only some of us never grow out of it.

PETER USTINOV

I'm for peace—I've yet to see a man wake up in the morning and say, "I've just had a good war."

MAE WEST

I was right where the bullets were the thickest! Underneath the ammunition truck.

LOU COSTELLO

The Generals' Game:
  1. Each general can choose as many babies as he wants from the pile.
  2. The generals hit each other with the babies until they get tired, and then go out for dinner.

B. KLIBAN

Let's go back to the '40s era when everybody was our gallant ally—except the people who are now our friends.

KENNETH HORNE

MX missiles—they changed their name. They call them the Peace Keepers. A multiple-warhead hydrogen bomb called the Peace Keeper. What do they call a sledgehammer? The Finger Massage? Is napalm now Dry Skin Remover? Let's be consistent. It's not mustard gas

—it's a really strong antihista-mine!

WILL DURST

You can't say civilization isn't advancing; in every war they kill you in a new way.

WILL ROGERS

It was the second day in the Army. The rookie missed mother and home. He wanted loving-kindness, but the sergeant didn't give it to him. They lined up and he turned to another recruit and whispered, "I've got a good mind to tell that sergeant off again."

"What do you mean, again?" the other asked.

"I had a good mind to tell him off yesterday too."

LEW LEHR

When I lost my rifle, the Army charged me eighty-five dollars. That's why in the Navy the captain goes down with the ship.

DICK GREGORY

I have the secret for world peace. And you know what it is? Nose jobs! That's right, nose jobs for the whole world.

Think about it. I have. Look around you! You'll see that once somebody has their nose fixed, they never get into a fight.

What's more, they'll do anything, but anything, to avoid a punch in the nose.

It's not like when you had your old nose. Your old nose didn't cost you anything, so you don't care. Once you've had your nose fixed, you're for peace talks. New noses do not stand up in combat.

Once the people in all countries start having their noses fixed, the economy in all countries will really zoom. Plastic surgery is not cheap.

SELMA DIAMOND

The terrorists are irrational. "Allah says die Yankee dog!" Whaddya gonna do? I think we can use this to our advantage. The Islam fanatics, their religion tells them they can't come into contact with pork. This opens up a whole new vista of warfare. We don't need guns. We don't need bombs. Ham grenades!

PAUL PROVENZA

Our bombs are incredibly smart. In fact, our bombs are

better educated than the average high school graduate. At least they can find Kuwait.

A. WHITNEY BROWN

If I was going to storm a pillbox, going to sheer, utter, certain death, and the colonel said, "Shepherd, pick six guys," I'd pick six White Sox fans, because they have known death every day of their lives and it holds no terror for them.

JEAN SHEPHERD

A German soldier in Paris, 1940. He takes the first girl he sees to a hotel room, has his way with her, and says arrogantly, "In nine months, you'll have a baby. Call him Adolf."

She replies sweetly, "In two weeks you'll have a rash. Call it what you like."

MARTY BRILL

Countries are making nuclear weapons like there's no tomorrow.

EMO PHILIPS

Weather

The temperature in any room is room temperature.

STEVEN WRIGHT

I always wondered what great scientists talked about when they got together. Can you imagine Dr. Fahrenheit and Dr. Celsius talking, and Dr. Fahrenheit would say, "Man, it's hot in here." And Dr. Celsius would say, "It's not that hot."

DAN FRENCH

Tonight's forecast: Dark. Continued mostly dark, with scattered light by midmorning.

GEORGE CARLIN

 Wedding

Wedding: The point at which a man stops toasting a woman and begins roasting her.

HELEN ROWLAND

I went to a wedding . . . I couldn't believe the groom was married in rented shoes. You're making a commitment for a lifetime and your shoes have to be back by five-thirty. I was the best man at the wedding . . . If I'm the best man, why is she marrying him?

JERRY SEINFELD

Your father just kissed a bride and got himself a black eye. I know everyone does it, but not seven years after the wedding.

CHARLEY WEAVER (CLIFF ARQUETTE)

Whistling

If you hate whistlers as much as I do, here are five things to say to stop them. Count them off with me on your fingers. Number one: Say, "Does your head have so much air in it you have to whistle?" Or, a simple question, "Is your head leaking?" You might be solicitous: "Are we playing Name That Tune?" Or number four: "Do you come equipped with headphones?" Or number five: "If you're going to imitate a whistling teakettle, go sit on a stove." These don't work all the time. So if the idiot keeps whistling you might want to take your five fingers and make a fist.

CY KOTTICK

Wife

Translations from the Wife:
"I don't know what you're talking about."
She knows exactly what you're talking about.
"It isn't what you said, it's the way you said it."
You have looked down the front of another woman's dress.
"Me? Angry?"
She. Angry.
"I don't want to talk about it."
Bring me flowers.
"I don't even want to discuss it."
Bring me a diamond bracelet.
"Men!"
You.
"I've been thinking . . ."
She's been brooding.

"It isn't what you said, it's the way you said it."

It isn't the way you said it, it's what you said.

ROBERT PAUL SMITH

My luck changed because of the little woman. I made my first million, and I owe it all to the little woman. She was two inches high. I sold her to a circus and made a million dollars.

DAVE KETCHUM

Leonard Box was arrested yesterday. Somebody told him his wife was as pretty as a picture, so he hung her on the wall.

CHARLEY WEAVER (CLIFF ARQUETTE)

If a wife does not cause all your troubles, she at least conveniently symbolizes them at times.

DON HEROLD

A man asked a private detective to follow his wife. After several days, the private detective came back with his findings. He said, "I have the proof —your wife is definitely cheating on you. What do I do now?"

The man says resolutely, "Follow my wife and that bum!

Keep on their trail nigh day, even if you have t them around the wor' then I want a complet on what he sees in he

MYRON COHEN

 Women

They don't make them like they used to. At least, I don't.

JOE E. LEWIS

It is a known fact that men are practical, hardheaded realists, in contrast to women, who are romantic dreamers and actually believe that estrogenic skin cream must do something or they couldn't charge sixteen dollars for that little tiny jar.

JANE GOODSELL

I hate women because they always know where things are.

JAMES THURBER

A woman's mind is cleaner than a man's. She changes it more often.

OLIVER HERFORD

255

A bimbo is a young woman who's not pretty enough to be a model, not smart enough to be an actress, and not nice enough to be a poisonous snake.

P. J. O'ROURKE

I believe you should place a woman on a pedestal, high enough so you can look up her dress.

STEVE MARTIN

Women just want men who'll share your hopes and dreams. If you don't, we'll bitch at you until you die.

STEPHANIE HODGE

Always begin with a woman by telling her that you don't understand women. You will be able to prove it to her satisfaction more certainly than anything else you will ever tell her.

DON MARQUIS

Women are the most powerful magnet in the universe. And all men are cheap metal. And we all know where north is.

LARRY MILLER

Do we know much about women? Do we? We don't. We know when they're happy, we know when they're crying, we know when they're pissed off. We just don't know what order those are gonna come at us.

EVAN DAVIS

Words

Why are hemorrhoids called hemorrhoids and asteroids called asteroids? Wouldn't it make more sense if it was the other way around? But if that was true, then a proctologist would be an astronaut.

ROBERT SCHIMMEL

Work

If you get to 35 and your job still involves wearing a name tag, you've probably made a serious vocational error.

DENNIS MILLER

In labor news, longshoremen walked off the piers today; res-

cue operations are continuing . . .
GEORGE CARLIN

I like work; it fascinates me; I can sit and look at it for hours.
JEROME K. JEROME

I got a job—looking for one. I been out of work so long I forgot what kind of work I'm out of.
ROBIN HARRIS

The typical successful American businessman was born in the country, where he worked like hell so he could live in the city, where he worked like hell so he could live in the country.
DON MARQUIS

Our experts describe you as an appallingly dull fellow: unimaginative, timid, lacking in initiative, spineless, easily dominated, no sense of humor, tedious company, and irrepressibly drab and awful. And whereas in most professions, these would be considerable drawbacks, in chartered accountancy, they're a positive boon!
JOHN CLEESE

I was a house painter for five years. Five years. I didn't think I'd ever finish that damn house.
JOHN FOX

There's no limit to the amount of work a man can do, provided, of course, that it isn't the work he's supposed to be doing at that moment.
ROBERT BENCHLEY

"How's your new job at the factory?" one guy asked another. "I'm not going back there." "Why not?" "For many reasons," he answered. "The sloppiness, the shoddy workmanship, the awful language . . . they just couldn't put up with it."
MELL LAZARUS

Work is the greatest thing in the world, so we should always save some of it for tomorrow.
DON HEROLD

I used to work in a bakery as a pilot . . . I used to take the bread from one corner and pile it in the other.
CURLY HOWARD

A man was late for work. "What's the idea of being late?" asked the boss. "Well, the alarm clock woke up everybody but me this morning."

"What do you mean, the alarm clock woke up everybody in the family but you?"

"Well, there's eight in our family and the clock was set for seven."

"SENATOR" ED FORD

The trouble with unemployment is that the minute you wake up in the morning you're on the job.

SLAPPY WHITE

The way to live longer is to fall in love with what you're doing, then you've got it made. Then you can't wait to get out of bed in the morning and get to work. Unless . . . unless you got someone in bed with you.

GEORGE BURNS

----

*W*riters

I suppose that this is another of those young writers who are

worth watching. Not reading; just watching.

DOROTHY PARKER

If writers were good businessmen, they'd have too much sense to be writers.

IRVIN S. COBB

I write for *Reader's Digest*. It's not hard. All you do is copy out an article and mail it in again.

MILT KAMEN

They don't even send him rejection slips anymore. All his stories come back marked "Opened by Mistake."

GEORGE PRICE

In addition to comedy, I'm a writer. I write checks. They're not very good.

WENDY LIEBMAN

It took me fifteen years to discover that I had no talent for writing, but I couldn't give it up, because by that time I was too famous.

ROBERT BENCHLEY

After being turned down by numerous publishers, he decided to write for posterity.

GEORGE ADE

My dad's a writer. His favorite expression is: "The pen is mightier than the sword," which I believed for a long time. Until I moved into the city. And I got into a fight with this guy. He cut me up real bad, and I drew a mustache on his face. And then I wrote him a nasty letter.

KEVIN BRENNAN

I tried phone sex and got an ear infection.

RICHARD LEWIS

Inflatable dolls—the ad says, "She never has a headache." But *you* do, blowing her up.

ROBERT SCHIMMEL

There has always been sex at the movies—only now it's up on the screen too.

DANNY THOMAS

If the purpose of pornography is to excite sexual desire, it is unnecessary for the young, inconvenient for the middle-aged, and unseemly for the old.

MALCOLM MUGGERIDGE

X Rays

You know what scares me? The X ray! What's the matter with those rays if the dentist has to hide in the next room? He's got this great big thing focused at you going *buzz* and he's hiding.

Then he hands *you* the plates to hold in your mouth. You know that awful scene: "Take this finger, hold it over

---------- -----------------------------

X-Rated Entertainment

Walking across town tonight I looked up and saw a club marquee that said, "Live Nudes." I thought: Good choice.

TOMMY SLEDGE

here, this finger hold it over here, this finger, hold it over here."

Then he comes back and says, "No wonder your tooth hurts, you have a finger chopped up in there!"

SHELLEY BERMAN

Yuppies

Middle class was defined by having certain values and only a certain amount of money. But this new middle class seems to have absolutely no values and an unlimited amount of money.

FRAN LEBOWITZ

By yuppie I don't mean "young urban professional." By yuppie

I mean: "Wanna earn money, wanna get ahead, wanna kiss ass?" "Yup yup yup yup yup!"

ALLAN HAVEY

Even her garbage was gift-wrapped.

JAMES KOMACK

There's one rich man in Chelsea who's so snobbish he won't even ride in the same car as his chauffeur.

DAVID FROST

I hate California. The trouble out here is that people you go out to eat with make you feel like scum. By eating healthy food! I usually order something New Yorky. Like "Give me a bacon cheeseburger and a plate of cigarettes." Then the guy with me goes, "Oh, I'll just have a Perrier and a motivational cassette."

RICHARD JENI

For most of history, baby-having was in the hands (so to speak) of women. Many fine people were born under this system. Things changed in the 1970s. The birth rate dropped sharply. Women started going to college and driving bulldozers and carrying briefcases and using words like "debenture." They didn't have time to have babies . . . Then young professional couples began to realize that their lives were missing something: a sense of stability, of companionship, of responsibility for another life. So they got Labrador retrievers. A little later they started having babies again, mainly because of the tax advantages.

DAVE BARRY

A yuppie wouldn't salute the flag if it wasn't 100 percent cotton.

MARK RUSSELL

Rich yuppies eat at sidewalk cafés and the dinners cost forty dollars each. But isn't the point of being rich *not* having to eat in the street?

RON SMITH

She was a rich girl—breast-fed by caterers.

BILL SCHEFT

A yuppie is someone who believes it's courageous to eat in a restaurant that hasn't been reviewed yet.

MORT SAHL

Zeal

We make most of our mistakes when we are optimistic.

DON HEROLD

I'm still suffering from shock from the last war. I was almost drafted! Luckily I was wounded while taking the physical. When I reached the psychiatrist, I said, "Give me a gun, I'll wipe out the whole German Army in five minutes." He said, "You're crazy!" I said, "Write it down!"

JACKIE MASON

Some of the charges the police use are a bit overzealous: "Loitering with intent to use a pedestrian crossing."

ROWAN ATKINSON

Zipper

The man who invented the zip fastener was today honored with a lifetime peerage. He'll now be known as the Lord of the Flies.

RONNIE BARKER

Airplane. Guy is sitting asleep, fly open, completely exposed. Next aisle, a guy's sitting there. He looks over and sees him. He gets the stewardess and asks her for a pencil and a piece of paper. He writes:

"Dear Sir: I'm seated across the aisle from you, and your fly is open and you're completely exposed. And I knew this note would avoid any embarrassment. Yours truly, Frank Martin.

"P.S. I love you."

LENNY BRUCE

A moment of agony that transcends all moments of agony. I hope this story is true, because it's too beautiful to be a lie. A man is at a long table. There are twenty-five people seated about this table, enjoying a formal supper. This man is meeting for the first time his prospective in-laws. It's a very stiff affair, white tie, he's trying desperately to behave tonight. At one point during the meal, he glances down into his lap and he notices that he has forgotten to do something terribly important. Very surreptitiously he reaches down and makes the adjustment. And everything is fine. A few minutes later he gets up to excuse himself. *And the whole tablecloth goes with him.*

SHELLEY BERMAN

Zoophytes

There are people on this planet who actually make their livings as sponge fishermen. There must be a real trick to that. You've got to get up pretty darn early to fool a sponge . . . Row out at dawn . . . Bait up a hook with a messy kitchen spill . . . Old guys sit around in the twilight of their lives swapping sponge tales: "He was huge! Biggest sponge you ever seen! Son of a bitch damn near absorbed me! Huge! Had Comet all over him!"

TOM McTEAGUE

Sponges grow in the o—
wonder how much deepe—
ocean would be if that dr—
happen.

STEVEN WRIGHT

index